When She's Pregnant

When She's Pregnant

The Essential Guide for
Expectant Fathers

To Jonathon
welcome to life's
greatest adventure

Jerry Shapiro

Jerrold Lee Shapiro, Ph.D.

To order additional copies of this book, contact:
Xlibris LLC
1-888-795-4274
www.Xlibris.com
Orders@Xlibris.com
552751

Contents

Also by Jerrold Lee Shapiro

Books

When Men Are Pregnant: Needs and Concerns of Expectant Fathers (1987, 1993)

The Measure of a Man: Becoming the Father You Wish Your Father Had Been (1993, 1995)

Becoming a Father: Contemporary Social, Developmental, and Clinical Perspectives (1995) Book of the Year Award from the *American Journal of Nursing* 1995

Finding Meaning, Facing Fears in the Autumn of Your Years (ages 45-65) (2012) Alpha Sigma Nu (Jesuit Honor Society) Book of the Year Award (2013)

Poster

Shapiro, J. L. (1994). *A Father's Declaration.*

Dedication

To my father, Myer Shapiro, who taught me gentleness in masculinity

To my wife, Susan Bernadett-Shapiro, my partner in life

To my children, Natasha and Gabriel, and my son-in-law, Aaron

To my grandchildren who inspired this edition, Will and Lydia

To all the fathers who participated in the survey and who freely shared their time, effort, and private feelings and to the fathers everywhere, my emotional brothers

And in memory of three patriarchs, my grandfathers Charles Wolbarst and Nathan Shapiro and my father-in-law, Faustino Bernadett

Introduction to the 2014 Edition

This book was first published in 1987, with the title *When Men Are Pregnant: Needs and Concerns of Expectant Fathers.*[1] A second edition appeared in 1993.[2] It has also been translated into several languages and published worldwide.[3] It has been out of print for some time, yet few newer books have been published on men during their partners' pregnancies. For this reason, many pregnant couples have requested copies in the twenty-first century. Inspired by my daughter and son-in-law (and two grandchildren) and with great emotional support and the cover design from my son, I decided to update and publish this 2014 edition, albeit with a new title.

In the three decades between the original survey of 227 expectant and recent fathers, I have conducted two subsequent (Internet) surveys of approximately one hundred additional fathers. The combined results indicate that a lot has changed for new dads and a great deal has remained the same.

Among the changes are dramatic shifts in birthing facilities and choices, a greater welcome to dads' participation in birth, an increasing age of both parents for the birth of the first child, and a significant increase in nontraditional family arrangements, including far more children being born to unmarried couples. There has also been a welcome cultural transformation of fathers playing a more active parenting role with infants.

What have not changed much are the relatively unaddressed needs and concerns of expectant fathers. That was the core of *When Men Are Pregnant: Needs and Concerns of Expectant Fathers*, and it remains the core of *When She's Pregnant: The Essential Guide for Expectant Fathers.* The quotes from the 2013 interviews are remarkably similar to those of men in their fathers' (and grandfathers') generations.

[1.] Impact Publishers, Atascadero, CA.

[2.] Delta paperback (Bantam, Doubleday, Dell).

[3.] Information available at www.jerroldleeshapiro.com.

Throughout this book, I have used the terms "husband" and "wife" to indicate the couple about to have a child. I mean no disrespect to any family form in using the traditional labels. It is clear that the number of children born to and living with their natural parents is dropping with each census report. Regardless of the forms of connection: marriage, cohabitation, single parents, or same-sex couples, the psychological issues remain the same.

For the purposes of this book, what is significant is that women have the child, and while a man's participation may last only a few moments, the vast majority of men take becoming a father quite seriously. Indeed, as you read this book, you will likely be as impressed as I am of how becoming a father may be the most significant event in a man's life.

It would be wise for us to understand that fact and to better understand why it's important to learn what goes on for men whether or not they are married to the mother of their children.

Notable Changes

Age of Parents. When the first research/survey was done, the average age of respondents was approximately three years younger than in the 2013 survey. This matches the national averages. The oldest first-time mother in the early survey was a statistical outlier at thirty-nine. In the 2013 survey, fully half of the respondents were in their thirties and forties. In the 1980s, celebrity dads such as Tony Randall, Warren Beatty, and Larry King were big news when their children were born. Nowadays, both moms and dads are much older.

Marital Status. A rising number of twenty-first century moms are not married. In 2009, nationally, 41 percent of babies were born to unmarried women—a percentage that has been increasing since the millennium. The largest percentage increase in such births has been to the thirty and older age group. By contrast, the percentage of teens having out-of-wedlock babies is less than half of the 1980 figures. Apparently, sex education with teens is having an impact—there is also a sharp reduction in teens with sexually transmitted diseases.

However, in 2010, close to ten million single moms were living with children under eighteen in the United States, doubling the figures from a generation ago.

Health and safety. The number of mothers and fathers who smoke, drink alcohol, or use drugs during a pregnancy has dropped precipitously. Similarly, car safety seats and certified strollers have become near universal. Toy safety and child protection laws have also become central to many parents.

Pregnancy rates. Fewer children are being born, and families are smaller. In 2009, pregnancy rates for US women (102.1 per 1,000 women aged 15-44) had been dropping noticeably for thirty years. The abortion rate continued to drop as well, and in 2009, it was lower than at any time since 1976. Pregnancy and abortion rates were also less than one half the prior generation rates.[4]

What the Changes Mean

Relationship forms and the sizes of families may change with the times, but becoming a father remains a remarkably significant event in the life of a man. His concerns, needs, and worries as he is thrust into new roles and responsibilities have gone significantly understudied. My hope is that this book will allow expectant fathers to become aware of more of their personal internal experiences and also help them understand what other new dads are experiencing. It may also help pregnant women understand better what their partners are experiencing and help them find new and more effective ways to connect with their partners.

Welcome to Life's Greatest Adventure

Preface to the first edition of *When Men Are Pregnant* (updated slightly)

Becoming a father was the single most powerful event in my life. Even though I was a clinical psychologist with a specialty in family therapy, I had little preparation in my past for the role of expectant father or daddy.

When I was first encountering my own emotional reactions to the pregnancy that produced my daughter, Tasha, I searched the existing literature for help in understanding some of my personal reactions. The lack of available resources and information was astounding. I began to talk with friends who had already been expectant fathers and was amazed at their insights and their willingness to share their deeply personal experiences. These informal conversations and long discussions with my wife, Susan, helped me become aware of and come to grips with my own experiences.

The informal questioning grew into a formal research project in which I interviewed 227 expectant and recent fathers from all walks of American

---

4.   All these data are culled from government census information, the CDC (NCHS) and the National Vital Statistics System.

life. Their open and frank expressions of their personal experiences are the cornerstone on which this book is built.

As any endeavor that is driven by deeply personal needs, *When Men are Pregnant* is in many ways the book I wished I had available during the nine months in which Susan was pregnant with Tasha. I hope it will serve you personally in that fashion.

This book is intended to help expectant fathers, their pregnant partners, and their counselors make better sense of the experiences of the earliest days of fatherhood. It is, I hope, a one-stop, complete psychological resource for men from the time they decide to have a child to the early days of being home with that child after birth.

A brief note about style: While the vast majority of expectant fathers are married, I recognize that a sizeable number are not. To avoid excess wordiness and confusion, I have referred to your pregnant female partner as "your wife" throughout the book.

Because of the intensely personal nature of the material garnered in interviews, the names of men and women who are quoted have been changed for purposes of privacy. However, personal characteristics and the content of their quotes are unchanged.

Jerrold Lee Shapiro
Los Altos, California
March 2014

Acknowledgments

Many people played a role in the development and production of this book. Among them, a few individuals stood out for their faith in me and the project. I especially want to acknowledge them for their support and assistance.

First and foremost is my wife, Susan, who gave time, love, and tremendous backing throughout the five years of research and writing. She read and proofread each chapter and made excellent suggestions for improvements. Without her, there would have been no book or experience of fatherhood.

My adult children provided support, inspiration, and help. My son, Gabriel, designed the cover of this book. My daughter, Tasha, helped with the latest online interview protocol and provided critical observations. My son-in-law, Aaron, offered me frank comments and the benefits of his experience as a recent dad. During the writing of prior editions, both Tasha and Gabe sometimes had to remind their daddy to stop writing and come out and play.

Dr. Michael Jay Diamond of Los Angeles also provided support and encouragement as well as theoretical discussions of the subject. As a close friend and fellow father and author of *My Father Before Me*, he has always been an inspiration.

My friend and colleague Dr. Larry Peltz of Santa Rosa, California, has long encouraged me and has been a model of what an excellent father looks like.

Two men were especially helpful during the long months between the completion of the work and original publication with Impact Publishers. Dr. Martin Greenberg of San Diego, author of *Birth of a Father*, was more than encouraging. He gave his time, expertise, and energy to a stranger who happened to share his interests. John McLain at Santa Clara University also gave his time and expertise to this effort. He worked tirelessly to help publicize the work and was responsible for the article that I published in *Psychology Today*. John went far beyond the call of duty on his job.

Dr. Katharyn May (later at University of Wisconsin), a pioneer researcher in the area of expectant fatherhood, was also generous with her time and research.

I am especially grateful to Dr. Robert Alberti of Impact Publishers for his considerable editing of the manuscript and prompt action in producing this book.

A special note of thanks is extended to my two former students and current colleagues Kate Wolf Pizor, who proofread and edited the final two chapters and extended her knowledge and caring in many ways, and Richard Kleiner, whose doctoral dissertation research provided a basis for some of the conclusions drawn in the study.

Support and reading of the early drafts of this work were also extended by my colleague Alan Scheflin at the Santa Clara University law school and by my brother-in-law, Dr. Tino Bernadett of Palos Verdes.

Many of my colleagues at the University of Hawaii School of Nursing and Santa Clara University Counseling Psychology Department also provided support and useful ideas.

Of course there would have been no book without the sincere, personal cooperation of the 227 fathers who were interviewed and who completed research scales and the many clients with whom I have been privileged to work as a therapist. While their names do not appear in the book, their influence and lives provide the color.

Chapter 1

The Lost Cord

People smile and tell me I'm the lucky one, and we've just begun.
Think I'm gonna have a son.
—"Danny's Song" by Kenny Loggins

The sentiment on the front of the pastel greeting card was innocent enough: "Congratulations on the birth of your daughter." The zinger was handwritten inside: "To the proud parents, especially the mother, who did all the work."

My wife and I received the message shortly after the birth of our daughter, Tasha, in a card sent by three members of my family, who lived six thousand miles away, people who at that point had never met my wife.

I shall always treasure their ability to encapsulate an entire cultural phenomenon into a few lines.

As a culture, we truly value motherhood, child-rearing, and reproduction. People pamper the pregnant woman. They show many signs of what used to be called polite manners or social graces. Adolescents will hold doors open for her. Strangers will offer your pregnant wife their seats on the train or stop them on the street or between aisles at the local supermarket to chat about their own pregnancies and children and theorize as to the sex of the unborn child.

When my wife, Susan, was pregnant with each of our children, she was approached by several strangers and acquaintances who said that they were certain that the baby would be a boy (girl) because of her facial coloring, because she was carrying the fetus low or straight out in front, or because of the content of their own recent dreams. Their ability to predict correctly seemed far less important than their sincere desire to make contact with

17

someone so close to the beginnings of new life. Our culture loses its paranoia and its boundaries in the presence of pregnancy.

This is surely as it should be. If your wife is pregnant, she probably feels more vulnerable as well as more special at this time. She is inhabiting a changing body, there is a new life inside her, her hormones are acting in novel ways, and she clearly deserves any extra support and care that is offered.

But what about you, *the expectant father*? Even though you do not have any authentic physical signs of pregnancy, you will soon begin to experience a host of emotional and psychological reactions, if you've not already. Psychologically, you are just as pregnant as she is. You soon will be just as responsible for the care of a helpless infant. In modern America, expectant fathers are expected to play an increasingly greater role during pregnancy, birth, and the early years of child-raising.

Where will you get the extra support, understanding, and caring as you go through this most important transition in your own life? How will you and your partner develop the teamwork necessary to handle the added responsibilities and duties that accompany this addition to your family? Will you be ready for the new emotions, roles, rules, status, and behaviors you are about to face?

How This Book Originally Came to be Written

From March 10, 1981, to December 2, 1981, I was an expectant father for the first time. It was an exhilarating, exciting, and wonderful experience. It was also a quite confusing and anxious time for me. I was entering for the first time into a world in which I barely knew the basics. I was surprised by the wide range of my emotions. As an academic, I followed a course normally easy for me when I am anxious: I read and ask questions of experts. When I attempted to resolve my concerns about expectant fathering in my typical manner, I experienced a rude shock. In searching the parenthood literature available in libraries and bookstores, I discovered that virtually 98 percent was devoted to *motherhood* and *childcare*. A growing but still quite small number of books describe the male experience of parenthood. (A listing is available in the bibliography.) But essentially, no attention was paid to the emotional and psychological aspects of *becoming a father*. Even Bill Cosby, in his hugely successful book *Fatherhood*, gives only passing reference to how fathers feel before the birth.

Most books on pregnancy present only a few pages or a lone chapter addressed to the expectant father. The predominant message given is that pregnancy is a time of stress for women and the new father's job is to help minimize this stress as much as possible. The primary focus of this literature has been on the importance of the new father actively participating in pregnancy, childbirth, and childcare. Substantial emphasis is placed on the need for the father to take on a larger share in the countless household tasks that accompany the arrival of a new child. Expectant fathers are encouraged to be present and assist their partners during labor and delivery.

There is good reason for this emphasis: it is excellent advice. Yet it was insufficient for my needs. Even within exceptionally valuable childbirth education classes, which encourage and teach active father participation, there was little recognition of the internal struggles, thoughts, conflicts, and emotions of the parental experience for fathers.

A curious paradox was building in me. Although I was receiving encouragement to be actively involved in the pregnancy, at the same time, I sensed less interest in what was happening inside of me. Any support or caring I offered my wife or our unborn child was eagerly welcomed. However, I was discouraged from expressing or even having anxieties or fears.

Susan was connected to our child through her body. Lacking any physical umbilical cord, my relationship with our unborn daughter had to occur in my own heart, mind, and soul. Sharing space with my joy was a multitude of concerns and a growing acknowledgment that nobody wanted to hear about them.

It occurred to me that if an experienced family therapist was only marginally prepared to handle expectant fatherhood, the problems could seem even greater for men who were untrained in psychology.

Since 1981, my professional career and my personal life have centered on the theme of fatherhood. From 1981-1985, I carried out a series of studies of expectant and recent fathers. These 227 men represented a cross section of new American fathers from all walks of life. They graciously completed paper-and-pencil tests and allowed themselves to be extensively interviewed in a most personal way.

From 1988-1992, I conducted a comprehensive study of *family genesis* (the metamorphosis from a couple to a family), then completed two more studies (2002 and 2014) on men who were becoming fathers. During that entire period, I have actively followed men's transformation to fatherhood in my clinical practice.

The original book, *When Men Are Pregnant*, and two subsequent books on fatherhood[5] emerged from these personal and professional experiences. I hoped that it will help expectant parents better understand and cope with some of the hidden difficulties in a pregnancy. Now over thirty years (and a

---

5. *The Measure of a Man: Becoming the Father You Wish Your Father Had Been* and *Becoming a Father: Contemporary Social, Developmental and Clinical Perspectives* (with Dr. Michael J. Diamond and Dr. Martin Greenberg).

son and two grandchildren later), the goal is to bring the insights of a host of expectant fathers to the generation of their sons.

A Cultural Revolution

The experience of fatherhood in present-day American culture is radically different than it was one or two generations ago. Fathers of men who were born between 1940 and 1965 probably had a clear perception of their parental role during pregnancy and beyond. As family therapist Dr. Richard Kleiner quipped,

> *The father's job was pretty much to deposit* some sperm *and then to pay for college . . . Unless it was a girl, of course, and then you had to pay for a wedding too.*

The prime concern for men of your father's and grandfather's generation was to provide financial security. They worked hard, often long hours, and felt great pride when their wives could be "free" to be homemakers and mothers. Family duties were more clearly divided, each partner playing a proper (culturally-limited) role in making the family a going concern. Child delivery was handled by a pregnant woman and her obstetrician, occasionally with help from female relatives. Child-rearing was essentially the job of the mother, whose workplace was the home. This division of labor left the "labor" of pregnancy completely within the female domain. The expectant father's role in labor and delivery was to make his partner as comfortable as possible, get her to the hospital in time, smoke cigarettes, and pace the well-worn circle in the hospital waiting room, anxiously awaiting the nurse's report on the sex of the child and the health of his wife and baby. It was rare for a dad to be present at the birth.

Stories of fathers who handcuffed themselves to their wife as she was being wheeled into the delivery room are still part of the folklore passed on to new generations through childbirth education classes.

As recently as the mid-1960s, only 10 to 15 percent of fathers were actually present at the birth of their children. Those who were not medically trained (or acting in an emergency) were greatly restricted. A man who insisted on being present for the birth of his child could find himself placed in a wheelchair or other restraints in the delivery room.

Today, however, husbands rarely plan to be absent. A 1982 Gallup Poll indicated that 85 percent of all husbands expect to be present for the birth of their children. They also expect to play a much greater role in childcare than their fathers did. "Help around the house" is no longer limited to keeping the family car in running order and the lawn well-trimmed.

It should come as no surprise that men of previous generations cannot comprehend the pregnancy experiences of fathers today or serve as effective role models. Pregnancy is no longer exclusively "women's work."

In a late 1980s *Cathy* comic strip by Cathy Guisewite, Cathy's male coworkers discuss a host of alternative birthing practices while their (older-generation) boss questions, "Whatever happened to the good old days when women were the only ones who got pregnant?" It would be an easy mistake to think that our own fathers were less concerned about their wives and children than are fathers today. Their absence at the birth of their children was culturally sanctioned, and their caring had to be expressed indirectly in terms of the kind of house and larder to which the new baby would come home. One man I spoke with on a radio talk show said that he just had the opportunity to be present at the birth of his granddaughter and realized how much he had missed. He also reported that during the delivery of his own daughter, he was "feverishly finishing the cradle so she would have a place to sleep." Let us not miss the fact of his own "labor." Other fathers of the forties, fifties, and sixties confirm the cultural expectations of their generations. One grandfather-to-be told his son,

> *I don't know how you could be in there (delivery room). You couldn't get me in there with a gun to my head.*

Another recent father was told by his father and mother that they thought it was wonderful that he would be with his wife but indicated that he should watch her *face* the entire time and not look "where the baby is coming out."

A man reflected to his son-in-law,

> *When your wife was born, I went bowling. I just kept bowling and bowling until my sister came and told me she and Ma (his wife) were both okay. Then I went and had a stiff drink and went to the hospital.*

Of course, many women who became mothers during the middle of the twentieth century may have been as psychologically distant from births as fathers. The vast majority of women were given general anesthesia, fell asleep, and woke up sore and with an infant. One woman who had her first two children under general anesthesia and the last one "naturally" said,

> *I think I'll always feel different about Jimmy. I felt him come out of me, and Gil (husband) was there. It was instant family. With the two*

oldest, it was different. I love them just as much, but their birth was more like a present than a shared experience.

Times have changed.

It is only natural that such major changes in cultural expectations have brought with them some new problems for fathers-to-be. From the moment he is aware of the pregnancy, a man is thrust into a world which is novel and alien. He is encouraged, instructed, and cajoled to be part of the pregnancy and birth process, something he typically knows little about. He is expected to become the "coach" or supporter of his wife, who has the leading role. There are no direct family role models since his own father almost certainly didn't do what he is expected to do. Indeed, his own father may well discourage participation by indicating how reticent he would be.

The Cord that Double Binds

These difficulties, while troublesome, can usually be overcome with care, education, and preparation. There is another problem, however, that is far more serious and confusing: a cultural double bind which I call *the Lost Cord.* On one hand, men are encouraged and induced to "participate fully" in the pregnancy and in the birth of their children. They are also—in virtual contradiction—given to understand that they are to remain outsiders. It is clearly indicated that the request for your full presence excludes the expression of any feelings that might upset "the little woman." Your anxiety, anger, sadness, or fear is unwelcome. You will also discover that little recognition will accompany your expected participation.

I experienced this personally during a childbirth education class I attended with my wife. As the class toured the labor and delivery rooms of the hospital, the instructor gave a thorough description of the facilities. She discussed the use of several surgical implements and tables, stressing how well the hospital was equipped to deal with emergencies. When we returned to the classroom, she asked, "Now doesn't everyone feel more comfortable?" It was apparent to me that several of the fathers-to-be were feeling uneasy. I ventured a reply, "Actually, I feel much more nervous now." Other men nodded in agreement. To my astonishment, not only was my comment ignored, but within a matter of seconds, the topic of discussion had shifted to female reproductive anatomy. When I subsequently queried the instructor about this privately, she responded, "What did you expect me to do, get all of those pregnant women upset?" The message was loud and clear: *fathers shall not express nervousness about childbirth.*

This example clearly illustrates a double bind: the difference between the spoken (conscious) message "please be involved" and the unspoken codicil "except for your negative feelings." To be truly involved, a new father must come to recognize his own feelings. When he does, he will soon realize that not all of them are positive. At times during the pregnancy, he will be as frightened, concerned, sad, and angry as his wife.

What can he do with this frustration?

He can retreat to a traditional male role and remain strong, silent, and distant from his wife and the pregnancy. Of course such detachment is viewed quite negatively by current standards. He is also very likely to feel abandoned and lonely himself.

He could take the opposite tack and express his "negative" feelings, but then he risks upsetting his wife and experiencing some unpleasant guilt.

It is not always easy to make a choice. For many men, knowing and labelling their specific feelings is quite difficult. Yet if you cannot share your concerns, you could well find an increasing emotional distance between you and your partner and a greater potential for loneliness and self-doubt.

There are solutions to this paradox, and they are addressed in detail in the later chapters of this book. For the present, it is important to recognize that it can be as difficult—psychologically and emotionally—to sit next to and try to comfort a person with morning sickness as it is to *be* nauseated. Neither person will feel able to do anything except endure and hope that it will end soon. A man who is culturally oriented toward action and competence might prefer the personal nausea.

Any sensitive person can understand that a young woman about to have her first child might feel frightened and ambivalent. She is going through a host of physical, emotional, and psychological changes. It is generally accepted that this is a time for her to be pampered, humored, and specially cared for. The physiological and psychological changes are carefully explained to her, and all of her changes are supported by biology. She is expected and allowed to be fearful, sad, angry, or confused about the pregnancy and is generally encouraged to express these feelings.

By contrast, her mate has neither the biological basis nor the social support for the changes and feelings he is experiencing. Should he express equivalent feelings, he is likely to be seen as selfish, inconsiderate, or chauvinistic. It is not a time for him to be pampered or to spend time developing a relationship with the fetus. He is encouraged to keep such feelings to himself and not to risk making his spouse any more uncomfortable than she already is. Instead, he is given the strong message that it is now a time for him to "man up" and care for her. He is thus discouraged from even feeling "out of sorts" for fear of the impact on the mother-to-be.

Some men unconsciously compensate for this by actually developing some physical signs of pregnancy. Generally speaking, however, men's "sympathetic" pregnancy symptoms (couvade syndrome) generate little sympathy and are treated humorously by family and friends.

The uncertain position men occupy in regard to pregnancy, birth, and child-rearing has its ironic side. Much of the increase in men's participation grew out of the push for equality fostered by the women's movement. Yet during this crucial transition in a couple's life—the beginnings of family—women are reinforced for being "the little woman," understandably a bit helpless, and men are rewarded for being the "strong, silent type." Both are anathema to removing sex-role stereotyping.

This is quite a trap for the man who is earnestly trying to be the perfect expectant father. If he refuses the new role of fatherhood and leans on traditional values (that pregnancy and birth belong to women), he runs counter to current cultural mores and will receive little reinforcement from others. By contrast, if he does allow his sensitive side to come out, he could well be reprimanded for potentially endangering his wife in her "delicate condition."

Your pregnant partner probably does want to know most of what you are feeling during her pregnancy. The problem is that she has other needs pulling for her attention as well. Unfortunately, expectant couples too often respond to a misunderstanding by partially withdrawing from each other during the pregnancy.

The dilemma is not unresolvable. Each chapter in this book contains specific advice for meeting these challenges at various stages of the pregnancy and birth.

Complications

Picture the young father struggling with his own impulses to be a son and to be babied. We find him sitting next to—but disconnected from—an exhausted woman with a slightly green complexion. Her shape is changing, and her eyes are closed, her hands resting somewhat tentatively on her stomach. She is focusing inward. It is hardly a surprise that they bypass each other and both feel somewhat lonely and isolated. Let's take a closer look at what they're going through.

The child is father to the man. It has been well-documented that expectant fathers tend to reexperience the feelings of their own childhoods. Two perspectives are common:

1. A reassessment of their own fathers, perhaps with more understanding than previously possible
2. Reliving the feeling of being a child

Many men strive at this time to reconnect with their fathers or with other significant males in their lives, searching for a role model, desiring to be close to things masculine, or building a bridge to a parent who may have been emotionally distant in the recent past. Attempts to get close to their own fathers automatically activate feelings of being a son.

If a man grew up with lots of rejection in his family, pregnancy is likely to rekindle feelings of *abandonment*. Conversely, if a man felt trapped in his original family, he might reexperience feelings of *suffocation*. In either situation, the pregnancy is likely to exaggerate any unresolved problems from his personal childhood.

For a man, pregnancy often reproduces a childlike feeling of helplessness. It's frustrating to have such a great deal of responsibility and so little authority to change anything. If a man grew up in a home where he never felt a sense of mastery and self-worth, he is likely to be greatly affected by this "lost cord" paradox. His wife feels a greater need to rely upon her partner and is responding to a maternal pressure to turn inward. She is beginning her relationship with the new child growing inside her. While asking her husband for more attention and affection, she has less emotional energy to give to him in return.

This is one reason that some marriages which already have serious defects may not survive the added stress of pregnancy. Indeed, in my years as a family therapist, I have observed that couples who try to "fix" a failing relationship by having a child are most often unsuccessful.

Abandonment. If fears of being ignored, rejected, or abandoned are prevalent in the psychological makeup of the potential father, the enforced solitude, caused partially by his wife's focus inward, can be a time of severe testing.

*   His spouse is not available emotionally.
*   She may also be unavailable physically or sexually.
*   He needs to reflect on the present and upcoming changes in his life,
*   He lacks friends who are sufficiently familiar with the issues and able/willing to talk about them.
*   He believes that he should be strong enough to handle these things without help.
*   He lacks awareness of what is making him uncomfortable in the first place. (i.e., he often will relate the discomfort to financial or job concerns).

This time is even more difficult if he comes from a culture or value system that embraces the traditional male role model or "macho" image. Over the course of many years, he will have learned a number of ways to keep these fears from his conscious awareness.

The normal person a man would turn to at this time is the person whom he trusts most, who knows him best, and who is going through a similar experience: his wife. However, it is at precisely this time that she is most unavailable. This is a serious conflict: both people are most vulnerable and most needy simultaneously. In a strong marriage, such adversity can bring them closer. In a weak relationship, it can be devastating. One phenomenon which can develop out of this conundrum is the all-too-frequent extramarital affair during the third trimester (discussed in detail in chapter 7).

Suffocation. Men who have no particular fear of being left alone, however, may have a history of an overintrusive or suffocating parent or partner. Their predicament can be just the reverse.

Thus, if a man treasures his freedom from any constraints, a newly needy wife may indeed be an ordeal, especially if he grew up in a home in which he had no real privacy. A man who has spent a good deal of emotional energy avoiding being trapped or suffocated might find the pregnancy a serious threat to his psychological well-being. As Tom, an expectant father and well-known attorney, put it,

> *What I liked best about Joan was her independence. She was the first woman I ever met that didn't need to be involved in every aspect of my life. She was a real independent woman in the best sense. All of a sudden, she's pregnant and crying a lot, always wanting to know where I am every minute of the day, and forgetting what I tell her . . . just sits around and wants me to hug her all the time. I don't think I have read an entire section of the paper without her sitting on my lap . . . It makes me crawl. I just want to escape.*

Like many men, Tom handled this conflict by getting especially involved in work during the pregnancy and "making himself scarce."

That doesn't always work. Liam reported that his pregnant partner would not let him work. He reported,

> *I am not exaggerating. Here, let me show you. Twenty-two texts from her in just over an hour. I keep telling her, I need to focus on my job, but then she just texts me back and says I don't care about her or the baby.*

The intimacy continuum and paradox. Two needs that are evident in humans shortly after birth are *security* and *freedom.* The ability to confront and deal with these needs is essential for true intimacy.

Abandonment	Freedom	Security	Suffocation

The two needs are shown on a single continuum. Extreme levels of freedom may result in feelings of abandonment, and excessive security can feel constricting and suffocating.

The art of intimate relating is in the balance of these two basic needs. Pregnancy can make it difficult to maintain this balance, particularly with a new family member to account for in the equation.

A successful pregnancy necessitates a close and intimate partnership between the expectant parents and a generally supportive environment. There are many pressures that will test a relationship during this time. In addition to unresolved conflicts of the past, there are a host of concerns that relate entirely to the present. These concerns are the primary focus of this book.

Chapter 2

Seven Major Fears of Expectant Fathers

It's a lot like walking into a pitch-black room and suddenly
thinking that there may not be a floor.
—a client describing his concern about
his impending new role as a father of twins

What feelings do expectant fathers keep private? The 227 men who took part in my original study and ninety-nine in follow-up interviews expressed several fears that were usually not discussed. I have grouped these concerns into four categories: performance fears, security fears, relationship fears, and existential fears.

Performance Fears

Queasiness

I want to be there, but I also want to be a million miles away. You know, I just don't do well with blood and stuff. I keep thinking I may faint or something.

That's how an expectant mental health counselor father described the most universally expressed fear. Men who genuinely wanted to participate in the birth itself nevertheless anticipated discomfort about observing the abundance of blood and other bodily fluids that are normal during delivery. The expectant father wonders about his ability to "keep it together" and truly help his wife through the process.

Niles, a computer salesman, became progressively paler even as he described his distaste for "messes." He must have alluded to "losing my cookies" ten times in a five-minute interview period. The significance of this concern was confirmed in other interviews with recent fathers. The typical man extolled the recent birth of his child, praised his wife's strength and courage, and then proudly depicted how well *he* came through the procedure (without vomiting or fainting).

Fear of nausea is really not surprising in our culture, given our penchant for avoiding and isolating unpleasantries and illnesses.

The medical establishment often helps encourage this fear. Many doctors and nurses show distaste or dislike for fathers' presence during delivery and frequently tell fathers that they may faint and get in the way. One already-nervous man was told by his wife's obstetrician,

> *Okay, you can be present. But if you faint, don't expect us to worry about you lying on the floor with all the blood and gore. We'll just have to kick you out of the way and go about our business.*

Other men told of obstetricians who demanded a guarantee that the husband would "not be a problem." San Francisco TV talk show host Ross McGowan recalled being strapped into a wheelchair "for his own protection" to prevent him from fainting or causing trouble during the birth of his second child.

Although these examples represent extremes, they do demonstrate common, and thankfully diminishing, medical attitudes about fathers being part of the delivery team. An expectant father concerned about his own ability to handle queasiness may become discouraged by such suggestions of horrors and become quite uncomfortable with the insensitive "black" humor common to hospital staff.

Marcus humorously quipped,

> *I was cool about being at the conception and went with her to some of the prenatal visits. [I] was okay in the classes when they showed those videos and am happy about having a child. The thing that I don't want is to have to be at the birth itself. I'll be a fine dad. I just don't want to have to see the kid coming out, followed by God knows what.*

Humorist Dave Barry famously noted that when asked if he wanted to see the placenta when his daughter was born, a punishment for a very serious crime would be to have to view some number of placentae.

In fact, it is a rare event for men to actually have difficulty in the delivery room. Of all the fathers we interviewed, only one described getting even the least bit light-headed, and he was in a hot delivery room during a stifling day in August, even the nurses were complaining about the conditions.

The reality that expectant fathers rarely feel queasy does little to diminish their concern. The fear of fainting is likely to increase if "complications" require surgical procedures such as Caesarian sections. Some hospitals deny fathers the right to be present at a surgical birth. A man who observes his wife being cut may indeed be more prone to discomfort, especially if he is unprepared for the surgery.

Caesarian births (and the special preparation necessary for them) are detailed in chapter 11. It is interesting to note here that some fathers are more relieved than upset by a surgical birth primarily because of the switch in responsibility from them to the obstetrician.

There are three sources of assistance for fathers who anticipate queasiness at the birth: information from experienced fathers, opportunity to discuss the fear openly; and preparatory films or visits to live births.

- *Experienced fathers.* Often, the most helpful information comes from veteran fathers. Prior to the birth of my daughter, one friend told me,

  I was really afraid of getting faint, but when I got in there, I was so into the birth and Marisol, I forgot to get sick.

- *Opportunity for discussion.* Men who fear light-headedness can benefit from discussing their concerns with others: their partners, medical or birthing people who are sensitive and unlikely to turn the concern into a joke, other men who share the concern, and recent fathers who have just gone through the experience without fainting. To discuss the fear may initially highlight it, but eventually, most men will be calmed by repeatedly expressing their concern and receiving an understanding or reassuring response.

- *Vicarious practice.* Of considerable aid in preparing fathers for their children's births are the excellent films shown during childbirth education classes. These films of couples experiencing both vaginal and section births can demystify the birth and let the father see exactly what he can expect and what he needs to prepare himself for. Some couples take an even closer step by actually attending the birth of a child before theirs is due.

Responsibility

One day, I was going along happy-go-lucky. The next day, I was the sole support of three people.

More than 80 percent of the fathers shared the feelings expressed by this twenty-two-year-old father of three days.

For many couples, prior to the first pregnancy, both husband and wife work outside the home and contribute financially. As the pregnancy comes to term, the expectant father realizes that he will be the primary (and at least temporarily the sole) financial provider for the family.

The change from an expectation that both partners will work outside the home to an awareness that the woman is limited for some period of time and that there is a helpless infant to care for can be quite powerful. Nothing brings out feelings of responsibility in men or women quite as much as becoming a parent.

Some men cope with this by increasing the amount of work they do around the house. Others take on a second job. Some men switch to more reliable jobs or engage in behaviors that represent "culturally appropriate nesting" for males.

When my wife was pregnant, I found myself allowing my carefully limited private clinical practice to expand. I began working longer hours to build a "nest egg"—a uniquely appropriate term under the circumstances.

A close friend chose the time of expectancy to switch to a more stable job from freelance work. Typical of many American men today, he did not quit freelancing. He simply added the new job and worked harder to "provide."

Having children often brings greater awareness and involvement in political and world events. Individuals who have expressed little interest in issues like political stability, schools, pollution, climate change, nuclear arms, or preserving endangered species may become very involved in movements designed to make the world better for children.

Finally, men frequently take on a magnified sense of responsibility for others in the world. Becoming a father to his own child can give a man a sense of fatherhood to all children.

It is important for an expectant father to recognize the shifting demands and responsibilities brought about by the birth of his child. Major financial, physical, and emotional adjustments will need to be made.

Security Fears

The Ob-gyn Establishment

Medicine that deals with "female" issues remains mysterious, discomforting, and alien to many men. Most men have little information about female reproductive anatomy and do not understand the relationship between a woman and her gynecologist. For years, feminists have written about the dehumanizing quality of much gynecological care. They cite the stirrups, positions for examination, and general attitude of many physicians as dehumanizing, embarrassing, and insensitive. Often, expectant fathers first experience these feelings during their initial contacts with an obstetrics and gynecology staff.

I found my own first meeting with prenatal care particularly distasteful. The nurse who did our initial interview neglected to ask how we felt about the pregnancy, what concerns we had, what we wanted from her and the hospital, or anything similarly helpful. Instead, she began her interview—with two people exceptionally happy up to the point of encountering her—by asking in a derisive tone, "What form of birth control will you be using after the termination of this pregnancy?" She didn't bother to find out whether we might have religious or other objections to such use.

For the first time, I experienced personally the well-documented dehumanizing and insensitive treatment possible by some ob-gyn medical personnel. In fact, only my wife's calm acceptance of the treatment and the firm pressure of her hand on my thigh stopped me from making several angry statements and gestures. Subsequent insensitive treatment by the administrative and nursing staff was consistent with this initial contact.

Our experience was not unique. Many of the men interviewed for the original study indicated similar experiences and feelings. Information was frequently withheld or presented in a degrading manner. Many expectant fathers told of how their expressed concerns about what to do were frequently silenced with looks that implied "Only a fool would ask that."

Several men who accompanied their wives to prenatal pelvic exams reported that they felt coldness and nonacceptance from the same members of the obstetrical staff who had previously praised them for being so involved. The men were often made to feel out of place in the examining rooms and offices. There was often no place for them to sit or stand out of the way to observe relevant tests or information.

Explanations for this go beyond the nature of the facilities or the infrequent attendance by males in this female domain. There are clear indications of an attitude that expectant fathers do not belong. During one visit, in the minute or two it took to weigh my wife, three nursing staff members carrying full bedpans "accidentally" bumped into me and said "excuse me" in the way that comedian Steve Martin has made famous, a way that indicated that I shouldn't have been there. Times are improving.

In the thirty years between 1980 and 2010, the percentage of female obstetricians has risen dramatically. Today, approximately 70 percent of medical students and residents with this specialty are female. This trend bodes well for pregnancy care and sensitivity to women's concerns. It may also indicate a change for more considerate treatment for expectant fathers.

In my most recent (2014) survey of forty-nine fathers, 60 percent of those who responded to the question reported that they felt welcomed during prenatal exams. Of the 40 percent who did not, the most prominent concern was that the staff either focused entirely on their wife, "As if I didn't exist," or shifted their full attention to the husband, ignoring all nonphysical needs of the pregnant mother.

Of particular interest were two comments by two expectant fathers whose wives gave birth at the same facility in California:

Carlos reported,

> They were very nice and considerate, and the doc really took her time asking both of us about what was going on. Then the nurse came in and, after doing the tests, turned to me and said with great understanding, "It's hard to your wife looking so uncomfortable and to see us draw blood from her. My husband says that he'd much rather have the needle himself than see me or the kids in pain."

Pedro's experience was quite different. He wrote,

> First of all, our appointment was at 2:00 p.m., and they kept us in a crowded waiting room till three while the staff laughed and gossiped behind the desk. Then they took us into the room, and there was one chair for the doctor and the exam table for Sonja, so I had to stand. Then the first thing the nurse asks is why do I have to be here. Is there a problem (abuse) in our marriage? Then when the doctor came in, the first thing she says is, "Are you here for a particular reason or just tagging along?" She may have been joking, but it wasn't so funny.

Questions of Paternity: Irrational Fears

> I was joking when I told my wife, "If that kid has blond hair and blue eyes, I'm gone."

What is surprising about this "joke" is that *more than 50 percent of the* men *surveyed acknowledged fleeting thoughts, fantasies, or nagging doubts that they might not really be the biological father of the child.* This disquieting notion is regularly enhanced by several sources in modern-day culture. Occasional reports in the news or on the Internet often exaggerate the numbers of husbands who are not the birth fathers to startling headlines and viral dissemination. There are daytime television programs that specialize in determining paternity through DNA tests and "outing" publically the couple. Women who are unsure of the biological father periodically ask advice columnists whether they should tell their husbands. Abby and Ann always recommend *against* disclosure.

In addition, many men insensitively react to news of a pregnancy or a child who does not look like the father, with unintentionally cruel jokes about the mailman or other workers around the home.

There are a significant number of couples who mistakenly try to resolve marital difficulties by having a child. If the marital problems included extramarital affairs, fears about another man being the biological father are obviously increased.

There is also psychological justification for paternity fears. It takes men longer to believe the pregnancy is real than it does their partners. Part of the reason for this, of course, is biology. A man must experience the pregnancy through his partner. In addition, the very notion of being partially responsible for something as monumental as the creation of life can be somewhat mind-boggling. Any personal insecurity will argue against the potency required for such an enormous task.

Gary, a chef and recent father, has bright-red hair, freckles, and a very unique appearance. His infant son has all the same characteristics. Despite the obvious genetic similarity, Gary reported his doubts:

> *Well, I'd never tell my wife this, but I really think that Scotty is not mine. I wonder about it from time to time, and it hurts me . . . I know she'd be real upset if I told her. I really do trust her. I know she has not had any affairs since we've been married. But I don't know. It still bothers me. I even think Scotty looks just like me, but somehow, it feels like someone else had a hand (or something) in it. I feel embarrassed even telling you. It's so disloyal to my wife.*

Men were not alone in harboring such concerns. Greta, a pregnant woman present for part of her husband's interview, volunteered,

I have had dreams or daydreams or thoughts that the baby is not my husband's, even though I have not had any other relationships since we've been together, and that's five years. It's weird.

Women also report a corresponding fear that the baby might not be theirs: they worry that the hospital staff has mixed up the babies in the nursery.

This question of paternity is not attributable solely to modern times. Aristotle, writing in the fourth century BC indicated,

The reason mothers are more devoted to their children is that they suffer more in birth and are more certain that the child is their own.

Do expectant fathers really question whether or not their wives have committed adultery? The answer is no. In fact, when we asked men who admitted to doubts about paternity whether they thought their wives might have been unfaithful, many of the respondents were downright insulted. This is a curious paradox.

If a man truly doesn't believe that his wife has been unfaithful and yet worries that he is not the father, there must be some very powerful feelings behind his uncomfortable thoughts.

The primary feelings of this type are *basic insecurity* and *humility*. "I doubt that I could really do anything as monumental as create human life. Surely, that is more a godlike than a manlike thing to do, and it would have to be done by someone far more potent and accomplished." Such beliefs may persist in the complete absence of rational evidence. They linger precisely because they cannot be countered, even by DNA testing. They are based on feelings of inadequacy (which may or may not exist in conscious awareness). Reason and rationality are very poor allies in the fight.

The feeling of *inadequacy to create life* also shows itself for men (and women) in "psychological denial" of the pregnancy—a phenomenon that lasts for some men until after the birth.

Such doubts—however unrealistic—may also be a reaction to a man's feeling of *being left out* of the pregnancy. The doubts provide him with an emotional buffer from the pregnancy and birth. If he's not sure the child is really his, he can gain psychological distance from the process by telling himself, "I'm just an observer here." This emotional protection may actually allow him to be a more active participant during the delivery.

The expectant father with paternity fears needs a generous portion of reassurance that he is loved and that there is no other man in the picture. His wife is best suited to give this support but often does not know that her partner needs it. He may be unwilling to risk hurting her feelings or insulting her with disclosure of these thoughts.

Questions of Paternity: Realistic Issues

What happens when the father-to-be *knows* he is in fact not the biological father? What additional complications may arise? I have had the opportunity to interview a number of men who became fathers without being biologically involved in the pregnancy. There were five different types of circumstances:

1) *Adoption*—Adoption is a social response to a biological dilemma. It is created when people who are biologically capable of producing children are not able to care for them. Other couples, often infertile, parent the children. Adoption presents particular problems for parents. A comprehensive examination is beyond the scope of this book. However, particular concerns of adoptive expectant fathers are addressed in each chapter. Adoption normally does not bring up paternity concerns for a man unless he is married to the biological mother. An example of this is Louis.

   Louis married Dianne when he was twenty-one years old, and she was 27. While they were dating, she became pregnant by another man. Louis married her "to give the kid a name and because I was lonely" and adopted the infant as his own. However, his concerns about her sexual relationships with other men continued well after the birth of their son. They spent a year in marital therapy working on this problem. Three years later, he became a single parent when she deserted him and the child for yet another lover.

2) *Artificial insemination (known donor)*—Some infertile couples are able to pass on one set of genes through artificial insemination. An arrangement is made for the woman to be impregnated with the sperm of a donor without sexual intercourse. Couples sometimes arrange for the sperm donor themselves. Men whose wives have been impregnated this way often feel uncomfortable and insecure. They have a tendency to compare themselves unfavorably to the donor. This comparison can become an obsession without lots of reassurance or counseling intervention.

   Frank lost his ability to produce sperm through a childhood disease. He and Mary Ann arranged for his older brother to be the donor, thinking that the genetic transmission would be closest to the natural match. However, his childhood competitiveness with his older brother surfaced during the pregnancy in feelings of extreme worthlessness. He successfully overcame these feelings of insecurity only after eighteen months of psychotherapy.

3) *Artificial insemination (unknown donor)*—This is usually easier for the father because "the competition" does not have a specific face or personality. However, the expectant father may have greater worries about the unknown characteristics that are passed on to his child.

4) *Sanctioned extramarital affairs*—Sometimes men agree to have their wives impregnated by another person via sexual intercourse instead of artificial insemination. A man who agrees to this may subsequently suffer insecurity and jealousy about the sexual intercourse and his wife's feelings toward the other man.

Some men who originally thought this would not be a problem for them expressed a lot of unexpected emotional pain when I interviewed them.

Some couples regularly and freely have open sexual relationships with other people. Normally, these "swingers" use birth control for such liaisons. I have interviewed two men whose wives did not know who the biological father was. Both men claimed not to be concerned about being the father of the child; however, neither relationship survived the pregnancy.

5) *Illicit affairs*—Extramarital affairs are an all-too-common occurrence in modern society. Women who engage in such affairs sometimes get pregnant and may be unable to provide reassurance when their husbands have paternity concerns.

Affairs almost always are a symptom of problems in a marriage. When the affair produces a pregnancy, the problems are intensified, and the couple needs the intervention of a therapist (or other third party) to help them unravel the issues. In my clinical experience, these pregnancies often are a way for a woman unconsciously to express extreme hostility toward her husband. Usually, her anger comes from a feeling of being neglected.

In summary, if a husband's fears that he may not be the father of his child are realistic, there is a greater obstacle for the couple to overcome. Few couples can surmount it alone.

Loss of Spouse and/or Child

One apprehension which does have a very real basis in the recent history of humanity is anxiety about the potential loss of a partner or a child. This fear begins to arise for most men during the second trimester and may be based on dreams, family history, or stories of other people. It may also be rooted in an expectant father's increased vulnerability and personal fears of abandonment (at a time of greater dependency than normal). When a man considers the creation of life, he inevitably contemplates the end of life as well.

One man responded,

> *All of a sudden, I am filled with fears of JoAnn and the baby not making it through the pregnancy. I think it started with the conversation with my mother and her reminder that my grandmother had died in childbirth. Now that I think of it, so did her sister. I just can't get these thoughts out of my head. Afraid to tell JoAnn . . . don't want to upset her. Why am I so worried? She's young, healthy, the hospital is good. Why am I so worried? I don't know how I'd go on without her.*

Brian, a thirty-year-old first-time father, talked about a nightmare:

> *I don't know what I'd do if anything happened to Sally. I had a dream one night where I was alone with the baby and she was gone. There was a funeral or something. The baby was tiny, and I didn't know how to hold it. It was crying and hungry. I became aware that the baby was my only link to Sally. I didn't want the baby. I wanted her.*

Jeff, becoming a father for the third time, confided,

> *The thought of Gerri dying made me want to die, but I couldn't. I had to take care of the kids.*

Pete, a very large man and a former professional athlete, who actually came close to losing his wife, confessed,

> *I feel so guilty. I was the one who got her pregnant. I wanted kids. Now she has to face all the pain and danger. I wish it was in my hands.*

This conversation took place while his wife was still in the hospital five days after the birth of their son. She had hemorrhaged after the birth and required almost two weeks of hospital care.

Pete's reaction is understandable, but why would so many men have such fears? We live in a modern society with advanced medical technology. The likelihood of anything really going wrong is quite minimal.

Actually, while most births are uncomplicated and "natural," there is some risk involved. In fact, the United States has a higher infant mortality rate (thirty-fourth in the world) than most other modern industrialized nations.

In addition, these concerns are deeply rooted in our cultural heritage. Only two to three generations ago, childbirth and its complications were the leading cause of death for women of childbearing age. Tragic stories and fears are normally transmitted down the generational ladder, especially when we have personal knowledge of these ancestors and their lives.

At a time of vulnerability, a man's fears are enhanced, and he tends to cling to relationships that are secure. However, in his yearning for additional security, he is faced with a pregnant woman who is emotionally turning inward toward the infant and away from her husband. At such a time, it is easy for his unconscious mind to exaggerate her temporary distancing into a sense of permanent loss. We know from a variety of sources that the death of a spouse or a child is the highest stressor in modern American society. Hence, the fear of such a loss is also very stressful.

This is another kind of fear that is hard to discuss with anyone else. Many expectant fathers are reluctant to add to their spouses' stress. Why trouble her with your concern that she or the baby might die? Might it be true, as many men feel, that bringing up such a morbid subject would actually increase the likelihood of its occurrence? Isn't your wife just going to tell you that your fear is irrational?

Your pregnant wife is in fact the best person with whom to discuss these concerns. She shares your fears of abandonment and special vulnerability. She will have her own concerns about the pain and danger of childbirth as well as a worry of being left alone should something happen to you.

One fear familiar to all expectant parents is the discomforting anxiety that something will be wrong with the child. It is a rare parent who neglects to count the newborn's fingers and toes. Apprehensions that the child might have severe physical or brain defects are quite universal. Indeed, as the age of marriage and parenting rise, the increased incidence of sometimes serious problems is also increasing. Recent studies indicate that it is not only the mother's age that is a factor. An aging father's genetic contribution may be a significant factor in the likelihood of autism and other inherited problems.

This is one concern that you are advised to discuss with your partner. You can share mutual support as you go through it together. Do some research in the library, on the Internet, in the hospital, or in the doctor's office. Read about some preventable problems and take dietary or other steps to reduce their probability. If, for example, you both are in a cultural group that have a higher probability of carrying a fatal illness such as Tay-Sachs disease, prenatal or preconception testing may be of great value.

Relationship Fears

Being Replaced

As I was talking to a couple about the upcoming birth of their first child, the husband told me,

> *The one thing that really scares me is that the best of our lives together will be gone as soon as the baby is born. In some ways, I'm already feeling displaced by the turtle (the couple's pet name for the fetus).*

His wife looked perplexed. As he looked at her, he said,

> *It's already harder to get physically as close. Also, I am less vigorous in our lovemaking. And when you become quiet and I know you're communicating with the turtle, I really feel left out. It's almost as if the primary relationship is with him, and I'm the fifth wheel.*

Many men expressed similar feelings during expectancy. In fact, they frequently described scenarios wherein they saw the husband-wife relationship as secondary to the mother-child bond.

Because most of the men in our original study had their own parents' relationship as a predominant model, it is not surprising that they have such fears. Many of the men who were becoming fathers in the late twentieth century had parents who lived through a period of great turmoil in marital relationships. Frequently, their own fathers were committed to the "earning-a-living" standard customary in the division-of-labor, mother-as-homemaker-and-child-rearer days of the 1940s, 1950s, and 1960s. In such families, the primary relationship *was indeed* between mother and children, with the father somewhere in the background. In addition, aspects of mother-son relationships were often Oedipalized ("When daddy's away, you're the man of the house"). Memories of such experiences can be quite powerful when these sons are themselves in the process of becoming fathers. After all, in their personal experience, daddy *did* get pushed aside by the mother-child relationship.

Furthermore, expectant fathers of today are more likely to have experienced the demise and divorce of their parents' marriage (or of their own prior relationships}. That experience can reinforce a concern that the marital relationship might buckle under the additional stress and changing role expectations created by the entrance of the third person.

This fear of losing the relationship and the security concerns already discussed play an important role in an infrequent but much-popularized and dangerous phenomenon: the late-pregnancy affair.

In my work as a clinical psychologist and researcher, I have interviewed twenty-seven men who have acknowledged having an affair during the latter stages of the pregnancy. Most of these liaisons had certain aspects in common:

- There was usually no history of previous affairs.
- The men felt particularly abandoned during the pregnancy.
- They had a strong need to talk to someone about the pregnancy and chose a woman because they found women more understanding than other men.
- The woman was usually someone the wife knew well (in one case her sister, in another her mother), someone who was also feeling estranged by the wife's pregnancy. Thus, the potential for a destructive liaison was enhanced.

Of particular interest was the fact that *each of the men described high sexual attraction for his wife during the pregnancy*. Feelings of rejection were more powerful motivation for such an affair than disinterest in a pregnant shape.

There is no way to excuse or minimize the impact of such an affair, despite the great sense of remorse and guilt reported by the errant husbands. Even with psychotherapy, it is very difficult for couples to overcome the devastation to the marital relationship and to the wife's trust in her husband and other women.

Existential Fears

Existential Issues: Life and Death

Of all the novel experiences caused by a pregnancy, none is so subtle yet so dramatic as the profound consciousness of the biological life cycle. Several men reported feeling closer to their own deaths as a result of being so intimately involved with the beginnings of life. Many considered their own mortality for the very first time. They also described an increased sense of connection to their own fathers and made efforts to become closer to them during the pregnancy if it was possible.

Modern American culture stresses youth, activity, and life, deemphasizing death and aging. We have managed to avoid the reality of death by sanitizing it and anesthetizing ourselves to it (by presenting it so casually and frequently on television, for example). We tend to live as if there were no endings. Most people regard death as something that happens to others and gradually learn to face death only as it strikes parents, friends, and others who are close emotionally or physically.

Since death is so much avoided and kept from daily awareness, while birth is expected to be such a happy event, most expectant fathers were surprised by their feelings about the fragility of human existence.

As they anticipate the birth of a child, however, men begin to ponder such issues. The very fact of becoming a father changes a man's generational position. Until he is a father, a man remains identified as a son. As a member of the younger generation, he believes that he has more time. If his own parents or grandparents are still living, he has a psychological buffer against death since he expects to outlive them. So long as they remain alive, he feels safe. However, once he becomes a father himself, there exists a new younger generation, one he cannot expect to outlive.

The fears of death are described well by one expectant father (a university professor), who said,

> I really never thought about death before or life and what it means. I was always interested in getting ahead, doing well, publishing, et al. When we got pregnant, all of that changed. I was so much more interested in what was inside Nancy's belly than in esoteric research. My previous work seems so insignificant by comparison, and yet I'm also so afraid that this magic of birth makes me vulnerable to tragedy beyond any scope I truly imagined. I am very much in touch with my mortality and how fleeting this mortal coil truly is.

A father of two sons expecting his third child remembered,

> I became aware when Carla was pregnant that I no longer had any right to die. That might sound weird, but it's true. I stopped taking such huge risks. I found myself driving slower, avoiding rougher areas of town . . . all for the reason that I was now important to this little thing and I couldn't die because he needed me.

Finally, a quote from a widower whose first wife had died in an accident while she was pregnant:

> I just tried to shut out all those thoughts when Cindy (second wife) got pregnant, and I was able to do it somewhat, but sometimes at night, I'd watch her sleeping, see the big tummy, and get absolutely terrified that somehow I would not be alive to see the baby born.

Issues such as one's own mortality and the generational connection between father and child are not understood or resolved easily. It does seem likely that this concern over life and death is in some ways basic to all the previous fears. Each in some ways represents an anticipated loss, helplessness, inadequacy, or limitation. As the ultimate limitation, death colors all of our life experiences.

Feelings, Fears, and Fatherhood

If it is as important for a father to get a solid psychological start on parenthood as it is for a mother—and I believe it is—then men need to have fuller acceptance for their natural fears during pregnancy.

Most of the fathers in my study dealt with their negative emotions in relative isolation rather than as they normally would have at a time of stress, turning to their partners for support. Believing that their worries were unique and afraid of making the pregnancy more burdensome for their wives, they kept these fears to themselves. Unfortunately, this further isolated the expectant father and made close emotional connection more difficult for both spouses.

Several factors play a role in increasing the number and intensity of the expectant father's concerns. Of prime importance is the health of the marital relationship. What will a child mean to the relationship between husband and wife? The child who is conceived to fill some deficit in the marriage will be experienced in a different way than a child who is part of a plan to enhance an already satisfying relationship. Few issues are laden with as much potential for a power struggle as is the timing or planning for a child. The father who is having his first child (or his fifth) because he couldn't say "no" to his wife or because he feels guilty and is making up by "giving her a baby" is likely to have great resentment toward the child.

Similarly, if the pregnancy represents a father's attempt to recapture his own youth, to succeed where he has failed at other life achievements, to replace or continue himself, or to eliminate personal loneliness, the child will fall short of expectations, and all will suffer.

Conditions that led to an increase in fears in the study included the emotional, physical, and sexual unavailability of his wife; the lack of friends or family with whom he could share his reflections and worries; a personal belief that he should be strong enough to handle these things without help; and the lack of awareness that the pregnancy was in fact the main source of his worries.

One fact which emerged clearly in my study was that *when men did share their concerns with their partners, the relationships deepened, and closeness increased.* Couples who sought short-term counseling for pregnancy-related stress also reported very positive relational benefits.

As men become more involved in the process of fatherhood, expanded understanding of their needs and fears is increasingly important. The father-to-be cannot be fully a part of the pregnancy and birth unless these fears are fully recognized by himself, his spouse, his family, and society in general.

The next eleven chapters examine the pregnancy experience for men, from the decision to have a child to bringing the new baby home.

Chapter 3

Maybe Baby

> *The difficulty in life is the choice.*
> —George Moore (1900)

With greater control over reproductive destiny and with an increased awareness of family and professional roles brought about by the women's movement, many couples today are much more conscious about the decision to become parents. Children are no longer an automatic by-product of marriage. You have a lot more leeway in planning the size and timing of your family.

Having greater freedom of choice, however, does not necessarily make things easier. Any freedom entails corresponding responsibilities. You have to face such difficult questions as follows:

- When is the right time to have children?
- Is our relationship strong enough to care for a child?
- How many children do we want to have?
- How many years apart should the children be?
- Are we ready for a child now?
- What about the impact on our careers?
- Can we financially afford to have a child now?

Adding to this uncertainty is the fact that pregnancies do not always come about on schedule nor cooperate with planning. Many fathers expressed concerns about timing, finances, career issues, notions of child-rearing, division of labor, ambivalence, and fears.

One father, reflecting on the differences in the decision-making process he and his wife went through before becoming pregnant with their second son and his parents decision to have him, concluded,

> *My parents laughed at the interminable discussions Cassie and I had about whether we wanted a child, when we would have one, the cost of children, the best ages for us to be when we had a child, how to space children, who would do what kinds of childcare, what would happen to each of our careers, and how to make decisions about schooling, religion, and discipline. My mom said all she and Dad did was get married and "do what came naturally." It was assumed that he would work outside the home and she would be in charge of homemaking and childcare. All the other decisions were pretty much a matter of the neighborhood we lived in, the church, and God's will.*

Laughingly, he added,

> *In a way, I think that life was easier on them because of that . . . I'm pretty sure that we'd still be discussing options if the diaphragm hadn't slipped (twice).*

Making Decisions: A Human Dilemma

Whether you realize it or not, you make decisions based on your beliefs, values, personality, past experiences, and the current situation. For some people, emotions are the ultimate guide, while for others, logic generally prevails. Some rely more on tradition, while others value innovative solutions. Decisions can be made as a way of making a statement to yourself or others or by contrast to avoid attention, shame, or embarrassment. Often, the nature of the decision determines the manner in which it is made. Some decisions are not made consciously at all. People simply "let events take their course and see what happens." For some of us, it seems that the larger the decision, the more it is left to chance.

Carl Jung, discussing the process of human decision making, stated,

> *The great decisions of human life have as a rule far more to do with instincts and other mysterious unconscious factors than with conscious will and well-meaning reasonableness.*

When a decision must be made by a couple, the process is complicated even further. Each individual's concerns, unconscious needs, and decision-making style are involved, as well as the manner in which the couple functions as a unit.

Decision Making for Couples

The way you and your partner make decisions will resemble some combination of each of your individual personalities. The ensuing hybrid will have a manner unique to the two of you as a unit.

Joe and Mary provide an example of this. For Joe to make a decision, all the factors must balance. He carefully weighs all alternatives and chooses the path that has the lowest likelihood of failure. By contrast, Mary, his wife, makes decisions more on the basis of her dreams of perfection and "going for broke." When they need to make a decision together, they typically do not develop a mutually determined solution. Their unconscious agreement is that the person who feels the strongest gets to make the decision with the other spouse going along. Sometimes their decisions are dominated by dreams and gambling and other times by safety concerns.

Frequently, at least one of them has misgivings and sometimes lingering resentment.

Dave and Sue have a different pattern. Dave's decisions are almost always based on his "here-and-now gut feelings." He is whimsical and changes his mind often. Sue, however, is particularly aware of social concerns and norms. She frequently consults with her mother and sister before making a big move and is always sensitive to other's reactions. Because of these differences, they seem to be in an almost-constant state of disagreement. The decision-making style that they have unconsciously worked out is one in which he continuously generates options and she vetoes any that she deems socially inappropriate.

Each couple must find ways of developing a workable "combined couple" mode of decision making. Both of your individual styles must be taken into account, with each of you having input into the final resolution. Both partners must feel that their perspective is being taken seriously, or an interminable *power struggle* and substantial resentment could result. Victory in such a power struggle is measured more by the choice of method that is to be used than it is about the specifics of the argument itself.

It is most important for an individual to stage the battle in his/her own ballpark (a psychological home-court advantage). Thus, in Dave and Sue's relationship, if the decision is to be made primarily based on feelings, Dave is much more the expert and will usually prevail. By contrast, if social concerns are to guide the choice made, Sue is the expert. Agreement about the venue of the discussion is the most important aspect of the struggle even on an international level. At the peace negotiations designed to end the Korean War, it took the conferees as long to agree on the shape and size of the table and relative seating as it did for them to agree on substantive issues.

If you and your spouse have vastly different styles, you may well spend a great deal of time jockeying for the *method* of discussion. Once this method is agreed upon, the actual decisions can be almost-foregone conclusions. In the most common situation, the husband reacts to his world primarily with thoughts and his wife more with feelings. The real argument will be to determine whether his cognitive manner or her affective one will be most influential in the final decision.

As more people become involved in any decision, negotiations become even more complex. When you are considering family issues, parents, in-laws, and extended family members can add both assistance and confusion. Decisions made by larger groups have that many more "home courts" beckoning. Certainly, anyone who has been involved in group decision making can appreciate the old joke defining a camel as "a horse designed by a committee."

The Decision to Have a Child

How does a couple decide that they want to have a child? The process is a highly complex result of their styles of decision making, along with their hopes, desires, fears, and pasts. Sometime ago, I saw two couples in marriage therapy who dealt with most of these issues in determining whether or not to reproduce. Let's take a look at their experiences.

The Baby Decision: Al and Judy

Al is forty-two years old. He is Jewish and is the oldest child of Holocaust survivors. He married Judy three years after his "painful" divorce from his first wife. He left his first marriage with three children, a vasectomy, and a deep mistrust of women. Al is "cautious in all things." In his work as an accountant, he has been able to effectively employ his natural personality. He considers himself to be a very rational person and tends to make most decisions in his life by carefully weighing alternatives and then choosing the option that has the "highest probability of success and lowest risk ratio."

Judy is twenty-nine years old, is a successful potter, and is married for the first time. She grew up as an Irish Catholic but left the church when she was fourteen and was feeling so sexual. "I just got tired of confessing the same thing every week." She tends to be very intuitive, feeling oriented, dramatic, and flamboyant. She describes her three-year marriage to Al as the perfect blending of reason and emotion. "I provide all the excitement and fun, and he sets the limits and explains why we enjoy it." Judy gets along with Al's three children and is described by everyone in the family as "the perfect step mother, although the first two years were rough." She is particularly close to the sixteen-year-old daughter who was the first to come and live with them. All three children now live primarily with Al and Judy.

They came into marital therapy following a few stormy months in which they had fought repeatedly about Judy's recent desire to have a child. She described her "transformation" when she realized that she would be thirty soon, and the noblest cause in the world is creativity, and the highest creativity is that of human life.

Al responded by pointing out to her that having a child involved a great number of responsibilities, that he had a vasectomy because he had his children already, that their financial situation with three children going to college in the next five years was unstable, that he was too old and tired to begin again, and that she had known all of this *before* they got married.

The more emotional her need became, the more rational was his disagreement. They were at loggerheads not only because they disagreed on whether or not to have a child, but much more importantly because they weren't even discussing it in the same language. She expressed her emotional and spiritual needs, and he talked in rational, conscious, logical arguments that resembled a carefully planned balance sheet. By speaking in such different languages, they were unable to ever talk directly to each other about the same issues. Only after therapy began were they able to sort out the emotional from the rational components and discuss the matter with (instead of at) each other.

The upshot of the therapy involved his agreeing to bring more of his own irrational unconscious decision making to the fore and her discussing more of her own logical needs to have a child. Once they did begin to really talk, three of his emotional issues surprised both of them: his fears of another operation (reversing the vasectomy), potential impotence (which he experienced for six months following the vasectomy), and infertility; his worries about how his own parents would react to having non-Jewish grandchildren; and his concern that Judy would not stay interested in mothering.

Judy, by contrast, talked about how having a child would solidify their marriage and reduce her fears that he might leave her and about her intense desire to fulfil her destiny as a mother by having her own children. She also expressed her wish to have someone else in the family provide some of the energy and excitement. "Sometimes, I wish Al would come up with just one crazy plan or adventure."

For Al and Judy, the decision to try and get pregnant involved many factors. On the surface, they have a major disagreement about whether or not to have a child. However, when we consider the unconscious components of their decision-making process, we can begin to appreciate the host of significant issues which must be addressed before they can make an informed decision about trying to have a baby.

Although their situation involves some special problems, the complex process that they have to go through to arrive at a decision is similar to most couples. Thus, while Al might make all his personal decisions in a carefully weighed conscious manner and Judy might make hers in a spur-of-the-moment emotional way, together as Al and Judy Green, they must make decisions mutually. Until they find their cooperative couple style, they will struggle over intangible and elusive concerns.

How did they resolve their dilemma?

Al did decide to have a reverse vasectomy only after talking to his parents about their feelings about grandchildren with a non-Jewish mother. Both of his parents cared so much for Judy that they indicated that the religious matter was his and her problem, but that they would welcome another grandchild. Judy also made it clear to Al that she would be an active mother. She looked forward to spending time with a child and could easily put her career on "half speed." In fact, the more they talked about her plans, the more Al was able to understand that Judy had very much thought through the details. With that in mind, they took the necessary steps. He was also able to enjoy making a decision that was *not* logical or rational, but that "felt right at the time."

After two miscarriages and twenty-nine months of trying, they had a daughter.

Mel and Lynn: One Decision, Two Issues

Often, one partner wants children, and the other does not. When I first met Mel and Lynn, she was thirty-five years old, a successful businesswoman, and for the first time feeling both the "pangs of unfulfilled motherhood and the ticking of the biological clock." She and Mel had been living together for five years and had discussed marriage favorably. Mel, who was also thirty-five, had always feared commitment. As Lynn talked about her desire to have a child, he found himself losing his sex drive despite describing himself as having a "high libido." He had begun to work long hours, coming home tired, uninterested in sex, and "needing space." In discussing the matter, he expressed anxiety about the fact that a child meant a permanent commitment. He was particularly concerned with being replaced in Lynn's heart by a new child. These feelings were not new to Mel. When he was seven years old, his sister was born, and his experience from that moment on was that he was automatically a big boy essentially replaced as the center of family life. He also had left previous relationships when the question of children or a permanent connection came up for serious discussion. For Lynn and Mel, their different desires necessitate that they struggle with this question until one of them changes or the relationship deteriorates. Furthermore, because of her age, a lengthy struggle is in effect giving into Mel's wishes to not have a child. For them, the baby decision also represented a decision about the relationship itself.

The Baby Decision: Couple Styles and Reasons

If you are to make a decision about your reproduction, you will have to face your negotiating process.

Will you and your wife each have equal weight in the decision, or does one have greater say? Do either of you have veto power? Will the decision be made by the person with the strongest feelings or the one with the most doubts? Will one of you decide and the other acquiesce? Will the force of tradition, spiritual belief, religion, moral conviction, or values be the telling factor? What role will the opinions of family members or friends play in the decision? If all of your social group are having children, what additional pressures will that engender?

Each couple makes the decision to have a child in their own unique manner. Some couples have a child as a means of fulfilling lifelong dreams or to reify an already-strong union. Yet others do so in a vain attempt to fix a deteriorating relationship, to punish or entrap a partner, or to pressure a partner to marry.

For some, it is a carefully weighed, well-timed, and planned choice, for others the result of a carefree, passionate encounter. Whatever the reasons, the decision to try to have a child has a long-term impact. Whether there is a successful pregnancy, a miscarriage, or a discovery of infertility, there are long-lasting if not lifelong implications.

Essentially, couples make the baby decision in one of three ways: careful planning, passive planning, and accident.

Careful Planning

Some couples plan to have a baby in the same prudent manner in which they make all other choices. They will discuss their options, examine the pros and cons, carefully evaluate the timing, and then go ahead and try and maximize chances of being pregnant. Mac expressed it this way:

> Sandie and I always wanted to have a family, but we also wanted to make sure that we were financially and emotionally stable first. She completed her education and worked for four years until she could get an administrative job that allowed for a six-month maternity leave, and then we decided to conceive. We figured that if we timed her ovulation properly we would be able to determine the approximate due date. We also decided to start in January because that gave us a three-month margin to conceive and have the baby in the (next) tax year.

Glenn, another expectant father, said,

> We knew we wanted at least two children, and we wanted them three years apart, and we didn't want Betty to be having any children after forty, so since she was twenty-eight and we wanted to be open for at least three children, we figured we had to have the first before she was thirty. The pregnancy came along during the fourth month that we were trying, so we're right on schedule.

Yet others have described using a basal thermometer, being abstinent prior to ovulation to increase sperm count and the probability of conception, taking childbirth and child psychology classes prior to becoming pregnant, reading, talking to parents, or fitting the birth into the couple's plans. Chuck indicated,

> We figured we'd get pregnant and then take off for Europe for a few months and really enjoy being together before there was a third person to be concerned with.

Even the best-laid plans oft go awry, however. Conception is not always predictable, nor is nature fully cooperative, as Chuck commented,

> We were ready, excited, prepared. Everything was all set. We even had the room arranged. Then the doctor told us it was twins. That was a real curve. We aren't ready for twins. I even remembered a show we saw on TV where one of the babies was aborted and for a moment entertained that thought. I couldn't do that, but this twin thing throws off all our plans.

Pat and Stan: The cautious-impulsive couple. Surprisingly, some couples who are careful and planful in most things have a more cavalier attitude especially with very large decisions. Pat and Stan are a good illustrative couple. As a computer programmer and a certified public accountant, they claim to be "conservative, careful, cautious, and moderate in all things." Changes are instituted via a "process of careful study, needs assessment, and joint problem solving. Then we shop around for the best deal we can get." What is particularly interesting is that while they use this discretion in purchases of popcorn poppers, curtains, toothpaste, and groceries, they have impulsively decided to buy a new house and have a child. Such caution, spiced with impulsivity especially around issues like getting pregnant, is not uncommon.

Passive Planning

Couples who make the decision by passive planning are those couples who do nothing to prevent a pregnancy or who stop using or inconsistently use birth-control methods. As one new father put it, "We stopped using *serious* birth control."

Jackson, an expectant father, said,

> Well, we started using penetration before putting on a condom. And sometimes when it wasn't exactly around the middle of the month, we would just go ahead and not put it on.

Haim described it differently:

> Our religion makes deliberate birth control out of the question, so we just assumed we'd have as many children as God wanted us to have. I got to tell you this is our third, and it seems a greater blessing than even the first two.

By contrast, Henry characterized the upcoming birth as

> a disaster. It's about the worst thing that ever happened. It's our third, and we can't afford any more. I've been laid off, she has to stay home with the kids, and she refuses to use birth control. I hate her and the kids and the priests and can't even walk out because this kid is now "in the oven." I think she knew I was thinking about taking off and got pregnant to keep me here.

Sometimes the planning is done by only one partner. One man told us that he was "deceived" by his wife because she was afraid of losing him. "She stopped taking pills without telling me." Another expectant father told his new (second) wife that the reversal of his vasectomy was definitely a failure, while medical reports indicated a slight possibility that it was successful. Yet another man said that he was aware that his wife had forgotten to put in her diaphragm and decided not to "remind" her. One husband who wanted another child woke his wife from a sound sleep to make love. In her drowsy state, she claimed that she didn't have the energy to make birth control arrangements. Another couple had their fourth pregnancy when the wife who was faced with the decision of going to work outside the home for the first time in her life managed to do some sexual things that the husband had been particularly requesting for years. In the excitement, she neglected to mention that there was no birth control.

Passive planning problems. This passive type of conception can create some great conflicts for couples. One person can feel betrayed or lied to, and the opportunities for misunderstandings are quite substantial. It is especially problematic when one partner did not really have a part in the decision.

Passive planning excitement. Several men reported that passive planning was also more thrilling since it wasn't a sure thing and it was really a possibility at any time. There was something about the "Russian roulette" quality that made for greater passion and excitement for the couple and greater thrill and joy over the birth itself.

Sunil told the interviewer,

> *I was so turned on during our holidays. We forgot to bring her diaphragm and just went ahead anyhow. It was as exciting as the first time we ever had sex. I think we spent more time in bed that week than in the six months before it. I know it sounds crazy, but the chance that we could have a kid made it wild.*

Later, he confessed,

> *I sometimes get so turned on by the thought of not having any protection that I figure out ways to set up situations where we can be away from the diaphragm. Last week, we made love at the beach, and I was as turned on by the fact that there was no diaphragm as I was by being out of doors.*

When queried as to whether he could talk to his wife about this, he replied, "I'd be afraid, because if she disagreed, then she'd be sure never to let it happen." Two days later, Sunil called to say that he had talked it over with his wife, and she was just as excited and had also been finding "accidental" ways of avoiding using birth control.

Accidental Pregnancy

There are a number of ways that a couple can become parents by accident. The most frequently reported of these are the inadequate use of or failure to use birth control, irregular ovulation, and incorrect information that one or both of the partners is in fact sterile. Such surprise children can occur as "postmenopause" pregnancies or after many years of infertility. In rare cases, vasectomies or some forms of female sterilization spontaneously reverse themselves. Finally, there are situations where the pregnancy is the result of a liaison between the woman and another man. Because of this possibility, paternity tests to establish genetic ties between the father and the child have increased dramatically in the first decade of the twenty-first century.

Birth control failure has been the subject of numerous jokes and statistical reminders that any form of birth control is only effective for some large percentage of people. Thus, if the pill is effective for 98 percent of all couples, you could be in the 2 percent of couples who use birth control pills properly and still get pregnant. Abstinence remains the only fully effective method of birth control. In addition, many couples (perhaps also falling into the passive pregnancy group) use birth control devices ineffectively, inconsistently, or improperly. One mother that we interviewed had a second child twelve months after her first because she believed that while she was nursing, it was impossible to get pregnant. Another young mother used a diaphragm that was not fitted by a gynecologist. In 1984, there was a frightening news report that a substantial number of counterfeit (ineffective) birth control pills hit the public market. That could cause accidents even for cautious couples.

Accidental pregnancies and feelings of loss of control. Couples who have accidental pregnancies are most likely to be unhappy about the pregnancy and most likely to have the largest number of pregnancies that are not brought to term. An accidental pregnancy makes both men and women feel particularly out of control.

A forty-eight-year-old expectant father described it:

> *I just didn't know what to do. Masako is 44, the other kids are ready to leave home. I was looking forward to travel and retirement and privacy. Now with a new baby it's starting all over again with diapers, exhaustion, loneliness and I'll be 70 by the time this one's in college . . . I can't even tell her I am angry and disappointed. It's hard enough for her as it is . . . I don't even know how she'll hold*

up through the pregnancy . . . This baby is going to be two years younger than my grandchildren . . . We both thought she already went through the change . . . I just don't believe it . . . You want to know the truth. I actually prayed for a miscarriage.

This man, an administrator with vast powers and responsibility in his work life, was feeling so out of control in this situation that he developed a variety of stress-related physical symptoms that were serious enough to require hospital attention and therapy. He really didn't believe that he could suggest an abortion to his wife or even discuss openly his displeasure with the pregnancy. When they did begin to talk it over in therapy, they discovered that their feelings were identical. It is interesting that they were both disappointed and greatly relieved when she had a spontaneous abortion (miscarriage) in the fourth month.

This ambivalence is not unusual. An accidental pregnancy is not necessarily an unwanted one. Often, couples leave such major decisions to fate and live with the results whatever they might be. Similarly, some couples find that the only way to make a decision this large is to avoid making any decision (including decisions about birth control). Many of the fathers who were in the study talked about themselves being "an accident," and many also talked with some pride or pleasure about the current accidental pregnancy.

Clearly, however, the unwelcome accidental pregnancy has a great potential for serious marital problems. If there is a basic fault in the marital relationship, the pressure of an accidental pregnancy is most likely to bring it into open conflict. Such accidents provide fertile ground for blaming one's partner and for feeling guilty. Many marriages actually break up in response to such a pregnancy or to an abortion decision.

Abortion

Abortion, the removal of a fertilized ovum or fetus prior to its ability to survive independently, is both a medical solution to an unwanted conception and simultaneously one of the most emotionally laden areas of conflict in American culture. It is rare when a decision to have an abortion is taken lightly and equally rare when such a decision does not have some long-term psychological implications for the couple. One of the most difficult aspects of the abortion decision for men is that they feel such a peculiar combination of emotional upheaval, value conflicts, and powerlessness.

Abortion: No man's land. In most Western cultures, the fertilized egg belongs to the woman. One recent exception to this is a 1987 court case involving "baby M" in which custody of the baby was given to the natural father instead of the surrogate mother. Generally, however, it is the mother's decision whether the pregnancy will come to term. After all, *it is her body*. Her body is no longer the property of her husband. Although in some jurisdictions, it is not in the hands of the family, even if the woman is unable to decide. In a particularly painful situation in 2014, a pregnant woman who had been declared brain-dead was being kept alive artificially until the fetus was viable. This decision was made by the state of Texas without input from the husband or the woman's parents.

There has been a major shift in cultural patterns and attitudes, along with the legalization and a far more sophisticated methodology for abortion. While there is no such thing as an "easy" abortion, this option is far more readily available today than it was prior to the famous Roe v. Wade decision in 1973. Because the fetus is part of the woman's body, the decision to have an abortion is completely hers. In most cases of abortion, this responsibility is appropriate. Sometimes, there is no man present to consult; or for a variety of reasons, the couple is no longer a viable entity. In most other situations, both partners agree that the abortion is acceptable under the current circumstances and go through the painful process together.

If the partners disagree, however, the father can only sway the mother's decision by persuasiveness. Many husbands felt that they did not have a say in their wives' consideration of an abortion for an unplanned pregnancy. In the rare situation where the male wants the pregnancy to continue and the woman wants to end it, he has virtually no legal say or influence. In the case where he wants to have the child that they conceived together, he must rely on her to not have an abortion. If he wants the abortion and she does not, he is ethically bound to provide emotional support and legally liable for financial support of the child, even if the woman has no intention of living with him.

Perhaps the most crucial aspect of this dilemma is that most men (including several mental health professionals) feel that *it can't be discussed*. Even husbands felt reticent about trying to influence their wives in making or changing her decision. Such a lack of communication can place an even greater burden on the woman and put her in a position where she feels that she has to make this gigantic choice without support from her partner. Such burdens doubtlessly create mistrust in the marriage. One woman, knowing she was pregnant and fearing any discussion of alternatives, kept it secret from her husband until the possibility of abortion passed. In order to hide the pregnancy, she also dieted, paradoxically putting the fetus at greater risk. When her husband was informed about the pregnancy, he was more enraged about the deception than the conception.

There is no easy solution to such a dilemma. Couples facing such a no-win situation should find effective counseling or therapy quickly to work on their feelings and manner of making decisions prior to trying to get agreement on such a serious life/death issue.

Abortions are not made and forgotten. Often, a prior abortion has a serious impact on a current pregnancy. Bill indicated,

> *Joan was pregnant before. When we first started to date, we had to have an abortion. When she got pregnant again, she wanted to have another, but I couldn't. I grew up Catholic you know. So we decided to get married and have this child. I'm not sure that I really should have done it that way, but I just couldn't handle another abortion.*

Ted also confessed,

> *Marge and I had an abortion, and then we had two miscarriages. I really believe that it is God's punishment for the first one. Now I worry every day about this baby. I have had dreams of a stillbirth or retarded kid. I know that we had to have the first abortion, but I'm so ashamed. She is even worse. She feels that we will be tested for it for the rest of our lives.*

An abortion decision may well be even more poignant if there is doubt about the paternity or if there is good reason to know that it is a high-risk pregnancy for the mother or fetus. Decisions to terminate a pregnancy may also be made if there is a high likelihood that the child would be born with major deformities or brain damage.

The Context of the Decision

The modern Western fairy tale script goes something like the following: boy meets girl (usually under surprising circumstances), he pursues, she demurs, (but not too actively), boy and girl fall in love and go through some trials together, They marry in June and live happily, and the following spring, the first progeny arrives. No decisions are made. Negotiations are limited to minor items. It all just seems to work out according to some divine plan.

This scenario is remarkably enduring in our culture, especially considering the infrequency with which it occurs in real life. The reality of timing in marriage and creation of a family in today's world is not only less predictable but also generally far more complicated.

Someone once described major life events as belonging to two groups: those that occur too early and those that occur too late. Having a child that can be supported, loved, and cared for frequently involves much more than letting nature take its course and waiting until spring.

Often, decisions are made and remade several times before, during, and after a pregnancy occurs. Here are two couples who had many "second thoughts."

Sandra and Gino. Sandra married Gino when she was thirty and he was thirty-eight after a long and often stormy courtship. Gino had been married and divorced, and Sandra had been in two lengthy live-in relationships prior to their meeting. During their fourth year of an exclusive relationship, they married, but not until he had severe doubts and actually called off the wedding twice. Last year, after five years of marriage, they decided to eliminate birth control measures and "see what happens." At the arrival of her next period, Sandra became very depressed. Gino was understanding and helpful but claimed to have no particular feelings of his own regarding the failure to get pregnant immediately. He talked instead about the percentages and the "poor sample test of only one month," etc. Six months later, there was a pregnancy. When Sandra returned from the doctor's office with the test results, she was in her words "bursting with joy but afraid to express it because of my fear that Gino would be very upset."

When she did tell him that she was pregnant, his reaction was complex.

> *First, I felt amazed, almost unbelieving, and very happy. Then I started to get real low, depressed really, and withdrew. Finally, I was all of a sudden noticing all of the things about Sandy that I disliked, from her looks to her personality to her physical being. It was almost as if my mind was finding all kinds of reasons to get out of the relationship.*

When Gino found himself at a party propositioning another woman, he decided that there was a serious problem. It was at this point that they came into marriage therapy.

The therapy began with Sandra talking about her feelings of abandonment and neediness as the pregnancy developed and him describing his (apparently opposite) feelings of entrapment, suffocation and loss of freedom. As the therapy progressed, the issues of commitment became predominant, and the importance of Gino's family of origin entered the picture. It became necessary for him to reassess his relationship with his own family and particularly deal with his feelings about his own father, whom he saw as a failure and a coward for not standing up to Gino's very powerful mother. Gino's feelings about his own youth, and his recollection of how life was for fathers led to so much of his current fears with Sandra. For her own part, Sandra grew up with a very withdrawn father who was incapable of expressing emotion and who was constantly "nagged by my mom for anything he did or didn't do." She became fearful that she (like her mother) would feel emotionally deserted by her husband. Pregnancy had amplified these fears and caused her to be needier and less able to give Gino the time and privacy he needed.

Couples therapy helped Sandra and Gino communicate their respective needs more clearly. They were also able to get a sense that the feelings they were experiencing were normal. In addition, Gino talked with his father about how he had felt while expecting Gino.

As a result of their new understanding, they were able to adjust successfully to the pregnancy and birth of their son.

If you and your partner have an impasse in your feelings about having a child, the predicament may well be fueled by unconscious and long-forgotten experiences. It is worth exploring these concerns with a professional before they develop into a serious marital problem. *Jeffrey and Liz.* Jeffrey and Liz were in the third month of their pregnancy when the first "regrets" began to surface. They had been married for four years and had discussed having a child at great length. Jeffrey was much more positive than Liz but "wasn't pushy about it." In time, she agreed to "see what happened without the birth control." Six weeks later, the pregnancy was confirmed. The couple discussed in considerable detail the various possibilities for childcare. Because both were involved in careers, it was decided that both would participate in the home and childcare. They also planned that Liz would go back to work two months after the birth. Among the concerns that they considered were finances (it was particularly important to him that she continue to earn money after the child was born), the primary responsibility for childcare (she was worried that he would not participate very actively), and family problems (both agreed that their in-laws were "difficult").

Jeffrey was especially concerned that Liz's mother was planning to help out after the birth, and he feared that he would be pushed out of his own home. She confirmed the likelihood of her mother "coming in and taking over" but nevertheless wanted to have her mother around for a short time. Another disagreement involved the location of the birth. Liz insisted on a home birth with her close friend, a midwife, as the birthing person. Jeffrey was worried about complications and very much preferred a hospital birth. One issue on which they both agreed was that she would breast-feed the infant as long as possible.

Two additional considerations weighed heavily on their decision to get pregnant. The first was the presence of twins in both families. Neither of them wanted more than one child. Second, Jeffrey had a brother with Down's syndrome and had serious worries about carrying those genes. Although they had agreed to have an amniocentesis, neither felt very comfortable with an abortion if there were evidence of Down's syndrome.

In the third month of the pregnancy, after a great deal of all-day morning sickness, they came into marital therapy, "wondering if we are doing the right thing."

The concerns that Jeffrey and Liz experienced were not unusual, although the number was somewhat high. They are particularly sensitive individuals and were more tuned into worries that many couples face. Like Gino and Sandra, their communication improved in therapy, and they successfully resolved most of the issues.

Jeffrey and Liz's son was healthy at birth and was fourteen months old when the first edition of *When Men are Pregnant* was written. Liz went back to work when he was a year old (regretfully yet eagerly). Because of the (not unusual) lengthier gap between their expectation of when she would return to her career and her actual date of return, they have faced a financial crunch that forced some alteration in their spending habits. Although he insists that the baby has had a far greater impact on their lifestyle than expected, he says they would "do it over again." Jeffrey has been very involved with their son, but both he and Liz wish he could spend more time with him. Finally, her mother was very helpful during the first week of her grandson's life but has been "a problem ever since." They are currently visiting her only at her house and not allowing her to visit them because "she criticizes everything."

Jeffrey and Liz's experience is indicative of many of the struggles that couples face in deciding to have children. They are quite happy that they have a son and have talked about having another child "sometime in the future" yet still regret the loss of their freer pre-pregnancy lifestyle.

Of course, not all couples make decisions and discuss things to the extent that Jeffrey and Liz do. Some couples do not have the opportunity to even make the decision to have children. Many marriages begin with children present or on the way. These relationships have to deal with the issues in much different ways.

We'll explore some of the key components of the baby decision in chapter 4.

Chapter 4

The Decision to Have a Child

The biggest problem with making a decision is giving up the
alternatives.

In the previous chapter, we explored the ways "typical" couples go about making a decision—or a non-decision—to have a baby. Now let's take a systematic look at the elements of that momentous choice: timing, readiness, finances, career issues, division of labor, social changes, child-rearing practices, natural childbirth, adoption, ambivalence, fear, commitment and permanence, and the option to remain child-free.

Timing

The Roman Hesiod (circa 700 BC) noted,

> *Observe due measure, for right timing is in all things the most important factor.*

Deciding when to have a child is based on a multitude of factors, including romantic beliefs, myths, emotional readiness, pressure from family and friends, finances, careers, and age of the couple. As one thirty-five-year-old, recent, first-time father described it,

> *There were so many things to consider. We were never going to be ready. If it wasn't my career, it was hers. If it wasn't money, it was in-laws. We weren't even sure that we wanted kids in the first place. I guess we just figured out that if we were ever going to have kids, we*

would just have to decide to try and have them. There were always
reasons to do it and others to delay.

Timing of a pregnancy seems to be a most important consideration. A child arriving in a family that is prepared and desirous of the addition is very likely to flourish. By contrast, an unwanted child, who cannot be emotionally or financially supported, entering a family that is in the throes of deterioration will have a much poorer chance of thriving.

Is there a right time for a child?

Young fathers in the survey described the special youthful energy they could share with their children. They talked about growing up together and playing together. On the other hand, they feared that their work and financial considerations would keep them away from home far more than they would like.

Younger couples have to juggle lower-income years, the pressures of starting careers, and incomplete schooling with childcare and beginning their own adult lives. Often, they were resentful of not having had the opportunity to be free and "just a couple" for a while.

By contrast, older fathers talked about having their careers and, to some extent, financial matters more stabilized. They also felt like they had already had an opportunity to "sow their wild oats" and looked forward to "settling down with a family." However, they expressed concerns about how much energy they could give to young children and stressed the organization of their current prefamily lives. Often, they wondered "if an old dog could learn new tricks."

Tyrone, a thirty-seven-year-old expectant father, talked about his thirty-two-year-old wife being

set in her ways. I don't think she's very ready to make changes.
Come to think of it, I'm more set in my ways than she is.

For younger couples, schooling and career is often postponed (especially for the mother) by having children. For older couples, careers are interrupted, and one's status or position in a job or career can be lost. It truly seems like there is always a difficult conflict with regard to the timing of children. Some have suggested that it would be best if the man was older and settled in a stable job and the woman younger and energetic enough to chase around after young children. While many couples have these advantages, there are some distinct problems for couples where the age of the partners is discrepant. There already is a gap between the older and younger member based on life experience and opportunity. If she is younger and postpones her career, that gap might widen, and the chances of her feeling equal will diminish. This may create greater rifts between the partners.

A closely related issue is the *spacing* of children—how many years apart a couple feels is optimal for the children and for themselves. Experts disagree on the "right" number of years between children. Figures of one to five years are consistently used as the benchmark. If children are close in age, parents have to face a massive dose of diapers and exhaustion all at once. On the other hand, if children are too far apart, starting over with an infant can feel like an overwhelming task. If the children are four or more years apart, they will be less able to be companions for each other. If they are too close together, however, they might never have the valuable developmental experience of total attention from parents. In general, it is probably best for the children if they are between two and a half and four years apart. "Best" may be quite different for the parents.

It remains for you and your partner to agree on the number of children and the age distance between them. Of course, your fertility has to cooperate as well.

Readiness

Often, there is no rational, comfortable, or convenient timetable for many couples to make the baby decision. One major emotional component of this decision is the issue of readiness to be a parent. Unfortunately, this readiness may not come to both partners at the same time.

Readiness is most likely to be a problem when spouses are of different ages or stages of personal development, in different steps on career ladders, when the woman's safe childbearing years are running out, or when external pressures influence the baby decision.

Marie and Joe: The ticking of the biological clock. Marie married Joe when she was thirty-two years old. Now three years later, the marriage is floundering in the sea of power struggles, money conflicts, and a claim by each of them that "you're not the person that I married." This is a good time for them to focus their attention on redefining and understanding themselves as a couple. Because of the unresolved couple issues, it is not a good time to be adding a third person to their family. However, Marie fears at thirty-five that if she does not get pregnant soon, she will give up any chance of having a child.

Joe is ambivalent about having any children. As an owner of a fast-food restaurant, he works long hours as his business is just getting "off the ground." At this point in his life, a child would be an added financial and emotional burden. The more he tries to defer the decision, the more panicky Marie gets. She is also very aware that continued lengthy discussion without resolution is a *de facto* decision not to have a child. She is so concerned that she has recently been considering leaving Joe and "finding someone who wants to be a father." For Marie and Joe, the baby decision has to be made before they have worked out an effective decision-making method.

Wilma and Bronson: "I've already had my children!" Bronson was forty-five when he married Wilma. At twenty-seven, this is her first marriage. They met while he was in the process of obtaining a divorce after twenty years of marriage and four children. Prior to their marriage, Wilma and Bronson agreed that they did not want any additional children. Now two years later, Wilma has changed her mind and very much wants to have a baby. Bronson feels that his child-raising years are behind him and does not want to begin again, "at least not until my youngest is out of college."

Financial complications in their lives include large child support payments and alimony. Wilma reports feeling resentful that she is working and living a poorer lifestyle than Bronson's ex-wife. The resentment makes Bronson feel guilty, yet he does not want to have a child

"for guilt or any other wrong reasons." He portrays himself as caught in the middle, being pulled

> *every which way, feeling guilty . . . and wishing a woman could keep to a decision once it's agreed on.*

Wilma feels that she has a

> *right to change my mind. I didn't know how much I would want a baby until I began living with a man I really loved. Right now I feel like I'm working just to keep Bronson's ex-wife at home as a stay-at-home mother. I want some of the goodies too.*

Lisa and Matt: The juggling act. Matt and Lisa are both in their middle twenties. They married just after graduation from college. He went into business with her father and has done very well. Lisa is in her third year in law school and is trying to do well enough to "make it to a big firm." Both of them want to have a family eventually, but Matt is pushing to begin soon. Lisa is afraid of not being able to complete her degree or of not making it big in law if she takes a time-out now. They have begun to haggle seriously, and both have at times flirted with other people who have more sympathetic values. These flirtations serve the purpose of creating enough concern about their relationship that a baby decision becomes a moot question. Another effective measure that they unconsciously use to delay a possible pregnancy is a marked reduction in the frequency of sexual intercourse.

For each of these couples, the differential readiness to having a child is having a major impact on their relationship. It is very important that they resolve the dilemma about having a child, but in each case, they must also resolve deeper problems which involve their method of making decisions and the way they each view the couple relationship itself.

Pressure about readiness does not always come exclusively from the couple. Sometimes, others also influence the decision. Several men indicated that the current pregnancy was related to family or other environmental pressures.

George said that there was so much pressure from his parents that "I think we got pregnant just to get them off our backs."

Wendell thoughtfully commented,

> You know, all of our friends were pregnant or parents, and it just seemed like the right time. I don't think that it was best for us right now, but we would be out of place with our group.

One couple described getting pregnant soon after there was a death in their family as "a way of defying death by creating life."

Finances

Closely related to timing is the issue of family finances. Statistics indicating that a child costs close to $250,000 in the first eighteen years are unnerving to most Americans. Many couples want to build a "nest egg" prior to the arrival of children. Furthermore, modern middle-class American life often requires two salaries to maintain a comfortable lifestyle. Even then, savings are not easy to come by. The arrival of a child has the immediate impact of eliminating one salary at least temporarily. One question that many couples of childbearing age struggle with is, "Can we afford to live on one salary, especially when now there will be three of us?"

Some couples try to determine some set amount of savings that would be enough to support themselves and a child without a serious drop in their standard of living. Questions regarding how much money is enough (and the ability of people to save money for something so abstract as a future family) often are very difficult for couples to settle.

For most couples, finances are a major area of conflict. Commonly, husbands and wives have quite different spending habits—as well as feelings about—and meanings they place on money.

Kevin and Marion, even though they grew up "next door" to each other, come from completely different budgetary backgrounds. Marion is a "saver." The watchwords in her family of origin were "a penny saved is a penny earned" and "money doesn't grow on trees." Marion's first impulse on getting her paycheck is to deposit it in the bank and to pay outstanding bills. Prior to marriage, she had never bought anything unless she'd already saved the money.

Kevin, on the other hand, remembers his father as a "gambler, who was always fond of saying, 'Eat, drink, and be merry, for tomorrow we may die.'" He also recalls his parents ridiculing neighbors for saving their money and then "being too old to enjoy it." Kevin buys everything on credit, is always at the maximum limit of his credit cards, and is frequently overdue with bills. His first impulse on receiving a paycheck is to go out and buy presents for Marion and treating friends for drinks or dinner.

When they were first married, there was no real conflict. With two paychecks and a lot of "honeymooning" in the relationship, Marion was able to become a bit looser about spending, and Kevin became more willing to have bills paid on time. It was when they began to think about children that the extra expense and potential loss of Marion's income began to weigh heavily on their relationship. Their battles became very intense, with her blaming him for "blowing our money and making it impossible for us to have a child" and his berating her for "penny-pinching." Until they were able to come to some agreements about saving and spending money, the baby decision was held in limbo, and resentment grew.

It is not surprising that "finances" are the single most frequently cited reason for marital difficulty. Having children does change one's financial picture, and most couples today have no choice but to face the money and spending questions.

It is important to understand that money has been referred to as *the last taboo*, the issue that many are least willing to share with one another or even their therapists. Perspectives on finances often mirror both internal and interpersonal values and conflicts. Naturally, when there is too little money, it is always a problem for a couple, but emotional and financial concerns also occur for the wealthiest among us.[6]

Career Issues

Two other major life tasks occur at precisely the same time as the optimal childbearing years: the completion of schooling and beginning to move up the career ladder. For women, the twenties are a time of greatest safety and fertility for childbearing. How do couples reconcile the balancing act that

---

6. A comprehensive exploration on financial issues at midlife and beyond can be found in Jerrold Lee Shapiro's book, *Finding Meaning, Facing Fears in the Autumn of Your Years (45-65)*.

must be done to maintain a family as well as two careers? Who delays their career to be home with the children? Who finishes schooling earlier and later? How long is the decision to have children delayed? In American culture, because of the differential earning power of males and females and the many traditional social values, it is normally the woman who delays career in favor of family.[7] It is important that couples agree on a tentative timetable for each person's completion of schooling, resumption of career outside the home, and family needs.

The balancing of schooling, finances, and family time is very complicated. Curiously, as our jobs become more and more specialized, there is tremendous pressure on individuals to be accomplished in so many aspects of life. Many authors have written of the "impossibility" of being a mother, homemaker, career woman, and sexual expert. The problem is similar for fathers. There is great pressure on men these days to be a career success, great father, partner in household tasks, and sexual performer.

Clearly, mastery of all these facets of life is impossible, and attempts to accomplish all of them simultaneously is a primary reason for the record numbers of men and women seeking escape, psychotherapy, and other forms of stress relief. Because of this, couples must work together to develop support and timetables for each of them to pursue their goals as individuals, as a couple, and as parents. This balancing act is constantly in need of alteration, revision, and mutual understanding and support. Should it become difficult for you to negotiate career and related issues, a third-party intervention can sometimes be of great value.

Division of Labor

A major aspect of becoming a family is the vast increase in duties that couples encounter. Richard expressed some of these:

> We were real hang loose, you know . . . like we would stay up late and sleep in on weekends . . . we would go out for dinner or nibble goodies any time day or night. I think we went out to movies maybe twice a week . . . You know, we'd just let things go around the house, and then we'd take one weekend, and both of us would cook and

---

[7.] As male unemployment has increased in the midst of and after the Great Recession of 2008-2010 and as company hiring practices have shifted, more and more families are supported by mothers and fathers are becoming the main childcare provider. This is still a minority, but it is expanding.

*clean and fix until it was done. Now with Patty (eight-week-old
daughter), there's so much to do, and it has to be done now.*

Richard, like so many other parents, has to face the reality of being
on someone else's timetable for the first time in their adult lives. With a
sharp increase in the number of things to do, a reorganization of the duties
is necessary. For many couples, these negotiations can be quite intense.
Will the wife quit work and bear the sole responsibility for childcare and
homemaking? Will she try and do all that and also maintain her career? Will
the husband take on extra work that will make up for the loss of her income
and consequently be away from the home more? Will he expect to go to work
and upon returning take over the childcare from his exhausted spouse? Or
will those roles be reversed? Will both of them try and keep up their careers
and add the extra homemaking and childcare to an already-full schedule? Is
it possible and desirable for each of them to work part-time outside the home
and part-time as primary caretaker?

Often, these questions and their negotiated answers will play a role in
the timing and desire to have children. Experienced fathers were much more
concerned with these questions than first-time fathers. These issues had a
greater impact in determining when and whether they wanted another.

Tanya and Alex had two children in fifteen months. They both have
careers, but she has cut back to handle more childcare duties, and he has
increased his hours at work, trying to get the next promotion that will make
life a lot easier financially. She is now lobbying for a third child. Alex is very
much interested in Tanya's happiness and recognizes her mothering skill,
but he is also sleep deprived and hasn't had time with his friends without
children for almost a year. What's more, his parents are encouraging another
pregnancy, and hers are equally negative about the stress that another
grandchild would bring.

Social Changes

Several changes in family lifestyle have occurred in the past two decades.
Many people living together in stable relationships prior to marriage use a
pregnancy as the reason to "make it official." Since the pregnancy for these
couples is less likely to have been carefully and consciously planned, the
decision process is often more a passive or unconscious one. Furthermore,
the two decisions to marry and to be a parent are made simultaneously. While
this is not necessarily negative, it can provide extra complications for the
couple.

Another change is that many people marry more than once. This has markedly increased the number of stepchildren. John and Emily Visher (*Stepfamilies*, 1979), James Bray and John Kelly (*Stepfamilies*, 1999), Patricia Papernow (*Surviving and Thriving in Stepfamily Relationships*, 2013), and many other authors and stepfamily groups report that as many as 50 percent of the sixty million children under the age of thirteen are currently living with one biological parent and that parent's current partner.

For many adults, marriage itself involves the simultaneous addition of a spouse and children. Step relationships are always complex and take time, patience, hard work, and great understanding to work through. There are also the complicated family relationships in which children from three different marriages live under the same roof. Such blended families including his, hers, and theirs must somehow create new functional family units. Furthermore, the numbers and members change based on full—or part-time living arrangements. Careful discussion of step families is beyond the scope of this book, but it is important to note that the decision to have a child may have far-reaching implications for many people besides the two new parents.

Responding to a college essay question on how she might adjust to living away from home in a dorm, an eighteen-year-old Andrea responded,

> *I have a brother and a sister, two stepsisters and a stepbrother from my stepmom, and four stepbrothers and a stepsister from my mom's marriage to my stepdad. For me, adjusting to dorm life will be a "piece of cake." My worries are how I will introduce my family to some guy I might meet at school.*

For Jack and Bev, the early years of their marriage were understandably difficult. His daughter (Sharon) by a previous marriage was eleven when her parents divorced and Jack moved in with Bev and her two children: Nick, six; and Alisha, four. After a tumultuous year of moving in and out and finally desertion by her natural mother, Sharon permanently moved in with Jack and Bev. Despite difficult adjustments, Sharon and Bev were able to work out their competition for Jack and other difficulties. The ensuing three years were comfortable for all.

In 1984, five years after the divorce, Jack and Bev decided to have a child of their own. As the pregnancy became more pronounced, both Sharon and Nick developed behavior problems. Finally, when Sharon had her own pregnancy scare and Nick was arrested for stealing a video game, the family was referred for therapy. As you might expect, the entire upheaval centered on the children's fears of being displaced by a child who would have biological claims on both of the parents. As an adolescent, Sharon was also embarrassed by the presence of a pregnant "mother" in her home. She felt that her role as the new "baby maker" would be usurped by her stepmother. Once the issues were all discussed and resolved emotionally, the family resumed a normal course.

Child-rearing Practices

It is important for couples to discuss and come to some agreements regarding how they expect to treat, train, teach, and discipline their children. Each member of a couple grew up in a different family with somewhat-unique child-rearing practices. Often, partners differ on such matters as religious training, discipline, demand vs. scheduled feeding, breast vs. bottle feeding, etc. Resolution of differences prior to having a family will save a great deal of future trouble. Often, the most that is ever acknowledged about planned child-rearing practices is "I just don't (do) want to do what my parents did." While many couples do wait until they have a clash of values after a child is born, *it is of great advantage for a couple to develop compatible child-rearing practices as part of the decision to have a family*. You may face some delay in having a family in order to successfully negotiate these issues.

Some of the problems raised by the expectant fathers included differences over academic and athletic success, learning through classes vs. learning through "hard knocks," the influence of in-laws and extended family in child-rearing, choices about the type and quantity of religious training, schooling, the amount of childcare provided by the parents themselves, the importance of other children, neighborhood of residence, and safety matters.

Each of these concerns is serious and significant, and every couple must discuss and work toward *agreement* on those matters that are pertinent to their values and lifestyle. Fathers who "read their wives' minds" and assumed that their wives agreed with them often experienced greater marital discord.

Natural vs. Adoption

The question of adoption usually comes up when there is infertility of one or both spouses, when there is some genetic aberration carried by one or both, or when it is a same-sex couple. For couples who would have a high-risk pregnancy, adoption is frequently a favored choice. However, there are also people who believe that they also have a debt to all children in the world. One of the interviewees for the study responded,

> *Jackie wanted to have our own kids, and I must admit that the thought appeals to me also, but I feel an additional calling. I was*

in the Peace Corps, and to me, providing a good home for a child that would otherwise perish is a higher calling than to add another child to this earth. I hope we can do both, but it is very important to me that we save a living child before we increase the population.

In the 1990s, when the fate of many Chinese or Indian girls was potentially quite unpleasant, even fatal, several American couples saw it as a mission to adopt an Asian child.

The decision to take in foster children or adopt is something that many couples encounter in the process of having and timing a family.

Ambivalence

When people have the opportunity to make choices regarding the timing of their family, they must also face a certain amount of ambivalence about that choice. No decision that is as impactful and long lasting as the decision to have a child can be made without some doubts. How the partners deal with this ambivalence has a great impact on the decision. Some couples have an unconscious agreement that as a couple they will always be ambivalent. Thus, when she is favoring having a(nother) child, he demurs and vice versa.

Fear

Becoming pregnant and having children often brings up lots of fears on the part of both spouses. Physical fears, emotional fears, fears of loss or death, fears recalled from one's own childhood, and concerns about commitment or entrapment all play a major role in the decision to expedite or delay parenthood. Often, couples worry that they are incapable of having children or being good parents. Putting off the beginning of a family keeps these fears in the background.

When couples are not fully conscious of these qualms, other "practical" reasons are always found to avoid the parenting decision. Psychological concerns such as these have a way of guiding our actions without our full knowledge that they are doing so. Many expectant fathers in the study reported fears about having a child which surfaced when they were faced with the baby decision and some form of outside pressure. Two fears which are particularly predominant in pregnancy decisions for men are the related areas of commitment and permanence.

Commitment and Permanence

Becoming a parent inevitably creates changes in the couple relationship. One of the major adjustments that usually takes place for the expectant father is a deepened sense of the permanent connection to his partner. Thus, fatherhood not only bonds the man forever to his child but also to the child's mother. They have shared an experience, have created a life together, and in some way, are now uniquely linked to each other. As one man put it,

> I wasn't sure that I wanted to be with Chris forever. There were a lot of problems in our marriage, and having kids meant that we were together for life. I guess it was the big commitment. Even if we got divorced after we had kids, the kids would be a living link between us. I really needed to be sure that this was the marriage I wanted to be in, not doomed to endure.

This sense of permanence can also have a powerful romantic element for many men, and they become very excited about their family ties. Josh, for example, noted,

> I looked at Penny in a new way when I realized that we could be parents together. It was like a completion or fulfillment of us. It's hard to put into words, but the marriage all of a sudden grew a permanence that would extend into the future. I still get teary eyed when I think about that. My life gained some new mystical meaning, and we were part of the future of the human race.

Other men noted that the permanent connection also provided a welcome sense of security for them. Dave is an example:

> I felt unsure with Patty until Bobby came along. It always seemed like she wasn't completely committed to the marriage. I even had questions about her fidelity. Now it's different. There is so much togetherness. So many things that we need to do together just to keep him diapered and fed, we have to be a team. I really like that feeling of belonging.

If the decision to have children is often seen as the equivalent of making a lifelong bond with one's partner, then the fear of entrapment in a poor marriage is also underscored by the baby decision. Worries about entrapment or suffocation often have a serious impact on timing and on sexual attraction to one's spouse.

The fear of being trapped in a painful lifelong commitment is more emotional than behavioral. Many men do leave relationships after the children are born or even during the pregnancy. The rapidly expanding number of single parent, stepparent, unmarried parent, and blended family households attests to that.[8] In fact, there is reliable evidence that indicates that over 50 percent of all children will live in a home during their school years with either a single parent or with adults who are not their natural parents. Despite overwhelming evidence for the instability of the nuclear family, men frequently report the sense of the marriage vows being "set in concrete" with the advent of a child. Perhaps this very sense of being trapped contributes to the eventual dissolution of many marriages.

While it is true that both men and women can physically walk out on their children, the potential for emotional or psychological freedom is diminished at the point of conception. One expectant father put it so well:

> *I couldn't leave now. I am so curious about how the kid will look. Will it look like me? Like Annie? Both of us? There's also the feeling that our lines (genetic heritage) are intertwined now and will be passed on to the future. In that kid is a totally unique link of Annie and me.*

Thus, because of excitement, curiosity, guilt, fear, or responsibility, a pregnancy links the parents and child in a tighter bond than before.

The Intimate Paradox

In chapter 1, the intimate paradox was introduced. It is the nature of the human species that we are born with certain basic fears and needs. Two such universal fears are of suffocation and abandonment. Similarly, we are also born with corresponding needs for security and freedom. An individual who fears suffocation and must seek freedom is apt to find himself too disconnected to others, perhaps feeling abandoned. Conversely, one who seeks to avoid his fears of abandonment by greater closeness to others must inevitably face the fear of suffocation.

These needs and fears are present in infants and stay with us in a variety of forms throughout our lives. In the course of growing, people come to grips with these apparently conflicting needs with variable success. In developing

---

8.   In the 2010 census, married couples actually fell to below 50 percent of adults. There is wide variation across ethnic groups.

a long-term intimate relationship, you must confront your need for security and safety as well as your needs for exploration and freedom.

Successful long-term intimacy requires that the conflict be resolved such that freedom is possible within the framework of security. An individual who does not feel secure enough will struggle constantly to gain security and avoid the terrible fear of abandonment and loss. By contrast, an individual who fears suffocation will strive regularly for freedom and not directly be concerned with abandonment. Resolution of this conflict is considered by many therapists to be the lifelong work of individuals in intimate relationships. Further complicating this basic conflict is the fact that our needs change throughout the life cycle. Sometimes we are very much oriented toward freedom, and at other times, the need for security must be stronger.

Security and freedom concerns frequently emerge for men as they contemplate fatherhood. Certainly, there is a potential loss of freedom in the need to protect, care, and be responsible for the new member of the family. There is also a well-documented loss of security experienced by many men when they find their wives turning inward and focusing attention on the fetus instead of being attentive to them. Men commonly state a fear during pregnancy that the relationship with their wives will never be as close as it was before, a fear that is often borne out in reality. Many expectant fathers feel pushed out and left on the sidelines. In extreme cases, some of these men felt so far out of their own family and so insecure that they had extramarital affairs.

Other fathers indicated that they felt trapped by the upcoming birth and longed for the opportunity to do something different. Many had fantasies of leaving and taking a trip alone. Some actually took some time away from their wives and the pregnancy as a way of reassuring themselves that they could do so if they felt the need or desire.

Whichever part of this conflict is least well resolved prior to the decision will be the most difficult block to deal with during the pregnancy. Thus, if a man has an unfulfilled need for security, the stress of a pregnancy will bring forth fears of abandonment and consequently a greater need for closeness and reassurance from his wife. A man who is prone to feeling suffocated will have to struggle more with his need to be free and his fantasies of flight.

This conflict seems to come to the fore as soon as men begin to consider a pregnancy seriously and may last for many years in some form or another. It is important to note also that pregnant women go through the identical conflict, although their needs and resolution will not necessarily occur in the same way or with similar timing to their husbands'.

Life and Death

Permanence in the relationship is not the only issue that emerges at this time. Indeed, far more reaching for many men is the emotional realization that they themselves are mortal. The advent of birth brings with it a sudden and newly certain knowledge of one's own death and that of loved ones.

It must be something of a cosmic joke that the moment at which men often feel most excited and alive—at the realization of their involvement in the creation of life—is so frequently followed by an equally powerful acknowledgment of death.

One father's journal contained the following:

> *When we made love this afternoon, I knew we made a baby. I could feel it. It was very different than ever before. I have created life, and my own life is now full of new meaning, and yet when I think of this, I am frightened. I am so aware that this brings me into a new perspective with my own father's death. How strange to have both feelings at the same time. How unfair that as the family grows, it also diminishes. How many second thoughts will I have about this decision? Am I shortening lives by creation, or am I assuring my own immortality?*

He concluded,

> *This being a father is complicated.*

Child-free Option

Many couples consider the option of remaining child-free. This choice is generally "socially approved" only for couples who are deemed incapable of conceiving and being good parents. This category includes those who are too old, too young, too handicapped, too culturally different, and homosexual. While there is pressure put on most couples to have children during the marriage, for many, the decision to remain child-free is the best choice. In spite of, or because of, social pressure, this option is difficult to make and to keep. People who continuously choose to remain child-free frequently feel pressure to justify their choice to themselves and to others.

Conclusion

With all the complications involved in making a decision to be a parent, it seems amazing that babies are ever born at all. Of course, the biological and emotional drives to become parents help a great deal, but it is also important to recognize that deciding to have a child at the right time and with the right partner is probably the greatest decision one ever makes in life, even if it is a passive choice. Deciding not to have a child is as just as important.

The decision does not need to be made entirely alone. Many birth information centers, neighborhood extension programs, and organizations such as Planned Parenthood offer classes with names such as "Maybe Baby?" or "Becoming Parents: Know Before you Go." In addition, many family therapists, marital counselors, pastors, childbirth educators, and psychotherapists have considerable expertise in helping people work with the blocks to making effective decisions in this area.

If making a baby decision is problematic over a long term, it is probably worthwhile to look for unexamined fears and needs. It is also of considerable value to examine the factors in the relationship and in yourselves that hinder making a decision. Often, the inability to decide is a solid indication that an objective third party is needed.

The major issues presented in this chapter are designed to underscore the impact of the lifelong decision. It is also meant to reassure you that you are not the only ones who are conflicted about when and if you should become or add to your family.

The next three chapters focus on the beginnings of this journey: the precious nine months of pregnancy.

Chapter 5

The First Trimester: Conception to Kicks

My whole outlook on life changed with these three little words: the rabbit died.

The early pregnancy process is a time of dramatic change in the life of a couple. It begins with conception and ends with perceptive fetus movement, visible body changes, a sense that the dangers of miscarriage are over, and an evolving understanding that this is "for real."

The first three months are characterized by transition and emotional and physical upheaval. Both men and women commonly experience euphoria and despair, pride and incompetence, almost contiguously. Couples begin to develop a deeper sense of commitment and "glue" and, almost at the same moment, fears of entrapment and concern for the viability of the marital union.

Physical Changes

From the moment of conception (the fertilization of the female ovum by male spermatozoa), an impressive and complex growth pattern begins. In successful pregnancies, the result, approximately nine months later, is a living human being. Within approximately one week, the ovum, fertilized in the fallopian tubes, travels down and implants itself into the wall of the uterus. During the next few months, this "embryo" will become a fetus (at about five weeks) and then a baby.

By the end of the first month, the embryo is approximately one-quarter of an inch long measured from its head to its "tail." Traces of many organs become differentiated and recognizable. The head is especially prominent and comprises over one-third of the entire fetus. Rudimentary perceptual organs—eyes, ears, and nose—appear. The tube which will form the heart produces a bulge in the body wall, and blood pulses through its microscopic arteries. Another tube extending from the mouth will become the digestive tract, and little buds which will become arms and legs emerge.

By the end of the second month, a clearly human form is beginning to appear and is approximately one inch from head to buttocks. It weighs about one-thirtieth of an ounce. The developing brain and head become disproportionately large and the mouth, nose, and ears less prominent. External genitalia become apparent, but the specific sex is relatively undistinguishable. Also, the tail reaches its greatest development before receding. This is the time that the embryo becomes a fetus.

In the third month, this fetus triples in length to almost three inches and adds thirty times its previous weight (to almost an ounce). Bone growth is apparent, and external genitalia begin to show. Fingers and toes with rudimentary nails are also evident. Sockets for the first teeth appear. Immature kidneys develop and begin to secrete small amounts of urine into the bladder. Movements begin, usually undetectable to the mother. During this third month, the placenta begins to produce hormones necessary for the uterus to keep and nurture the developing child.

As the fourth month dawns (thirteen weeks since last missed menstrual period), the fetus begins to develop full-term proportions. The head is about one-third of the body length, the ribs become visible, characteristic facial features evolve, and the arms and legs begin an almost-constant motion. In a few weeks, the first kicks will be felt.

At this point, the likelihood of miscarriage or abortion is substantially reduced.

Emotional Changes

As great as the physical changes are, they are no greater or more significant for couples than the emotional changes brought about by pregnancy. Emotional adaptations engendered by the knowledge of a pregnancy range from denial to obsession, from joy to fear, and from minor to major lifestyle and value changes.

Psychologically, it is a very interesting time for expectant fathers. You may find that the pregnancy remains quite intangible until your wife is "showing" or you feel the fetus moving in her abdomen. However, you may have surprisingly intense emotional reactions to normal life events. You may cry at a movie, become excessively safety-conscious, or become unusually sensitive to the plight of others. Implausible reactions that seem out of character probably represent an initial emotional awareness of the pregnancy.

Discovery

Women often plan, fantasize, and dream about "the moment." The typical expectant father in our survey was surprised to discover that his wife had thought about and rehearsed the way in which she would let him know about the pregnancy. By contrast, men seemed not to have given as much thought to how they would be told as to the news itself.

The popular media (especially television) has a standard depiction of the way in which a man discovers that he is about to become a daddy. The scene is at the living room of their home. He comes home to find her looking like she has a secret and doing something that represents a clue (like knitting booties). He then gets to speculate in a bumbling and ineffective manner what the secret is while canned laughter on the sound track from the (nonexistent) audience indicates that his ineffective guesses are humorous. His reaction on finally discovering the truth is often silly as he foolishly rushes to overprotect her.

This representation of the good-natured, bumbling male is fairly typical for sitcom and general TV fare. The announcement that the baby is about to arrive is treated in much the same way.

Some of the real-life fathers interviewed in the survey were in fact very much surprised at the news, while others "knew" about the pregnancy before their wives did. Very few were bumbling or incompetent. They found out in a variety of individual ways that ranged from hyperawareness to complete astonishment. Since the surprised male most fits the media mold, we will begin with him.

"Are you sure?": The surprised father. One father-to-be indicated that he came home from work to find his wife anxiously pacing the floor and crying. Another man found out by getting a congratulatory phone call at work from a cousin. His wife had not found the "right moment" to tell him, and she had confided in others. Similarly, Reed discovered the news on his Facebook timeline. His wife has posted it, and he got the news only after "likes" and comments from most of her friends and family.

Steve described his learning of the pregnancy this way:

> I was dog tired that night when I got home, and all I wanted to do was take a hot shower, have a beer, and watch the tube. As soon as I got in the door, I knew something was wrong. I thought, "Oh no, what is it this time?" She had that look on her face. The last time it was because the plumbing broke, and all I wanted to do was turn around and go the other way. I remember asking her, "What is it?" and she said, "Guess." Well, one thing led to another, and we had this big fight, and she went crying off to the bedroom. I just went in

*and took my shower and got a beer. About an hour later, I went in
there, and we made up, and she told me. I was so happy, I just forgot
about how tired I was.*

Joe, an air force sergeant temporarily stationed in Okinawa, got a
long-distance phone call at 3:00 am. He said it was relayed by a ham radio
operator who told him, "Wake up, have you got some good news coming." The
next thing he heard was his wife exuberantly telling him that he was about to
be a father for the first time. He commented, "I think I woke up everybody
from the base to Naha City."

Many men are amazed by the news even though they had participated in
the decision to not use birth control. Frequently, these men were not aware
of any signs or symptoms in their wives or of her trip to the doctor for tests.
They had a variety of different responses to the news. Some were happy, some
excited, some sad, while others were stunned, scared, or angry. Most common
was a sense of disbelief.

A few men were shocked because they had simply been unaware that
their wives had decided to try and get pregnant. This was often true for
second or third children, where the wife wanted another child and the men
were less keen on the idea. One of these wives who decided to take matters
into her own hands reported,

> *He would say no, so I just decided to go ahead. I knew he wouldn't
> say no afterwards.*

Other men were shocked by the failure of their birth control methods:

> *She dropped the bomb at my house one day after we broke up. I was
> planning to marry her, only not so soon. She got pregnant on the
> pill. We beat the ninety-ninth percentile.*

"I knew it first": The exceptionally aware father. Not all men were
surprised. Another type of father was keenly involved in trying to become
pregnant. He was aware of his wife's menstrual cycle, and his moods, hopes,
and expectations often rode a roller coaster which coincided with it.

Carl was indicative of these men:

> *I was always watching for sign of her period, and each month when
> it arrived, I got a little down. I was always hoping that this month
> would be the one and we would begin our family. It really took a
> long time, and when the real one came, I was almost afraid to ask
> her aloud if she was overdue. When she missed it by three weeks, I*

just went out and got one of those home pregnancy tests. We were so disappointed when it showed up negative. Well first, we were excited just to be trying the test and then disappointed. But three weeks later, still no period, so I insisted that she go to the doctor, and we found out that the first test had just been wrong. Jan was almost two months pregnant. I can still remember the smile on her face when I picked her up at the doctor's office.

Vigilant fathers like Carl craved fatherhood. They were so keenly aware of their wife's physical condition, often more so than she.

One expectant father wrote in his journal,

I became a father today. I knew it was happening. There was just something sooo different. When we were making love, everything seemed open, and the feel was just different. I told Susie right afterwards. She doesn't believe it yet I know, but it's only a matter of time till she finds out. I really feel funny . . . like I'm the only one in the world with this great secret, and if I tell anyone, they won't believe me.

David Early, a newspaper feature writer, was interviewing me about the expectant fatherhood research and asked about men finding out about the conception. When I told him that everyone seemed different and that I personally had been aware of the moment of conception, he broke into a big smile and said that he had been aware of the moment for his own child and had never really discussed it with others who had a similar experience. It made for a wonderful moment between two strangers.

Yet another father indicated,

I had a very strong intuition . . . Within twelve to twenty-four hours of making love, I had a vision. There was an immediate difference in the feeling tone in myself and in the relationship . . . It's really hard to put into words . . . a very strong emotional knowledge.

"I thought something was up": The ambivalent father. Men who are less happy about becoming a father were often somewhat aware of the potential pregnancy yet somewhat surprised as well.

One new father told the interviewer,

I guess I knew she was late, but I just sort of put it out of my mind. Like, I didn't want to know. I was just hoping she was late, you know. Sometimes she isn't that regular, but I also thought that she

*might be hapai (pregnant). I just took a wait-and-see attitude . . .
When she went to the doctor, I guess I knew; and when she told me
the test was positive, I told her, "Ya, I thought so." Now that my boy
is here it's different, you know. I'm glad he's my boy, but the whole
pregnancy was a downer.*

"That's your opinion, let's examine other perspectives": The denying father.
Many men simply hear the words but do not fully register them for some time.
On being congratulated by a friend, newly expectant Larry responded,

*Thanks. I guess Clarice is going to have a baby. I haven't thought
much about it yet. It really doesn't seem real to me. No thunderbolt
out of the sky. She came home and said she was pregnant, and then
it was business as usual. I think I'll have to get used to the idea for a
while. Right now, it doesn't seem real to me . . . Oh, I meant to ask
you, did you catch the Dodgers' score last night?*

In order to get digesting time to incorporate the news, Larry kept his
fatherhood at an emotional distance. During the nine-month pregnancy, he
will have the opportunity for the full awareness to sink in, and he will be able
to accept and respond more fully to the news and changes in his life.

"Is it really true?": The dilemma of the adoptive father. Adoptive fathers
belong to another group. Men who adopt want a child very much but are
somehow unable to have natural children in their marriage. Their notification
comes not from physical signs, lab tests, and a doctor, but from a lawyer or a
social worker. Typically, the adoptive father is told that a baby is (or will be)
available at a certain date, and he and his wife are asked whether they want
this child. These fathers tend to react somewhat differently than other fathers.
They get excited at the news and then get very worried almost instantly. The
worries come partially from the fact that there is no absolute guarantee that
the child would be theirs to keep. Adoption produces an additional difficulty
for couples in that there is no normal nine-month preparation period to get
used to the idea of having a new child.

Adoptive couples do not have to deal with many of the physical
discomforts of pregnancy, but the price they pay for that is the greater sense
that the whole thing is a fantasy. For many adoptive fathers, the baby simply
appears, as if by magic (or stork). Such men showed a tendency to deny the
acknowledgment to a much greater extent. They often did not experience
many feelings about the upcoming delivery, living life with a "business
as usual" appearance until the baby was actually present. Some adoptive
parents keep their reserve until after the adoption is final, six months to a
year after they have the baby.

Acknowledgment and Denial

Arthur and Libby Coleman (*Pregnancy: The Psychological Experience*, 1971), pioneers in the modern understanding of the psychological aspects of pregnancy, state, "The main issue of the first trimester, for male as for female, is the discovery and acceptance of the pregnancy."

Emotional acknowledgment has particular significance for fathers. There is no question that once the pregnancy is confirmed, men whose wives are pregnant can tell others that they are expecting a child. However, there can be a considerable lag before the emotional impact is fully experienced. The pregnancy can be largely denied psychologically.

Mothers usually accept the pregnancy earlier than fathers. After all, she can begin to experience a plethora of internal manifestations of the pregnancy. Her breasts enlarge, she has morning sickness, and she literally feels different. She also has been conditioned by our culture for this event. Despite many welcome modern changes brought about by the women's movement, there remains a powerful ethic in our society to revere motherhood. She may also be a doctor, lawyer, engineer, or riveter, but motherhood continues to be a recognized pathway for a woman's fulfillment and achievement.

By contrast, the elevation of fatherhood to such heights of esteem and achievement is limited. Often, the only thing that happens is some locker room joking or insensitive speculation as to whether or not he is indeed the biological father. On revealing the conception to friends, men often hear "joking" questions such as "What does the mailman look like?" Furthermore, there are no biological changes to support a man's knowledge of the event. He must receive the information secondhand. The biological child that women carry is manifested in her mate by what Sam Bittman and Sue Rosenberg Zalk call the brainchild (*Expectant Fathers*, 1978). His pregnancy at this early stage is with the concept of the baby. It is therefore not surprising that it takes him longer to feel the emotional impact of approaching parenthood.

Each expectant father encounters this differently. Some men will be more involved in the early pregnancy than their wives, others equally involved, and many far more detached. The manner in which they react is usually some combination of the extent to which they are surprised by the news, how much they want to have children, how long they have been waiting, their personality style, the way in which they are told, their wives' desires and attitudes, and the context of the news.

One father of four said,

> *Mary has the worst timing in the world. The first time she gave me the news, I had just been sideswiped by a truck, and was trying to find my license and insurance information. And then with Jenny*

(our third) she called on the phone and told me when there were six visitors in my office. I just couldn't have a reaction. This last time was better. She arranged a big candle light dinner at home, and told me after a glass of wine. This time I was very excited, at least until I knocked over her glass of wine.

Dr. Katharyn May of the University of Wisconsin, Madison, a pioneer researcher on fatherhood, has described a pattern or "trajectory" of male acceptance of the news. She concludes that most men need a "moratorium" after the initial acknowledgment. Involvement increases as the birth gets closer.

The timing for emotional impact varies. From our survey, the most frequent time for genuine emotional acknowledgment was the occurrence of movement (the beginning of the second trimester). The second most likely time was the birth itself, followed by the announcement and acquiring of some toys or pieces of apparel for infants. When my sister-in-law Ann gave my wife and me a few infant outfits during the second trimester, Susan and I passed a private look, which could only be translated as "Hey, this is getting serious."

There is no true single moment of full awareness. It is more of a progressive thing with specific memory landmarks. In fact, men's reports of the emotional benchmark change depending on when the question is asked. When we asked *expectant* fathers to identify the moment of emotional acknowledgment, they responded with statements like the following:

- *When she told me we were going to have a child*
- *When her friends gave us some of the baby clothes*
- *When I felt my first kick*
- *It's interesting that you should ask that, I don't think it has hit me yet.*
- *When we went to the (childbirth) classes. Seeing the hospital and the other pregnant women and the preparation and breathing really brought it all home to me.*
- *I don't know when this happened, but all of a sudden, I started to be a father in dreams.*
- *Nightmares, especially about my wife dying and me being left with a baby.*

However, when we asked *recent* fathers, they all indicated that it was the birth itself. Apparently, that experience is so powerful, that all others retroactively pale by contrast. It is clear from the research that emotional knowledge of a pregnancy is not a clear-cut phenomenon, but rather, it occurs in stages, with the birth event itself by far the most influential.

Men who accompanied their wives to the prenatal exams often had a heightened awareness of the pregnancy. A small, but increasing percentage of expectant fathers actually go into the pelvic exam with their wives. Many that did were fascinated, disturbed, felt out of place, upset, courageous, and humbled. They often reported experiencing for the first time the infantalization that many of the feminist writers have described for decades.

If you do accompany your wife and if you leave the waiting room and go into the examining room with her, I suspect the psychological reality of the birth will be hastened.

Once the general acknowledgment develops, there are a variety of secondary reactions. Men have described several of these:

Pride. Fathering a child does fulfill one traditional masculine role. In many cultures, men are judged primarily by the sheer numbers of children they can sire. Several men in the survey reported a sense of strength, accomplishment, and potency, as well as feelings of helplessness and fears of the unknown.

Nurturance. Many men described a rush of nurturing feelings toward their wives that was different from anything they had known before. There is frequently a desire to assist her, to comfort her, and to care for her in new ways. Some men begin to do housework or increase the amount they do. Others try to build greater financial security as providers. A husband who cares for his wife while she has morning sickness is also probably rehearsing parenting his child.

There is a delicate line here. As a newly expectant father, you must be sensitive to your wife's (sometimes rapidly) fluctuating needs, but you cannot treat her as an incompetent or an invalid. You need to practice and get used to the nurturer role without overdoing it. It's like the old joke about the overzealous Boy Scout who helps the elderly woman across the street whether or not she has any interest in being on the other side. Often, it is a novel experience for a young man to be the caregiver. As with any new role, you may have to test it out a bit before you get it right. Moreover, if you nurture without receiving anything in return, you might grow to resent it. You must also let her know what you need and let her give you some nurturance also, if for no other reason than it gives her a chance to practice too.

Fears of loss of sexual partner. Many factors play into this fear: physical withdrawal by the wife who is understandably less interested in sex while she is nauseated, turning inward by the wife to focus more on her own body and the life inside than on her partner, a need by the husband to put some psychological distance between himself and the pregnancy, and beliefs that are held by the husband.

The first three of these factors are discussed later in the "relationship" section of this chapter. Men's beliefs about pregnancy and their fears are most relevant here.

One of the major questions men have about early pregnancy is what effect sexual intercourse might have on the baby. Many people incorrectly believe that sex can harm the fetus and have a tendency to refrain from sexual contact for weeks or even months. The early stages of a pregnancy are a special time in the life of a couple, demanding a greater than normal amount of closeness. For many men, this closeness is most readily expressed sexually.

One belief that can get in the way of healthy sexual relating is that sexuality serves only the purpose of procreation. Thus, once a pregnancy is confirmed, there is no need for sexual intercourse.

Some men psychologically divide the world of women into mothers (often referred to as Madonnas) and sex objects (whores). Once your pregnant partner is in the process of becoming a mother, you may begin to associate her with all mothers, including your own, and be repulsed by the suggestion of incest.

Jealousy. Some men exhibit a strong sense of what is sometimes referred to as womb envy during a pregnancy. The jealous feelings are twofold in origin. One source is the sexual envy at the woman's ability to have a child grow within her body. Many ancient myths address this envy (Tiresias who has to experience life from the perspective of each sex and Zeus who is so jealous of Athena's ability to have a child that he swallows her in an attempt to incorporate this talent).

Another source of jealousy comes from suddenly being thrust into the background and having to relinquish the center-of-attention role to one's spouse. For some men, this is a relief and a pleasure. For others, it is quite disturbing. Gordon described it this way:

> *I kinda got the impression that things were different when my mother, who claimed she would never get over my choice of a marriage partner seven years before, shifted from ending 30 minute conversations with, "Oh ya, tell Helen I said hello," and began phone calls with, "Hi, Gord. How's Helen? Can I talk to her?" My own mother! Since we announced the pregnancy, nobody actually seems interested in me at all.*

A certain amount of envy or jealousy is normal and healthy as long as the couple discusses it and shares their sensitivities. If the jealousy is persistent or strong, it is well worth seeing a therapist or other third party to help resolve the underlying issues of mistrust and low self-esteem.

Of Fathers of Sons of Fathers

One of the interesting paradoxes of becoming a father is that men feel both more like a son to their own fathers and more like an adult. The discovery of a pregnancy can bring to men a desire to know more about their own childhood and their fathering.[9]

The feelings of being out of control and helpless about the pregnancy may stimulate an unconscious reversion to former times. You might feel things that were more customary in your boyhood than in your manhood. At such times, it is natural to turn to a father figure for assistance. In this way, the act of becoming a father reconnects you to the feelings of being a son.

Many long-lost experiences are revived, and dreams become vivid. Fantasies about alternative lifestyles occur, and some serious questioning takes place. Questions such as "Who am I? What am I becoming? What do I know of fathering and what do I know of my father?" all become very important. The experience of closeness to other men (particularly fathers and especially one's own) become more central, even for men whose close friends over the years have been female. I remember being so driven to contact important male friends from my past that I wrote letters to two men that I hadn't been in contact with for several years. What a wonderful surprise when they both responded with warmth and caring and also shared recent experiences with me.

The search for meaning. Becoming a father involves a redefinition of one's roles and a rethinking of future goals. Many men begin to ruminate about the meaning of their lives and ponder the immense responsibility they have to the future of their world. These feelings and thoughts germinate here and bloom and grow throughout the pregnancy and the first few months after a child's birth. It is particularly significant for a man to question the meaning of this child and the changes in the life of his family.

One man concluded that he no longer had "the right to take (his own) life so lightly." Another expectant father expressed beautifully the change in his own consciousness:

> *I always was the outsider, the nonbelonger. But with Glenda pregnant and the child on the way, I think I can't do that anymore. I'm linked by this kid back to the human race. Something passes from my parents to him through me, and I'm part of the chain . . .*

---

[9]. Two books that explore this are *My Father before Me* by Michael J. Diamond and *The Measure of a Man: Becoming the Father You Wish Your Father Had Been* by Jerrold Lee Shapiro.

I'm not sure I can take belonging . . . It's unnatural. It's also enticing.
What else will this little bugger get me into?

One factor that seemed related to all of these psychological factors was the age of the father. Younger men seemed less worried, less ambivalent, and less involved in the pregnancy than did older fathers. Men in their middle thirties to middle forties seemed to experience these phenomena that we're discussing with much greater intensity.

Relationship Issues

Discovery of a pregnancy affects the relationship between a man and a woman in a number of ways. There is added stress from the time pressure, fears for the health and safety of everyone, excitement about the miracle of creating life, financial concerns, and the reappearance of psychological considerations long buried and forgotten. When a couple becomes a family, it gets far more complex. Not only are the number and types of interactions multiplied from a two—person to a three-person system, but in-laws and extended family also begin to play a different role. Freedom is necessarily curtailed in some ways, and security needs to be reassessed.

When a couple becomes a family, generally, *all the things that are good get better, and all the things that are bad get worse.*

The advent of parenthood often has a major impact on the nature of communication between the spouses. There is more of a future orientation and a partnership based on a living being who will share their characteristics. In addition, any planning must take into account a third very dependent person. Strong values which up to now were irrelevant, such as beliefs about discipline, money, religion, schooling, and the extent to which a family is child—or adult-centered, emerge and may well clash. In some ways, the pregnancy begins to influence every conversation between husband and wife. It will also affect the nature of conversations with others. Strange new emotions need to be addressed, and new feelings seem to come up at unintended and inconvenient times, both to the chagrin and joy of the individual.

For the most part during the first trimester, the woman is more involved in the pregnancy than her husband. There are many cultural and physical reasons for this. She is, after all, carrying the child. It is her body that is changing and being flooded with hormonal alterations. It is she who is nauseated and running to the bathroom. Her husband can only experience the pregnancy secondhand at this stage. As one expectant father put it,

> *It's hard to get too excited yet. My wife is sick all the time. Our sex life is gone. Nothing I can do pleases her. She is subtly trying to get me to get into it more, go to her prenatal exams, and it's all over this two-inch creature with a tail that's stuck to her uterus.*

Despite all his protests, he is involved already, if only on a reactive level. His wife and his marriage have changed. There are at least subtle pressures on him to participate in the pregnancy with his wife, but there is not yet any role for him. Dr. Katharyn May indicates quite clearly that the ultimate level of husband involvement in the pregnancy is predominantly dependent on the wife's attitudes and behaviors.

Morning Sickness

It is a fact of pregnancy that there will be tremendous hormonal and physical changes throughout. These changes are magnified during the first few months. Along with all the physical and psychological changes is a phenomenon which is euphemistically called morning sickness. This is not a universal experience for all pregnant women. In fact, one-third to one-half of all women have no signs of nausea, vomiting, or listlessness. Some women experience this only in the morning or during a part of the day, while others have the symptoms all day long. Normally, the symptoms do not extend into the second trimester. But for some couples, the fabled and anticipated healthy, rosy-cheeked pregnancy is not to be. Some women are simply ill throughout the nine months.

Morning sickness has been attributed to many factors from chemical (low blood sugar) to physical (extra sensitivity to smells and aromas) and psychological ones (ambivalence over the pregnancy). Whatever its cause, it is a time of substantial physical discomfort for pregnant women and difficulty for expectant fathers. No matter how well-intentioned and supportive a man can be, continual interaction with a slightly green-complexioned woman who seems to have a cracker box attached to her hand and who is unresponsive to any efforts of good cheer will take its toll on him. Expectant fathers need support and demonstrations of caring. However, it is particularly difficult for their wives to provide such support when they are fighting off nausea. Several men commented on the morning sickness.

Jack, a thirty-six-year-old first-time father, said,

> *I was real scared about the pregnancy, and I wanted to talk to Betty about it all the time. Every time we began talking though, she was running to the bathroom, throwing up. I just gave up after a while.*

Bill wrote in his journal,

> *When we decided to give up the diaphragm, our sex became so awesome. It was new passion and very exciting, and when she got pregnant, it was even more exciting, and now . . . nothing. Since the second month began, it's been like I was a total creep. She doesn't want anything to do with me. All I have to do is suggest sex, and she gets sick. I sure hope she hasn't given up on sex forever.*

Harvey told the interviewer,

> *The worst time of the whole pregnancy was the second and third months. I felt like I was living with an invalid. She didn't want to do anything and wouldn't try to help herself. I brought home food, dry crackers, took her for walks, gave her high protein snacks for nighttime. She just kept saying her mother was sick for all of her five pregnancies and she was just like her mom. It was very frustrating. I felt so helpless. I even started to resent the baby. I just kept thinking that if it weren't for the kid, you know. Then I felt so guilty. I mean, how do you justify being angry at someone who is sick or a fetus that is only half an inch big?*

One couple came for marriage therapy in the throes of three months of constant nausea. During the first therapy hour, the wife told the husband that she wanted an abortion, a divorce, and sterilization. After a few sessions of therapy (and a subsiding of the nausea), those requests were remembered as a bad dream.

Often, the best resolution to the problem of morning sickness is time and patience. Normally, the problem diminishes or ends at the beginning of the second trimester, along with the excitement of quickening (first movement). However, it is still important for the husband to convey to his wife that he feels for her in her discomfort and equally important for her to express her unhappiness at not being able to comfort him.

You can help by walking with your spouse, encouraging her to eat several small meals a day, telling her how important it is for you to feel her support, and trying to discuss these matters during parts of the day that are better for her.

One method for alleviating morning sickness is distraction. Often, if people can keep busy, they are less aware of the nausea (at least temporarily). Meditation, vacations, and work all serve to help in this regard. I was able to assist my wife with her considerable morning sickness through the use of hypnosis. The most effective hypnosis technique was helping her create a state of deep relaxation and then suggesting that she was at a favorite spot on a beach in Hawaii. My wife, who is a both an avid swimmer and an excellent hypnotic subject, found that the nausea subsided as she experienced the natural rhythm of swimming in her body. Since this was a temporary solution and I was not always available, I put the hypnosis on a tape that she could use when I was not present. While such methods do not guarantee complete alleviation of the symptoms, any temporary relief is welcome.

The Couvade Syndrome

Sometimes, husbands share more than empathy with their nauseated wives and have symptoms of pregnancy themselves. This phenomenon called the couvade syndrome is well known by anthropologists and has been described primarily in research of primitive cultures. A great deal of recent evidence, however, indicates that many men in modern cultures also experience a number of pregnancy-like symptoms during the course of the expectant period. During the first trimester, the most common of these are nausea, loss of appetite, stomach distress, weight gain, and tiredness—symptoms that are called morning sickness when they occur in pregnant women. One of the most interesting aspects of couvade is that it is rarely diagnosed properly, so men rarely attribute it to the pregnancy. This is not surprising because even the man who does seek medical help may never be asked or think to volunteer that his wife is pregnant.

Nurturing Your Wife

One of the first places that men get involved is in trying to help their wives become more physically or emotionally comfortable. Jerry described it this way:

> I felt so good when I could make her a small meal and get her to eat it. It sure felt good to take care of her that way. I also did some of the housework. It was great when she noticed it and commented. Then we got really close together.

Jerry's caregiving was very important for Sachiko and for himself.

Even if you are not yet able to feel the full impact of the pregnancy, you can recognize that your wife is needy at this time, and you are the best person to fulfill this need. What is also important is for you to tell her what she can do for you as well.

Not all couples can use the experience to get closer. Bob's frustration is evident in the following entry in his journal:

> *Sarah is so moody and out of sorts lately. I want us to be so close with this baby, but she seems so wrapped up in herself and her body. I want her to be as excited as she was when we found out that we were pregnant. We were so joyous. Ten years of marriage, and she seems like a stranger to me these days. I think this is just a stage and will pass. Will (his father-in-law) said that Sarah's mom was like that for a few weeks too and then bounced back. I feel frustrated. I want to do something and don't have any idea what to do.*

Turning Inward

Soon after she becomes aware of the pregnancy, a woman will begin to turn inward and focus more intensely on her body. In addition to the innumerable physiological modifications, emotional and spiritual factors are also at play. During the first trimester, she frequently begins an intense maternal bonding with the baby based on her dreams, fantasies, and spirituality. While very important for her relationship with her child, this can be difficult on her husband, as Tim's comments suggest,

> *During the second month, she was totally self-absorbed for five weeks or so. I was in a lot of grief: loss of our partnership, loss of our closeness. Until that time, we always did everything together. I really had to face my dependency and work that through. My dad had died just about that time, and I was feeling the loss of him and of my wife. One night, I just told her how sad I was. I felt like I had lost her. I just held her, and we cried for a while together. I just kept thinking over and over, Lindy is never going to be there for me again.*

Many men indicated similar feelings. They experienced their wives' turning inward as a rejection. At a time when they were trying to cope with their own ambivalence about the baby's imminent arrival, they began to have doubts about the marital relationship. If this was accompanied by an equivalent lessening or cessation of sexual activity, the rejection was perceived more poignantly.

Here's how one father remembered this painful time:

I felt like I didn't get enough attention. I felt so left out . . . like I had to do everything around things that concerned her. Nobody was interested in what concerned me. She was so involved with her own changes, there wasn't a spare moment to ask me how I was doing. The thing that saved me was my men's group.

This can be a hard time for a husband and wife. Both feel her divided loyalties. Talking about it and even arguing about each other's relative needs are important in creating a solid base for the relationship to allow room for the infant. Couples who do not take this opportunity to work on their relationship can have significant problems later.

As she becomes a mother, a woman's turning inward is not solely related to the baby. She may need to reassess her relationship with her own mother in finding how to be a mother herself. She may become closer and more dependent on her mother than she has been since her husband has known her. Her mother's influence on her may increase.

This relationship can be disquieting for her husband. He may feel excluded from the pregnancy. If the mother-in-law has wanted greater closeness to her daughter, she may also participate in strengthening the mother-daughter bond at the expense of husband-wife closeness. This is at a particularly unfortunate time for him. He is not yet totally involved in the pregnancy, and his ineffective attempts to get closer to his partner may paradoxically push her away from him and toward others. He could end up feeling more distanced, competitive, and envious of her relationship with the baby or her mother. If this is the first child, he has no way of knowing that his wife's internal searching will end and her need to reunite with him will intensify.

The husband will also begin turning inward as he reexamines his relationship with his own parents, especially his father. His attempts to make closer contact with his father may be somewhat more difficult than his wife's search. Cultural blocks to men's closeness can deter him. In reaction to this, he may regress to more typical masculine roles he felt comfortable with as a younger man.

Many couples drift apart at this time, and thoughts of the relationship ending may intrude and often alternate with lifelong family plans. It is a shaky and needy time, a time for women to draw men into the pregnancy and for men to indicate firmly their desires for partnership with their wives.

"I Want to Go Back": Other Regressions

In addition to the need to reconnect with parents, there is a related temptation to live in easier times—when the rules were much clearer. Thinking about having a child brings up thoughts and feelings about one's own childhood. These "regressions" serve two purposes:

1. attempts to escape from the demands of parenting and fears of the unknown
2. attempts to identify with the baby you are about to have

This will be accompanied by some "surprises." Attitudes and values of previous times will suddenly be thrust into the marriage, often contradicting more current beliefs.

Joseph complained,

> *When we met, one of the things I was attracted to was her radical stand against the crazy teachings of the church. In our town, that was rare. I was impressed that I wasn't the only one who pulled away. Now all of a sudden, she's wanting to go to church with her mother and talking about baptizing the kid. I told her I won't stand for it, but really, I can't stop her.*

Fred sought marital counseling during the third month of the pregnancy because his career-minded wife seemed quite different:

> *It's like overnight her whole brain changed to mush. One day, she's a conservative, professional woman; and the next, she's acting like an airhead who only wants to go dancing, put on makeup, and talk to her girlfriends on the phone. It's like being with a teenybopper who needs to be with the girls and her mom 14 hours a day and sleep the rest.*

Nancy, his wife, described him as

> *a stick in the mud . . . who can't have any fun and only thinks all day of work, work, work. I think he's trying to be like his German father, twelve hours of work on the job and eight more when he came home. He considered sleep a waste of good work time. Whatever happened to midnight runs to the all-night pizza joint? Or making love in the morning and going to work late?*

Resolution to this dilemma came slowly. First, they had to learn to stop blaming their partner for behaving like one of their parents and to stop reacting as if to that parent. Second, they began to recognize the characteristic process of their dilemma: as he became more stern and serious, she naturally filled the gap and became more of the fun producer; and as she became "less responsible," he became more parental. Both were behaving as they had when life seemed simpler, more certain, and predictable because both needed the partner to take more care of them. When they were able to talk about how scared they both were, the roles soon rebalanced.

Practical Considerations

It may seem premature to make too many practical changes with the baby still half a year away, but those six months can speed by. If this is your first child and you are like most men, your knowledge of birth options is minimal. There are as many options available for the birth as there are on a new car. Do you want "natural" childbirth? Do you want an obstetrician or a midwife delivering the baby? Will you be there as a participant, an observer, or a coach? Will your baby be born at home, in a hospital, or at an alternative birthing center? Will you use Lamaze? Bradley? Leboyer? How will you pay for the birth?

You will probably be exposed to these options and choices for the very first time.

Choosing the Birthplace

Several considerations go into the choice of a birthplace. The most important is your wife's and your own comfort. You want to make this birth best suited to your mutual needs. There are basically three options:

1. *Hospitals.* Hospitals have the advantage of being prepared for emergencies. They have the disadvantage of being associated in our minds as places to go when we are ill. Sometimes the staff at hospitals treat birth as an illness rather than a natural and joyous event. Hospital procedures, layouts, and conditions often preclude many choices regarding the way you may want to have the birth.
2. *Alternative birthing centers* are often located close to hospitals and offer parents greater flexibility in choosing how to have the baby. Labor and delivery rooms tend to be more like bedrooms with soft light, better provision for the husband, a less sterile atmosphere, and the

possibility of a midwife as the birthing person. The costs for delivery are usually less than half of a hospital birth. The disadvantages are that some obstetricians will not deliver babies in these settings, and there can be some delays in help in case of an emergency. Many couples are choosing these centers because the birthing process seems more humane and "natural." In fact, the success of these alternate birthing centers has encouraged many hospitals to recreate this environment on obstetrics floors or in adjacent buildings. This is normally more based on fiscal considerations than enlightenment.

3. *Home births* are chosen by the fewest number of couples. The advantages, of course, are the naturalness of the environment and the couple's comfort in the setting. The disadvantages can include access and availability of the birthing person at the crucial moment and the distance to a medical center in case of an emergency.

The primary consideration must be the comfort of the mother and secondarily that of the father. If there is any increased probability of a Caesarian section or other dangers to the mother and infant, a more conservative choice is probably wise.

Spend some time learning about the options in your community. Interview parents who have used the facilities recently and ask for their honest reactions. Educate yourself as to all the possibilities and discuss them with your wife. Most people will make the final decisions by the end of the second trimester, so the time for gathering information is now. The couples I interviewed who were pleased with their choice arranged it so both of them had input into the decision, with the woman having the final say.

Choosing the Delivery Person

Most babies in modern America are delivered by an obstetrician. Normally, your wife will have a gynecologist, who is also qualified in obstetrics. She may have a relationship with her ob-gyn and want this physician to deliver the baby. If so, it is your job to get to know this person as well.

It is not always so simple. If your wife is a member of a health maintenance organization (HMO) or a preferred provider organization (PPO) or goes to a clinic, she may not have a personal gynecologist. Sometimes, the physician you want will not have privileges at the center in which you plan to have the baby, or this physician might have several partners who work on a rotating shift and cannot guarantee who will actually be on duty and available for the birth. You will want to find a birthing person who will meet your personal needs as a couple.

In such a search, it will be important for you and your wife to determine how you want the birth to go and to seek someone who will adjust to your decision. This determination will take a lot of talking and exploring with your wife. Some of the questions you can address about the birthing place include the following:

Are episiotomies typical?

What procedures are normal for anesthesia, if any?

Do they allow rooming-in for the infant?

Do they allow for demand feeding?

Can the husband be present even in the case of a Caesarian section?

What percentage of births at the center are C-sections?

Will your wife be allowed to breast-feed immediately after birth if she so chooses?

Once you have found the person who will allow for your choices, you need to be certain that the birth center will not find ways to override your obstetrician or alternative birthing person and yourselves.

Remember, hospitals and alternative birth centers are businesses. They do as many births in as efficient a manner as possible. You and your wife are the only people who will see to it that *your* experience is the way *you* want it, and your wife may be in no condition to argue with a nurse while she is in labor.

Financial

If you are covered by insurance (particularly a group policy) at the time of conception, you are probably covered for some or all of the costs of the birth. Check on your policies or call the benefits officer at work to get accurate information. Births and hospital stays can be expensive. The going rate for a normal vaginal birth in a private hospital in the San Francisco Bay Area in 2013 can run from $2,500 to $5,000. C-section births characteristically cost $2,000 to $3,000 more. Most people have insurance that covers most of the costs for the birthing center, prenatal and postnatal examinations, and mother and baby care.

Try to arrange for the hospital to bill the insurance company directly and save yourself the headache of dealing with either bureaucracy. If you are not covered by insurance, you will have to pay for it out of pocket. Shop around. Inexplicably, differences in charges can measure in the thousands of dollars. Most important, quality care is not necessarily related to cost. In some communities, there are frequent "price wars" among different hospitals. You may have heard radio or television advertisements paid for by birthing centers. You can work out a payment plan in advance. Don't get caught at the last moment arguing with an admitting clerk at the hospital while your wife is in labor.

Premature Termination of Pregnancy

Not all pregnancies produce children. Some pregnancies end before term via miscarriage or abortion. Nature has a way of protecting the species such that only the fit members survive. One such example of nature's process is the miscarriage. Miscarriage is the natural death of an embryo in its mother's womb (usually a spontaneous expulsion of the fetus prior to its viability for life outside the uterus). Generally, this occurs during the first trimester of the pregnancy and is considered by most medical people as a sign that the fetus was not sufficiently fit to survive. Whether this is a convenient fiction or an accurate understanding of the process of nature, a miscarriage can have a substantial emotional effect on the expectant parents.

For parents who were ambivalent about the pregnancy in the first place, a miscarriage brings up the conflict to the fore a lot sooner than expected. For couples whom the pregnancy was greatly desired and awaited, there can be a deep experience of loss and failure. Men whose wives miscarried respond in a variety of ways ranging from profound loss and sadness to relief, accusations, and guilt.

Several men who had experienced a miscarriage spoke about the experience.

Brent talked to us during the second trimester of the pregnancy:

> *I guess I'm just beginning to get used to it. Gillian's had four miscarriages since our first was born, and each one was worse than the last. I got so disappointed. I started to think we couldn't have any more children. Each miscarriage was like a death to me.*

He began crying at this point. When he composed himself a few minutes later, he continued,

> *I don't know what I'd do if we lost this one. But the doctor said that everything was going fine, and Gillian always lost the others before the second month. We had an amniocentesis, and we know this is a girl. We've already decided to call her Anita, after my grandmother. I only hope that everything goes well. We pray at every grace and also sometimes in the evening.*

Once again, Brent began crying. When he continued, he said,

> *Boy, I didn't know how much those miscarriages still hurt. I think a lot about how nice it will be to have a daughter.*

Brent's recent losses have placed him in a very sensitive and precarious position in terms of his faith in the success of the pregnancy. It is of importance to note that Anita was born to Brent and Gillian and is now a very healthy four-year-old.

Mel had a quite different reaction to the miscarriage he and his new wife experienced. He confided that he and his wife of two months had married

> in a hurry because the baby was on the way. We probably would have done it anyway, but then on the honeymoon, she had the miscarriage. Actually, I was relieved. I wasn't ready for a child, and now I can figure out if we really have enough in common without a baby to be married. I think Tess feels the same way, but we haven't discussed it much . . . Sometimes I do wonder if we would have gotten married if there wasn't a pregnancy.

Joel described his reactions about a second miscarriage in quite a different manner:

> I just told her that I wasn't happy about the whole thing. I know it happened because she doesn't take care of herself. I told her to exercise, but she just doesn't get on a program and stay on it. She must be five or six pounds overweight now, and it's been two months since the miscarriage.

He projected his hurt and frustration onto his wife and blamed her and her physical condition for his disappointment. She also believed the miscarriage to be entirely her fault despite medical information to the contrary. Had they not entered marriage therapy at that point, the marriage might have failed completely.

Abortion

Sometimes, a pregnancy is terminated by conscious design. In this case, the termination is called a therapeutic abortion.

When abortions are considered, they are almost always during the first trimester. Despite the political wrangling and posturing about late-term elective abortions, they are actually quite rare. If the pregnancy is unwanted by the couple (or at least by the woman), they may opt for termination of the pregnancy.

There is no issue that is so clearly divisive in American culture as abortion. And there is no such position on abortion as "no opinion." Indeed, everyone has a strong conviction about abortion, and feelings are even stronger when a personal decision is involved. The debate about legal abortion has now been going on for decades and will no doubt continue into the foreseeable future. For present purposes, abortion will be considered as a fact of life, a very difficult decision, and a potential consideration for a pregnancy.

Since you are reading this book for expectant fathers, you have probably decided not to have an abortion. Some of the men in the survey had previously experienced an abortion. They discussed their reactions in depth. Some of these observations were presented in chapter 3.

When a couple learns they are pregnant, they must decide whether they want this pregnancy to continue. Because all pregnancies come with a certain amount of ambivalence, there is no real way to avoid thinking about not being pregnant. This feeling is often intensified during the first few months if the awareness of the fetus as a child has not taken a firm hold and if the woman is experiencing a substantial amount of physical distress.

Ten Tips for the First Trimester

1. Spend some time alone with your thoughts of being a father. See what emotions and thoughts emerge as you explore the possibilities. If you are not feeling the impact of the pregnancy, give yourself some time to consider it further. Many men don't fully experience it until the actual birth. What do you think of when you think of a child? Maybe jot down your thoughts in a journal or diary.
2. Examine what the conception means in terms of your life goals, plans, and relationships. Consider the spiritual and emotional as well as the pragmatic impact.
3. Talk to your wife about all your feelings—the excitement as well as the anger, sadness, and fear.
4. Begin getting as much information as possible on the manner and options for birth in modern society and in particular those which are available in your community.
5. Consider the added responsibility of financial and emotional pressures.
6. If your wife has morning sickness, do what you can for her to make her as comfortable as possible. Some distraction like talking about the future or things you both enjoy might be of help. Recorded relaxation exercises and meditation classes are available and may help. Try to understand that she is feeling quite miserable and cannot be very attentive to your needs. Attempt to broach your feelings when she is able to hear them.

7. Seek out men who are recent fathers and talk to them about their experiences.

8. If you begin to wonder about your own past, birth, or parents, try to get whatever information you can from parents, relatives, and neighbors. Some of the negative feelings you may experience are due to forgotten events that you personally suffered. Share with your partner your ruminations about your own childhood and parenting and the desires you each have to reconnect with your parents.

9. Read a few books on what is going on inside your partner.

10. Try to maintain as good an affectionate and sexual relationship as possible.

Chapter 6

The Second Trimester: Showing, Growing, and Moving

Wait! Was that a kick? Oh my God!
I can't wait to post the ultrasound picture.

For our present purposes, the second trimester of the pregnancy commences with the beginnings of perceived movement of the infant and concludes with the woman becoming large enough to have her own movement restricted. It is a time of contrasts. While the fetus is growing relatively faster than at any other life period, the parents undergo a period of consolidation and less active participation beyond the family. Such pragmatic considerations like specific practice for the birth or preparation of the nursery are still somewhat in the future, as are the performance fears which dominate expectant fathers' consciousness during the third trimester. You may know that the big "push" of activity attending the third trimester and birth are coming, but you are unlikely to be feeling the bulk of the pressure quite yet.

The second trimester is primarily a time for you to get used to the pregnancy and try to grow close, unite as parents and partners, and discover ways to function more as a family. Expectant fathers begin developing a deepening recognition of the reality of the pregnancy. Both expectant mothers and fathers usually experience excitement over the fetal movement (kicking) and about the preliminary decisions regarding birth options and family life.

You can also expect to lose some privacy as the pregnancy becomes public.

Physical Changes

Baby. For the growing infant, the second trimester is the time for the greatest relative physical growth surge in life. During this period, the fetus will grow from approximately two inches to a foot in length and from an ounce to close to a pound in weight. The greatest growth spurt takes place around the fifth month of pregnancy.

Changes inside the mother support this growth. During this period, nourishment comes to the fetus from the placenta rather than directly through the uterine wall. The placenta functions as a very efficient viaduct which brings everything from the mother's system to the baby and vice versa. Moments after the mother eats or drinks something, she shares it with the baby. This is one of the reasons that the mother's diet and intake of caffeine, alcohol, and other drugs are so closely watched today. The placenta is emitted after the baby during delivery and is called the afterbirth. When cut at birth, the umbilical cord which connects the infant to the placenta will ultimately produce the belly button.

During the second trimester, the baby moves and floats in the amniotic fluid receiving food and oxygen from the cord and the placenta. Pictures of the fetus resemble photographs of astronauts floating in space, hooked to life-support systems.

Mom. For the mother, the changes involve the showing of the pregnancy and frequently a welcome reduction or disappearance of exhaustion and morning sickness that marked the first trimester. Not every woman who has morning sickness loses it during this time. Some carry it throughout the pregnancy. However, the majority of women begin to feel healthy, energetic, and strong during this middle phase. The well-known "rosy glow" of pregnancy is often descriptive of women at this time. For these reasons, and because there is nothing that immediately needs to be done, the second trimester is often called the honeymoon period of the pregnancy.

Cravings

This is also a time when dry crackers cease to be the only inoffensive food to the mother. Strong and highly variable appetites emerge along with desires for apparently unusual combinations of food. Often, pregnant woman are the object of teasing for these cravings. It was during one of these times that I discovered in 1981, the curious fact that no restaurant in all of Honolulu served cream of asparagus soup before 5:00 p.m. Renowned desires for novel, specific dishes or for anything that is unavailable at home during the late evening have probably contributed greatly to the nationwide proliferation and success of convenience stores.

Late-night cravings provide a situation wherein a pregnant woman can be dependent on her husband. What kind of a husband would allow his pregnant wife to go out by herself to an all-night store? It can be a curious way for your wife to test whether you love her enough to indulge her at this time. Most men react to such cravings with good humor, enjoyment, and the knowledge of the mileage that they will later be able to get from telling stories about how they dragged out of bed at midnight to get the "little woman" a peppermint stick ice cream cone with a dill pickle chaser.

It is also a time when men, joining their wives for these late-night snacks, may begin to eat more and start putting on as much weight as their wives. The most common "couvade" symptoms reported by expectant fathers during the middle phase of pregnancy are weight gain and gastrointestinal distress. A third of the fathers interviewed admitted to gaining some weight during this period—none more effectively than I!

The Kickoff

Perceived movement (also called quickening) marks the beginning of this time period. Once it occurs, it normally increases throughout the pregnancy and beyond. As most parents will attest, the second trimester marks the beginning of a realization that the phrase "sleeping like a baby" signifies abundance rather than lack of movement.

The movement also brings a dramatic change in consciousness about the pregnancy for the parents. It is very difficult to deny the actuality of life when that life is making its presence felt in such a dramatic way. Most parents remember clearly the moment that they experienced the first movement. One father described it in his journal:

> We were making love today, and it was vigorous and very nice . . . middle of the afternoon . . . feeling very close, and just when we were done and were stroking each other and feeling loving, it happened. It was unmistakable, yet dreamlike. He kicked twice! The first time, Trese said, "I think I felt a kick." Then seconds later, I put my hand on her stomach, and there was a second one. I really felt it! I seemed like a pencil under the skin poking back at me. We looked at each other in joy and disbelief, and I remember joking and suggesting that it was a protest against disrupting his home with the intercourse. I knew then that our lives, even our sex lives, would now have to account for a third person. The little guy was talking

back to me. I seem to be walking around in circles today. Thoughts run through my mind and jump out, only to be replaced by new ones. Songs about daddies and sons (funny, I don't think of having a daughter) keep fleeting across my mind, especially Tom Paxton's "Marvelous Toy" . . . I wanted to call my dad too and tell him and ask if he remembers the first time I moved.

Another dad laughingly described his frustration with trying to feel his baby's movement:

When I came home that day, she told me, "The baby moved." I was stunned and immediately put my hand on her belly. She giggled and said, "Not now, he's sleeping now." Later that night, she told me, "He kicked again," but all my efforts to feel the kick were thwarted. It was almost like they had a conspiracy to play only when I wasn't looking. It was about a week before I actually felt it myself. Every time I tried, the kid would just fake left, go right, and I missed him. I even tried to put my hands on her whole belly at once and fell asleep like that. If that kid turns out to be a momma's boy . . .

Emotional Changes

Awareness. While some men become aware and involved in the pregnancy around conception and others at birth or later, the reality of the pregnancy hits the vast majority of men soon after they perceive some fetal movement. It is hard to describe the multitude of feelings that accompany the experience of the first movement. Often, it is the most powerful experience in a man's life to that point.

One father described it this way:

It hit me that I was part of God. I had a part in life and the human race. I would pass me on to the future. It took weeks to begin to digest that. I felt so potent and powerless at the same moment. I was a part of the grand scheme and also minuscule and meaningless at the same time.

Another dad described the moment of movement:

There was a ripple across her belly. I asked, "What was that?" and we both said together, "Was that a kick?" It was incredible. I am a father. My father is a grandfather. My life is now changed.

Early arrivals. Emotional realization of the pregnancy can be highlighted by early gifts or infant clothing. Within moments of receiving some infant outfits from Susan's sister, the reality that a person would soon be wearing those cute little clothes with the snaps hit like a ton of bricks. This child already has possessions. She was definitely more real than just a few moments before.

Many men reported a sense of sudden realization of their impending fatherhood brought about by some infant's object. Andy reacted,

> *It was the little shoes. They were about big enough for my thumbs. I took one look at them and then another and then another. It came like a splash of cold water in my face. Someone's going to be wearing those soon . . . and I'm responsible for them. I was proud.*

He continued with a quizzical smile on his face,

> *But I also started to think, maybe we're rushing into this, maybe we should wait a few years. I'm too young to be a father.*

Delays in arriving. Emotional awareness may be particularly delayed for expectant parents who need to await the outcome of amniocentesis, CVS, genetic, or sonogram tests. While the CVS tests are taken during the first trimester, results are not usually known until the second. Amniocentesis is done late in the first trimester or early in the second trimester. These tests are normally used by older mothers or those with a greater risk of genetic birth defects such as Tay-Sachs disease to assure that certain types of birth defects are not present in the fetus. Parents who must wait for the test results often put their emotional acceptance of the pregnancy somewhat on hold until they are certain that the pregnancy is viable.

Miguel, the father of a two-year-old, responded,

> *Until we get the test results back, it doesn't even seem real to me. My wife is 37 now, and we just need to wait. I think she's already connecting to the little one. She did the first time too. I'm more protective. I want this kid, but I won't get my hopes up until I'm sure I can have him.*

Daddy as protector. Yet another factor for men during this time is a growing concern for the safety of the fetus. In our culture, men are traditionally cast as the providers of security and protection. These concerns begin to intensify for most men during this time. In interviews of over 250 men, only seven said that they had not thought about the baby's health considerably during the pregnancy. Oftentimes, expectant fathers confessed to their friends that they had grave concerns that the baby be "born with the right number of fingers and toes." The specter of possible brain damage or other birth defect was so great for most of these men that they often felt that they could not even discuss these concerns with their wives. Rationalizations for avoiding discussion of these apprehensions ranged from fear of "jinxing" or "cursing" the child to "not wanting to upset the little woman."

There is no evidence that your concerns for the safety of your child will reduce later on. Fathers tend to be increasingly concerned with the health of their children. Indeed, the most common worry expressed in retirement communities and nursing homes is the health and safety of the children, who by now are often middle aged. The health concern for expectant fathers is sometimes expressed indirectly by an increased interest in environmental issues, education, world and political issues, and the future. Sometimes men express their caring more surreptitiously. Recent dads tend to check as frequently as their wives to make sure that the newborn is breathing. They just tend to do so when nobody else can see them.

The expectant father still lacks any direct physical link to his infant during the second trimester. He must get his contact secondhand. If fears for the safety of his unborn child surface, he is dependent on his wife for reassurance or information. Delays in receiving such data can encourage speculation about the worst possible scenario. Because in American culture, most men reduce anxiety by *doing* something, the absence of a clear plan of action may cause anxiety to escalate. Many men feel like Greg:

> *If I could touch the kid and feel him squirming around, I'd feel more in control . . . safer . . . If anything went wrong, I could catch it in time and fix it or something. Not that I know anything about babies you understand . . . just that if I know something is wrong, I can act.*

Universal father. In fact, a man's concerns for the safety of his own unborn child may generalize substantially.

Just as it is common for some women to take on the role of "earth mother" or "mother to the world," many expectant fathers customarily become father to all the world's children. A 1981 entry from my personal journal illustrates this phenomenon:

> *I was driving to work and listening to a newscast when I heard that Travis John, the young son of baseball pitcher Tommy John (then a member of the hated New York Yankees), had fallen and been seriously injured. At that moment, the boy's safety and his recovery became terribly important to me, almost as if it were a member of my*

own family who was in danger. It was almost as if it were my own unborn child. Somehow, I had become father to all children without ever noticing a change had occurred. It wasn't an isolated and sad news incident anymore. It was empathically my own tragedy, and all the feelings were almost as strong as if it were. The fears for his safety and the sadness and tears were very real even as I was driving through traffic on the way to the office. When I arrived at work, I was able also to talk with (a friend); and when I told him of the incident, his own eyes became moist as he related a frightening experience he had with his own son a few years previously.

Becoming "father to the whole world of children" is not a unique phenomenon. Ask a man who is about to have a child and listen carefully to the way the answer becomes personalized. One second-trimester expectant father told the interviewer,

I read people differently now. It's real important how they relate to children. I notice how people are with their own kids and whether they smile at other kids or just brush them aside. When I see someone who is insensitive to their own kids' feelings (like whacking them in the supermarket), I get real upset and angry now. It used to be that I just thought that they were stupid. Now it's like I feel protective of the child. It's the same as when we go out and see someone looking at my wife's belly. If they smile, I feel close to them; and if they don't, I get real defensive.

A dramatic public example of the father of this phenomenon comes from the world of baseball. During the 1982 baseball season, a young boy was struck by a foul ball and apparently injured. Jim Rice of the Boston Red Sox went over to the stands, jumped over the railing, picked up the child, and carried him to the clubhouse for medical aid. There was no apparent thought of the ball game or of himself or his profession at that time, only concern for the child. Interviewed later, Mr. Rice commented only that he saw the child hurt and that it could have been his own child. If it were, he hoped that someone would do the same. At a moment of crisis for Jim Rice and for the thousands of other men who have acted similarly in a variety of situations, emotionally, it *was* his child, and he acted appropriately.

When one's own child is in fact in danger, this feeling and impact is multiplied exponentially. Many men interviewed have stated that they would willingly sacrifice their own lives for the safety of their sons and daughters. They also volunteered that no such sacrifice had ever occurred to them prior to becoming a parent.

Some men who have experienced the tragedy of actually losing a child have contacted me during the course of doing this research. They indicated that even the great fears they began experiencing during the pregnancy underestimated the horrible reality. The loss is so severe that even the earliest fears during pregnancy are justified.

What Kind of Father Will I Be?

It is common during this period to begin to speculate about what kind of a father you will be. Many interviewees commented that they really had no idea what it was like to be a father. They lacked models and practice. Several men commented,

> *I never knew my own dad. He was always on deployment somewhere, and then when he came home, he always wanted to be the boss.*

> *My father was very strict with us kids. I hated him as a kid. I do not want my kids to hate me that way.*

> *I've always been pretty selfish and done things my own way. I don't know if I'll be able to put anyone else first.*

> *My wife was the oldest girl in a big Catholic family. She knows all that stuff. I was an only child. I don't know step 1 about fathering.*

In fact, men are actively discouraged from participating in the care of young children by much of traditional culture. Dads are "supposed" to come home from a hard day at the office (store, mine, factory), sit down with a drink or at dinner, and play with the fed/washed/pajamaed children for a few moments before they are sent off to bed perhaps with a story. On the rare occasion that mom would go out with another woman to go shopping on a weekend, dad might be expected to be a babysitter.

No matter what kind of a past you personally had, you will likely have fantasies about how you would like your children to feel about you. Do you want to be a strong, silent, distant role model or an involved, feeling one? Will you be the disciplinarian or the "easy mark" for your kids? Is it your desire to be involved in every aspect of your child's life, or do you want to provide a home, safety, and food and leave the rest to others? Do you want your children to have a life like yours, or do you want them to have something different?

Final answers to such questions will not be forthcoming at this time. It is the pondering about the questions that is of especial value. It is especially constructive to match up your fantasies about how you wish to father with your partner's notions about mothering.

Emotional Stress

In addition to feeling excitement about the reality of the life growing inside your partner, you may also become increasingly tense about the pregnancy during this period. An increase in stress naturally exacerbates any problems that may already be present. If you have a tendency to drink alcohol as a way of relaxing, you might find yourself drinking more during this time. If you have problems with drug use, gambling, or fidelity, you might be particularly susceptible during the middle trimester. This can be disconcerting for your pregnant wife and problematic for your marriage. During pregnancy, your partner will feel more vulnerable and dependent. If the person on whom she is leaning is unsteady, she has particular problems.

In attempting to face such problems and resolve them, many expectant fathers enter counseling or therapy for some kind of habit control during the pregnancy. They rarely see the pregnancy as a major issue unless the therapist focusses in on that area and the time frame for the presenting problem. The following interchange occurred in a session with one such man who was referred for a recently developed fear of heights:

JLS: *When did you become aware of the fear of heights?*

Client: *I've always been somewhat afraid, you know high anxiety or vertigo.*

JLS: *And when did you notice it getting worse?*

Client: *I don't know, maybe a few months ago.*

JLS: *What made it bad enough for you to seek help from me?*

Client: *Oh, I don't know. I guess it got really bad about four months ago.*

JLS: *And what was happening in your life then?*

Client: *Well, I moved to an office on a higher floor last July.*

JLS: *That was several months ago. What happened around four months ago?*

Client: *Nothing to do with heights.*

JLS: *What else changed in your life four months ago?*

Client: *Let's see, four months ago was December. Christmas, New Year's. Nothing very out of the ordinary except, well, I don't see how this has anything to do with it, but my wife got pregnant in December. She's due in about four months.*

JLS: *And how is that for you?*

Client: *Well, I'm excited. This is our first.*

JLS: *Any other feelings, concerns, fears about the pregnancy?*

Client: *I don't know what that has to do with the fear of heights?*

JLS: *Well, maybe nothing, but if both events occurred at the same time, they may be connected in some way.*

Client: *Well, she's had four miscarriages before. She was married before, and every time, she lost the kid. I really don't want to bring that up and talk to her because I'm afraid she'll worry and it could happen again.*

JLS: *So you haven't been expressing that fear?*

Client: *No, I avoid it by not thinking about it.*

JLS: *It sounds like you do think about it. You just don't talk to her about it. Do you talk to her about the fear of heights?*

Client: *Yes, she's very helpful with that.*

JLS: *So you not only avoid worrying her with the fear of a miscarriage, you also may be providing her with some other concern that she can focus on and help with and keep her mind off the miscarriage.*

Client: *That sounds a bit far-fetched, but now that you mention it, I remember the first time I felt the fear was one morning going to work after she told me she was spotting. When I got afraid, I just came home.*

JLS: *So the fear also gives you a good reason to be home to take care of her if she needs it?"*

Client: *I never thought of that.*

Two weeks later, he returned with his wife and discussed the phobia and the fear of miscarriage with her in the office. She was very relieved that her husband cared so much for her and their child that he would go to such lengths to show the caring. The acrophobia began diminishing at that point and disappeared entirely during the eighth month of the pregnancy.

Not all phobias are a result of such concerns, nor are all problems so easily and clearly defined. It just seems that any symptoms that are manifested prior to a pregnancy have a tendency to increase in intensity during the pregnancy.

Relationship Issues

The second trimester is a time for the couple to make preliminary emotional and practical preparations for the arrival of their child. One of the most important components of this preparation is the need for them to bond together as a team of future parents.

Teamwork

In the absence of pressure for major physical preparations, the couple has the opportunity to work on their emotional readiness. In addition to individual preparedness for the intricacies and demands of childbirth and parenting, you need to lay the groundwork for a more complete and flexible working arrangement. This is a very important time for you and your spouse to join together and develop patterns of operating as a unit. Most couples do not have as great a need for such cooperation prior to the birth of their first child. There is considerable freedom that comes from the knowledge that your partner is an adult capable of taking care of herself. Should you occasionally be unable or unwilling to satisfy her needs, she has a number of optional sources for help. Infants, however, cannot care for themselves or find other sources for gratification. As an adult family member, you'll be involved in a complex interdependence of roles.

Whether this is a first child or a subsequent one, changes in the relationships will occur. Couples who fail to prepare for these changes by working to make their relationship more functional and cooperative are often shocked later to find themselves unprepared for the rigors of childcare. Such couples are prone to resentments that can actually threaten the continuation of the relationships itself.

The excitement over the first kicks and increasing emotional realization of what you are cocreating may naturally produce a shared sense of closeness. As one father exclaimed,

> *All this stuff is unnerving and frightening. The only consolation is that we're in this together.*

Many couples sense their growing mutuality in practical, emotional, and spiritual ways, but it is rarely without complications. There are several factors that can hinder this enhanced couple bonding.

Nature of the original decision. Couples who did not make a mutual decision to try to have a child may find their relative acceptance of the pregnancy a cause for distance and resentment rather than closeness.

Timing of the pregnancy. Even if you and your partner made a joint decision to try to get pregnant, your expectation of when it would actually happen might not square with the timing of this pregnancy. Lee reported for example,

> *Well, when we decided to get married, we talked about also wanting to have a child. Since everyone we knew was trying for months, even years, we assumed that it would take us some time also. It took almost 20 minutes for us to conceive after making that fateful decision. We even had to move up the wedding to beat the birth . . . I don't regret any of it, you understand, but it took some real getting used to.*

Bret's situation was different, but his reaction was quite similar:

> *Me and Li, we must have tried for four years to have this pregnancy. We decided that if it didn't happen by March, we'd take the tests, you know fertility like that. Then all of a sudden, she's hapai (pregnant), and I'm having all these second doubts like, "Wait a minute, it's too fast."*

Differences for men and women. Most women begin bonding with the infant earlier than their husbands. When the first movement is felt, their bonding accelerates. Generally, husbands operate somewhat differently. They begin their acknowledgment process of the baby at the announcement of the pregnancy, but then they have what Dr. Katharyn May calls a "moratorium" in which their communication about the pregnancy is primarily internal and indirect. When they first feel the movement through their partner's abdomen, men often begin directly to come to terms with the pregnancy itself. If you begin getting used to the fact of the pregnancy while your wife is accelerating her bonding with the infant, you will likely be out of synchronization for a time. This can cause misunderstanding and distance in your relationship.

Teamwork timing. The research on expectant parents suggests that the woman plays a primary role in determining how involved her husband will be in the pregnancy and birth. Biological, chemical, and cultural reasons provide women with a greater number of expectations than their husbands. Whereas most women report thoughts, plans, and fantasies about being pregnant and about the nature of the birth of their children long before a pregnancy occurred, very few men ever gave the matter much thought until the pregnancy was viable and emotionally acknowledged. Frequently, men reported that they would be at the birth of their children, go to childbirth education classes, and participate and coach at the birth to the extent that their wives wanted them to do so. Being together and doing something that was important for their wives superseded any personal concerns.

Because of this and the physical differences, your wife will probably be far ahead of you in dealing with the pregnancy and childbirth planning. It is probably best to let her take the lead and to help her by contributing your feelings as they do occur. You will likely be in a position to advise, but she will be making the final decisions.

No generalization ever applies to all men or women. Some men will mastermind the pregnancy, controlling each and every step of the way, arranging for the childbirth preparation classes, buying all the books about birth and childcare, and imposing pregnancy dietary and exercise rules on their wives. Even if you are one of this minority, it is crucial that you recognize that your partner has probably thought and fantasized about pregnancy and childbirth prior to any imminent birth. Do both of you a favor: include her in any planning.

Another male/female difference is found in studies of dreams of expectant parents. While most women reported dreams and fantasies of childbirth and infants during the second trimester, their husband's dreams tended to be much more centered on young children (five to six years old). Such dissimilarity probably reflects an equivalent desire to be close to one's child in a way that is most comfortable. Men appear to relate better to school-age children.

Whatever method of planning you jointly choose, it is crucial that you participate as equals. You may adjust to the pregnancy slower than your partner, but that doesn't mean that it will be less profound for you.

Where did you go honey? Your wife's internal focus of the first trimester will probably expand when she first begins to feel her baby's movement. She will communicate with the life within and bond more deeply with her child emotionally and spiritually. This internal connection may be quite pronounced at times and is very important to the later development of your child. It is important to understand the profoundly personal nature of the relationship between the mother and the life growing within her. Quickening presents mothers with an awesome reality. She is sustaining another life with her own body. Your partner may feel oneness with this other individual beyond anything she has ever experienced. Pregnant mothers are often deeply impressed with the enormous responsibility of keeping themselves healthy and safe. They feel both more vulnerable and more protected by the pregnancy. The "glow" frequently attributed to pregnant women may be partially a function of this intense intimacy (and a realization that the morning sickness is gone). Women who are happy about being pregnant find this a profound and joyful time.

But what of you, her husband? The new closeness between the mother and his child has to be somewhat gratifying, yet it also distances you from them. Many men describe feeling like a "fifth wheel."

An expectant father also needs to connect with the fetus, but his progress is limited by a lack of direct access to the fetus and by cultural expectations. In this way, the pregnant woman acts as a gatekeeper. If she is available and welcomes his bonding with the child, the father is free to develop a closeness to his unborn child that is similar to hers. He also develops a greater sense of connection with his wife and enhanced bonding as a family unit. Many fathers discussed how they would talk or sing to the baby through their wives abdomen or stroke the extended abdomen in an attempt to make tactile connections with their child. When the wives both allow and encourage this "secondhand" bonding with gentle humor and a feeling of togetherness, the family unit begins to incorporate the new member into its system. At least one 2013 study in the Netherlands confirms a significant relationship between the expectant father's prenatal bonding and the later father-child attachment.

Harvey said,

> *To Grace, the whole thing's a joke. She thinks she's just humoring me, but I am getting through to our baby when I play my guitar at night and when I talk to him. It may seem funny, but I know that he can hear me. She believes too, because last week, one night, she said, "You forgot to play your music," and we both laughed and cuddled.*

But what happens if the gate is not left open to the expectant father?

If your wife withdraws deeply into herself to bond, she may feel your attempts to get in as disruptive and intrusive. If a competition develops between the child and the husband for the wife's time, later problems can be created.

Mark, a father with grown children, expecting the birth of the first child of his second marriage, confessed,

> *When Shirley goes inside and ignores me, I fall directly into depression. It's just like when Alice (his first wife) took off and left. I know she's only trying to get close to the infant, but it seems like desertion to me, and I feel like the best part of our lives together is already over.*

Steve indicated similar feelings:

> *As soon as the baby began kicking, Mary had no use for me at all. I felt like I was divorced. I was relegated to the role of provider, and there was no room for me in that tandem they had. I even began to hate the baby—my baby—for taking her away. When I complained about it to her, she told the whole family, and now even my own father is telling me to grow up and not be so selfish. It makes me wonder about what it was like for him when I was in utero.*

Several men indicated that they thought that their spouses deliberately kept the "kicks" from them as a way of maintaining a separate intimacy between woman and child.

For some men, the experience of their wives' occasional distance was a welcome relief from their dependency. It allowed the fathers to gain some respite from the pressures of their lives, especially the extra stress created by the pregnancy. It also provided them with a temporary escape from their own ruminations and internal confrontations about the meaning of the pregnancy. Irv said,

> *Well, yes, I have noticed Judith turning inward, but I understand. I mean it's all part of the process of pregnancy, don't you think? Well, it does get to me sometimes a little bit, but nothing serious you know . . . more of a slight irritation and a sense that I'm being kept out of something that doesn't really involve me. I guess I deal with it by working longer hours and not having so much time at home to notice it. One good thing is that Judith doesn't bug me about watching Monday night football. She just sits next to me on the couch and spaces out.*

The majority of the men surveyed had the opposite reaction. They felt thwarted in getting close to their spouses and blocked in their attempts to bond with their growing infant. These men felt abandoned and at the same time guilty about being so needy. Furthermore, when they did discuss their feelings with others, they often got feedback that they were selfish and needed to "grow up and take care of their wives' needs. After all, she's the pregnant person."

Peter's experience was very typical:

> *I think something is very wrong with me. I have been feeling more and more needy as this pregnancy progresses. I also feel that I can't reach Tina at all. She doesn't want to talk much, and when we do, I feel like she drifts away. It's like the baby will replace me in her heart. I so wanted the baby as a way to solidify our love and our marriage. Now it seems like the marriage is between her and the baby and I'm on the outside. I know that having a child changes the marriage, but it seems that the changes are too big for my tastes. Maybe I'm just neurotic, but I want this pregnancy to be shared.*

Jim was much more resentful:

> *So far since the pregnancy began, I picked up an extra job to make up the money that we lost when she quit, have begun to do more than my share of the housework, run out at all hours to buy her pistachio ice cream, and she won't even talk to me about the baby or iron my shirt for work.*

When asked whether they had discussed this feeling of rejection with anyone, most men said that they hadn't because they felt guilty about being so "selfish." Some men indicated that they had discussed it with friends or relatives and were told to forget it. Others discussed it with their wives and claimed that they felt better after that.

Not all men are directly aware of these feelings. Sometimes the feelings are symbolically represented. George revealed the following dream:

> *I don't know what it's all about, but I have had repeated nightmares of being abandoned in a dark tunnel, and I'm very small, maybe five years old or so. Then this woman comes by and offers to help me out, but somehow, she leaves me there. The woman is my mother and also my wife. I wake up still feeling desperately alone.*

Dreams of one's birth and symbolic representations of birth like George's coming through a tunnel are frequently reported. They often represent the unmet needs of the expectant father. In George's case, being helped through the tunnel and being connected to his family was very important.

The crucial part of this for you is that at the time when you are just beginning to become emotionally aware of your impending fatherhood, experiencing a plethora of mixed feelings and especially looking for support, your partner is accelerating her move away from you and inside herself. There is nothing wrong with either of your desires, but there is a lack of synchronicity.

At the time when a woman becomes emotionally aware of her pregnancy, her partner has not yet begun to react personally. By the time he does begin to become aware of the pregnancy and his own needs, she has moved to a new stage and is now actively pursuing the relationship with her baby. This paradox causes a great deal of marital stress. When she needs the closeness, he is not sufficiently involved in the pregnancy to be fully present for her; and when he needs the closeness most, she is most interested in another interaction. This is commonly described by couples as a particularly difficult component of the pregnancy process.

Sexual Complications

The second trimester of pregnancy would seem the ideal time for enhanced sexuality for the couple. There is no need for interruptive or uncomfortable birth control methods. The morning sickness is gone. The woman typically feels healthy and energetic. It is the last chance before her increasing size will necessitate limiting positions and comfort. Sexual expression can be a particularly healthy and meaningful way of enhancing feelings of connectedness and union. Feeling sexually desired can help dispel a woman's self-consciousness about her changing shape and help prevent a deterioration of her self-image. The husband's performance concerns about the birth and providing for children are usually not much of a distraction yet. Physicians, pregnancy books, and the popular press all describe this period as a time of increased sexual activity. Indeed, for many couples, this is a time of considerable sexual expression.

It is therefore a puzzle that many couples in the study describe this period as a time of lower sexual interest than prior to the conception. What could cause this?

At least one explanation has to do with the differential speed and style of bonding. A couple that is not synchronized may well have a difficult time being open and free in their sexual expression. If they are competing over the baby, loving may represent a loss of power in their struggle. If both are feeling in need of their partner's understanding and affection, they may well find it hard to be giving to each other.

If you do find yourself competing with or distancing from your pregnant partner, increased affection and sexual expression may be a bridge to bring you closer. If you find yourself turning away from sexuality, it is definitely a time to talk and build links with your wife. It is important to tell her if you feel pushed away. Be clear about what you want instead of expecting her to read your mind or going away resentfully.

If you have the belief that sexual activity might hurt or impair the infant or have a notion that sexuality and parenthood are somehow incompatible, you need to discuss it with your partner and possibly with an expert in marital counseling.

A rift at this time may persist and grow. Feelings of distance and being left out of the pregnancy can foster a potentially devastating late-pregnancy affair.

Bonding Names

Many couples begin giving the child names during the second trimester. Joke names exist for most couples at this time. One couple named the child "Attila," a clear reference to the morning sickness of the earlier stage. They hastened to add, "Unless she's a girl, of course, and then it's Attila Hunny." Books of names for babies begin appearing, and couples try out both serious and humorous options. Names like junior, little guy, thing, lizard, squirrel, beaver, queen, baby x, and pinhead were reported and offer a humorous look at the unconscious fears that are common for couples. These first names are usually part of a shared secret and special closeness for the couple. Such private language is rarely made public.

Are You Pregnant? The Secret Is Out

During this trimester the pregnancy becomes known to the world. If people were not told previously, they now become aware that the woman is pregnant. Congratulations and maternity clothes soon follow, as does the welcome (or unwelcome) status of "pregnancy." There is generally lots of approval for pregnant women. Along with her enhanced status comes a corresponding lessening of social attention paid to the man. If you are comfortable with this and can enjoy her time in the limelight, it may well be an enjoyable period.

If envy is experienced, it can be both positive and negative. If it leads to greater identification with your partner, a desire to be closer to her and the baby, and to become more involved in the pregnancy yourself, it can be quite rewarding. By contrast, if the envy grows into jealousy at her ability to grow children, increased competition between you, or rejection, it can create problems in the relationship.

Once the pregnancy is public, the sense of a shared secret may lessen, and you may feel a loss of some of the intimacy with your partner. Sometimes the attention from family, friends, and strangers may feel, intrusive. It is very important to share these feelings with your partner and to adjust to the changes together. Sometimes, conscious limits must be put on how others may be involved. Cameron related,

> When our friends and family found out that we were expecting, a few of them were all over her, touching her belly, talking with her as if they were privy to the most private parts of our life, and making plans for us . . . mostly her. We shared in the discomfort and decided that we had to be more clear on what was okay and what was (intrusive).

Return to the Future

Reconnection. The attempts to reconnect with your parents, which began in the first trimester, continue along with an evaluation of your own childhood. Many expectant fathers become aware of their poor paternal role models and reexperience conflicts and feelings that have been dormant since they were children. These feelings can provide a basis of empathy and sensitivity for the child's experience of the world and allow you to be a better dad when your child is born. It can also help you begin to understand what it was like for your parents when you were about to be born.

For men, the attempt to connect with their own fathers often activates ambivalent feelings. Many men recalled experiences like Seth:

> My old man was a tragic figure. He didn't belong in the house with us kids. He and my mother had a terrible relationship. All he did was work and fall asleep on the couch watching TV. I wanted him to pay attention to me a lot, and I think he really cared for all us kids. He just couldn't admit it. I used to be so frustrated when people at the plant would tell me how proud he was of me. Why couldn't he ever tell me himself?

Several men interviewed had to grow up without fathers. J. T. replied,

> I know it was bad with him and my mother. She was an alcoholic. I think he was too. One day, when I was seven, he just showed up with his girlfriend, picked up his stuff, and split. I didn't hear from him again until four years later. He sent me a birthday card on my

*brother's birthday. After he left, she had the "uncle of the month"
franchise. Lots of jerks and lots of drinking and abuse. I did contact
him later and heard his side of the story, but I don't want him to
have anything to do with my kids.*

Other expectant fathers remembered losing their fathers to divorce,
accidents, war, drugs, alcohol, or illness. These men often had poor or no
role model to help them with their own parenting. Their efforts to reestablish
paternal contact during the second trimester often represented an attempt to
find the fantasy perfect father who was all things to them.

By contrast, Chaim said that he didn't think he could live up to the
standard set by his father:

*He was the ideal father who coached the little league team, always
knew what to do to soothe hurt feelings, could figure out any school
problem, fix anything, and told the best stories. I guess he always
had time for us kids, and we all felt like a top priority for him.*

As you and your partner both recall your experiences as children, you
have the opportunity to nurture and protect each other, fulfill some old needs,
and resolve conflicts with parents which affect your current feelings.

In addition, as your parents approach their impending grandparenting,
both sets of parents may actually begin to play a larger or different role in your
life than they have in recent years. Some inevitable in-laws issues may begin
to emerge here. Thus, the reconnection may bring with it a new closeness
or a rediscovery of the reasons why you had distanced from them in the first
place. These "déjà vu" experiences serve a most valuable function. As you
recall your own childhood feelings, you are beginning to develop a necessary
sensitivity and empathy for your child's experience of this oftentimes-baffling
world.

Practicing parenting. The second trimester of the pregnancy, with its
lower pressure and higher energy, provides an excellent context in which the
couple can explore and rehearse with each other the parenting styles that
they bring from their respective pasts.

If they discover through this practicing that certain influences from their
families of origin clash or are inappropriate for their current values and
lifestyle, they can begin a search for more consistent parental models.

Couples who do not experiment with different parental roles might be
courting larger problems later. Thus, if the wife has an image of a mother
as a weak, homebound, helpless individual who is dependent on her strong
husband and the husband has a corresponding notion of the father as a
domineering, authoritarian provider for all of his family's needs, they might

easily play out this "traditional" pattern and evaluate how well it fits them now. If she believes in the helpless-female stereotype and he falls into the role of child with all mothers, they have a relationship that has no parents. They can begin to recognize that they will have to take turns being the nurturer and receiver.

Expectant parents who believe that parents are or should be unconditionally loving and supportive of their children without regard for their own or their partners' needs might well begin to develop eighteen years' worth of resentment toward their children or find their own relationships deteriorating. By contrast, some couples believe that parenthood involves a little more inconvenience than adding a car seat and a backpack to their existing lives. They are in for a revelation.

Although it is useful to experiment with alternative parenting and family styles, you do need to be cautious not to have the roles harden and persist. Should you get stuck in playing daddy to your wife's little girl or little boy to her mommy, you will experience several difficulties. A marriage that is maintained as a parent-child relationship can develop serious sexual dysfunction. Sexual problems can also arise if either or both of you hold to rigid beliefs about the nature of women. The so-called Madonna-whore complex involves a conviction that women are either good or evil. Your wife will never seem more Madonna-like than when she is beginning to show her pregnancy. Should you find yourself following strict role patterns and losing sexual interest in your wife, it may be worth consulting a marriage therapist. Of course other factors can inhibit sexual feelings such as ambivalence over the pregnancy, reduced energy caused by increased demands of working harder and helping out more around the house, and stress.

Pragmatic Considerations

Among the issues that must be confronted during this period are

- preliminary preparation for the actual birth,
- finances,
- planning for the infant's living space,
- expectations about relative duties in and out of the home including childcare,
- development of a timeline to address each of these issues.

Birth options. The midpregnancy is the time to firm up plans for the birth itself. Will you both participate in childbirth education classes? What birth options will you choose? What part will you play in the birth, Dad?

Serious investigation of options should take place during this trimester, and discussions between spouses are important. Your choices will determine what sorts of preparation you will have to make during the third trimester. It is important to identify your own and your wife's needs early so that conflicts can be recognized and resolved prior to the birth itself and not cause later problems.

Generally, men tend to take their lead from their wives. Women often have much stronger feelings and expectations for childbirth than their husbands, and most men try to go along with his wife's desires. If you want to have a say on how you will be involved in the pregnancy and birth, you will have to do some research with your partner and explore options for the birth that are best suited for you. Once you have all the information, you will be in a position to better negotiate with your partner for what you want.

It is definitely a time to discern where you want the birth to occur, who will deliver the baby, which childbirth education classes you will attend, and what sorts of maternity and/or paternity leaves you will be able to take.

Childcare groups in many communities publish extensive comparisons of the childbirth options available locally. These publications are usually free or at minimal cost and are available online or at public libraries, birthing centers, and childcare and birthing education centers.

Finances. Financial concerns begin to grow for many men at this time. Many take steps to counter this anxiety: a large number of men in the study changed to more stable jobs, while others added overtime or moonlighting jobs for extra income to take up the slack.

By contrast, some men took on greater financial burdens during the midpregnancy. Quite a few bought a home for the first time or instigated a move to a bigger, frequently far more expensive, home. Many men bought new automobiles (particularly cars that stress safety, like SUVs). There was also renewed interest in both investments and gambling for the "big score."

The focus on financial matters serves two purposes. It helps men feel like they are playing a significant role in providing for the baby. It also allows them to focus on something besides the pregnancy. They can avoid dealing with matters with which they have no direct influence and at the same time be busy coping in a traditional masculine way.

Whatever your fiscal resources, you will likely have to face some of your financial concerns during this term. It will be important to share your apprehensions and recommendations with your wife and ask for her help in understanding the part of the burden you will be carrying.

Financial concerns may be especially prevalent for couples in which the male will be doing the lion's share of the childcare and the woman most of the wage earning. Kyle Pruett's book *The Nurturing Father* is an excellent resource for couples who choose or are forced into this parenting style.

Womb with a view. Another concern for couples during this time is fixing up the room to house the baby. Often, this is an opportunity for couples to work on a project together and to cooperate in "family" activities. The preparation of the living environment for the child is one place where fathers can have a full sense of involvement. One father indicated the role he anticipated playing:

> *She gets to provide the kid's bedroom now (pointing to his wife's abdomen), but after he's born, he'll have a room made by Daddy.*

Another father informed us,

> *I feel so out of it with all this baby stuff, but I'm a builder. I just put my energy into making the crib, cradle, changing tables you know. I know what I'm doing there.*

A man who did no work with his hands took an opposite route. He read, researched, and generally became the family expert. Accumulating information helped him feel more connected to the pregnancy and helped him reduce his anxiety. What one father accomplished by making a crib out of boards and nails, another achieved by finding the best, safest, and most reasonably priced crib.

One couple described their inability to move. They could not afford to relinquish their rent-controlled apartment, especially because she was planning to take a year off from her job:

> *The place is really way too small. It was fine for Katie, but then I moved in a few years ago, and now we are expecting our daughter. So I got a storage shed, and we cannibalized the large closet to make a baby-sized baby room. We will have to deal with the space later, but for now, I am working on remodeling every night after work.*

Preparation timing. Every individual works a unique personal timeline, and each person has a different need for advance preparation. There are people who have everything including bottles and diapers lined up and at the ready in a completed, perfectly functional nursery during the fifth month. Others prefer to wait until the baby is actually home before they consider what needs to be done to accommodate this new member of the family.

Cultural factors often affect this timing. Among Jewish and Irish Catholic expectant parents, there is often an uneasy feeling about making too many specific preparations until after the birth of the child. In the roots of both cultures, there is a belief that premature preparations could jinx or cast an evil spell on the baby's health. Americans with a Pacific Island heritage commonly name the baby only after it is home for some time. Expectant parents who have roots in such subcultures often are importantly influenced by them.

Timing for preparedness is not usually a problem unless the parents have widely divergent styles. When a compulsive early planner happens to be married to a crisis-oriented reactor, they are likely to view each other respectively as a hopeless neurotic and a lazy bum(mette). Recognition of these differences and careful negotiation is often necessary to prevent some serious rancor.

Making sure baby is adequately equipped. When men do accept and try to involve themselves in the pregnancy, they often go to some extreme lengths to make a special connection with the baby. It is not unusual for men to go out and buy a ball and bat for the fetal Willie Mays. They might buy a stuffed animal or toy that a preschooler would appreciate. One expectant father was certain to videotape the baseball All-Star Game in anticipation of sharing future "good old days" with his own unborn child.

Ten Tips for the Second Trimester

1. Pay close attention to the physical changes in your wife. Make an effort to be involved in the changes by discussing them with her and by maintaining close physical contact with her. Try to feel the kicks through her abdomen.
2. Allow yourself to grow increasingly accustomed to the reality of the pregnancy. Notice your emotional reactions.
3. Keep an open channel of communication with your partner and discuss your feelings and hers as much as possible.
4. Investigate the birth options available in your community. Evaluate them with your partner. Make plans for the kind of childbirth education and other necessary preparations.
5. Make a comprehensive accounting of your finances and especially develop some sense of income and expenses. Evaluate carefully with your partner any changes that can be made.
6. Take the opportunity to reconnect with your own past. If possible, talk to your parents, relatives, friends, and neighbors about your boyhood. Pay particular attention to your relationships with your father and other important men in your past.
7. Try to find some quiet time to reflect on what is happening for you and what the baby means in terms of your life. Respect your wife's internalizing also, but let her know if she is so far inside herself that you feel deserted.

8. Focus on your dreams for your child and try to implement any that are practical. Take part in plans for creating the baby's future living space.

9. Take especially good care of your partner. Honor her cravings and listen to her feelings. Pamper her when she's most vulnerable. Do not lose sight of her as a sexual being and your adult partner.

10. Share your fears and concerns with her if possible and let her care for you. Try to find a buddy with whom you can also share deep concerns.

Chapter 7

The Third Trimester: Preparation for Birth and Fatherhood

Death and taxes and childbirth! There's never any convenient time
for any of them
—Margaret Mitchell (1936)

The final third of the pregnancy is very much the period of preparation for the birth itself. It is often marked by the end of the "honeymoon" portion of the middle trimester and by an increased awareness of impending parenthood.

Physical Changes for the Woman

The pregnant woman now begins to get much larger and less mobile. The radiant health (glow) of the previous few months may begin to give way and be replaced by some physical discomfort. Whereas the physical discomfort of the first trimester is primarily due to outpouring of hormones, the later-stage discomfort occurs more because of the growth of the fetus and the changing size of a woman's internal organs. Her expanding proportions makes mobility a problem, and by the end of the eighth month, there is also often difficulty in accomplishing such previously automatic endeavors as getting from a lying position to a standing one.

As the pregnancy comes to term and the uterus continues to expand, the woman's stomach is pushed upward and compressed, and there is less room for food. This often produces heartburn and indigestion. In addition, the disproportion formed by the enlarging uterus, also makes digestion slower and can lead to irregular bowel movements or constipation.

Women who are prone to retaining fluids might experience swelling and become bloated. Other symptoms include varicose veins (most frequent in mothers who have had several previous children), hemorrhoids (a secondary symptom of the problems caused by the constipation), shortness of breath, frequent urination due to a compressed bladder and limited capacity, as well as dizziness, muscle cramps, and headaches.

An expectant mother will begin to tire easily from the growing "extra package" she continuously carries. Moreover, much of her nutrient intake is going to the baby. Her sleep may also be disturbed. She may suffer from insomnia. She may find her enlarging body difficult to get into a comfortable position for sound sleep, and if the baby is active, she may even experience the feeling of being "kicked" awake.

Add to this a substantial number of psychological factors regarding body image, sexuality, career and role changes, and her perception of her own femininity and the result is that these are difficult months for the pregnant woman. Indeed, one of the things a husband least understands is the ability of his wife to feel most feminine and to be thrilled by her changing shape and almost simultaneously to fear that she has lost her sex appeal and to perceive herself as misshapen and "blimpy."

Emotional Changes for the Man

Things are also not so easy on the husband. As the deadline approaches, your sexy, competent wife is becoming needier and less able to do her share of the necessary chores. If she is awakened during the night, your sleep is also likely to be interrupted.

A man who is unaccustomed to sharing in homemaking tasks might find himself in a situation where they have to live with a less neat, clean, well-run household or he might take over some of those duties himself.

If you have increased the amount of work you are doing outside the home in order to provide financial security, you might also be prone to tiredness and irritability.

Other emotional concerns and troubles you are likely to encounter include dissatisfaction with the sexual relationship, performance anxiety, pressures of financial responsibility, and discomfort with the lack of privacy that a pregnancy can bring.

Existing problems in the basic relationship between the partners tend to become significantly aggravated during this time of increasing stress.

Almost a Father

All of the stresses and tasks unique to this third trimester are leading to one major event: the upcoming birth. Psychologist Alan Gurwitt has creatively labeled this period as "coming to term(s)." This pressure can become quite intense for expectant fathers. Men are about to enter a world where they have little control and knowledge, and as the big day approaches, they become increasingly aware of this. They are also about to enter a world in which they will experience untold delights and excitement.

Tim described it:

> *I think I'm losing my mind. I get all excited about the big day and about being a daddy, and then I feel like crying. Then I get real scared and dream about running away. I think I should shout "I'm too young to be a parent." I still want to be a kid.*

Josh also described being very sensitive and emotional at the least provocation. He described a phenomenon that was very common among expectant fathers:

> *I don't know how to describe it, but I just start crying at the dumbest movies . . . especially about kids and parents. The more (melodramatic and) ridiculous the story is, the more I cry. The worst was the films we saw at the (childbirth education) class. I just welled up with tears at every birth as sort of anticipation of what was happening for us. It was also scary too, worrying about something happening to the baby. I keep having a dream that I'll be left alone with the baby and that something will happen to Marge.*

Carl talked about his own crying during this period:

> *I think my tears were a cry of anguish and pain all mixed with the joy that comes with becoming a father.*

Reality

While there are some men who can continue to deny the upcoming birth until the baby is actually born, most expectant fathers begin emotionally acknowledging that the baby is real and imminent during this final trimester. There are many signs to tell him that this is so. His wife's shape has changed markedly, and the pregnancy is quite public. His own feelings also have begun to change. The baby is becoming something more of a reality and less of an "abstraction," and he begins relating to the infant as a person. Names are chosen, and the joke names that a couple has for their infant begin to slide away.

The father's dreams also begin changing. Many men reported that they had a variety of nightmares of something happening to their pregnant partners. Many men also reported symbolic birthing dreams. George, for example, described a dream of being caught in a long pipe and having to squeeze his way to safety like James Bond in the movie *On Her Majesty's Secret Service*.

Fathers also become acutely aware of other children and think about child-rearing. Often, they become intensely involved in preparing a home for the baby. They may build or buy a crib or cradle or help create a nursery room and layette. Many expectant fathers begin practicing their parenting role by caring more for their increasingly needy wives. Safety factors also begin to enter into the expectant father's consciousness. Many men bought gifts for their wives and babies during this time. In a sense, the father begins to catch up with his pregnant wife in "giving to the baby."

In addition, many expectant fathers reported seeing the world around him in new ways. One of the most significant alterations that occur is that he begins to perceive himself as the family's representative to the outside world. Two significant ways in which this is expressed are in his roles as provider and protector. Many men reported feeling particularly sensitive to threats of intrusion or lack of safety for their families. This was particularly shown in attempts to provide a stable financial setting.

Thus, even as the woman is becoming preoccupied with the life growing within her and with the advent of motherhood, the expectant father also begins to refocus and redefine himself as a father. Many men, who prior to this time seemed almost unaware of the pregnancy, begin to catch up on learning about pregnancy, childbirth, and child safety—learning about the details of bringing the baby home, including the awesome array of car seat information. It is also common for men to reflect on their own fathers and the fathering they received as children. Often, their circle of friends begins to change as they seek out other men who are about to be or who are already fathers.

For many men, the pattern was first to do something related to fathering and only subsequently to become aware of fatherly feelings. Several men reported that "it didn't really hit me until I felt amazement that my parents were about to become grandparents."

Isaac was interviewed while he worked on finishing touches for the cradle he had built for his child. He was working on his patio, and there were three little neighborhood boys watching him intently. They seemed honored when he would ask them to hand him a tool. The due date of birth was only two weeks away. He was justifiably proud of his work when he remarked,

> You know, this is the first thing I ever did with my hands that came out right. I've always been the one to bring it to the repairman if there's any problem. But I've really labored on this, and it's okay . . . This is my first with Rachel, but I already had two kids before. It was different then. I don't know. The times weren't right or I wasn't, but my kids are grown and away, and I hardly knew them . . . I know these kids (motioning toward the three boys on the patio) better. They're my new friends. I just met them when I started to work on this . . . I never really knew any kids. When mine were little, I was busy making a living. Well, this one will be different. I'm going to be a major part of her life.

The interviewer asked how he knew it would be a girl. Isaac replied, smiling,

> I just know. Besides, I already have two boys. It's time for a girl . . . I've been looking in toy stores lately. I'm going to make her a whole bunch of things. Swings, wooden cars . . . I want to name her after my mother. How do you like the name Ruth? Rachel prefers Roberta, after her father . . . It's funny, but I feel like I already know her. I think about her so often. I sleep with my hand on Rachel's tummy and wait for the kicks. She's an active one, I tell you.

Isaac and Rachel's son (named Robert) was born less than a week after the interview. Isaac reported one week after the birth, "It seems totally natural to have a boy. It's something I'm used to." Bobby was already the apple of Daddy's eye.

Like most fathers, Isaac adjusted to this surprise quite well. However, in the process of adjustment, some unexpected events can be quite problematic. In "coming to terms" with the final trimester of pregnancy, expectant fathers must come to grips with changes in sexuality and preparatory anxiety.

Changes in Sexuality

Changes in sexuality are so crucial to the process because the birth is a result of sexual relating. It is not surprising that problems would also occur in this area.

One change that frequently accompanies the final stage of pregnancy is an alteration in the frequency and type of sexual activity. Although some couples stop intercourse almost as soon as the pregnancy begins to show and others joke about making love in the hospital on the way to the delivery, most couples do report a considerable lessening of sexual activity during these last months. As the woman gets larger, of course, positions and types of sexual activity need to be modified. The freedom of the middle trimester when couples are feeling healthy, sexual, and free from birth control concerns must give way to the changes brought about by the progressing pregnancy. The missionary (man on top) position for sexual intercourse will often become uncomfortable and awkward, and couples need to adjust to this. Often, couples experiment with other positions that bring great satisfaction (and continue long after the children are born, grow up, and leave for college).

Some couples seem to believe that intercourse during the latter stages of pregnancy might hurt the infant. While this notion is completely unfounded except for couples with unique medical problems, these couples frequently stop intercourse at this time and find themselves suddenly without any sexual outlet. It is important to work this out in some mutually satisfying way to avoid resentment and seeds for larger problems later.

Two recently divorced fathers told of sexual problems that began during the last trimester became very serious. Joseph angrily reported,

> As soon as she began to get big, she just cut me off and sent me out of the bedroom. I can't believe that I actually slept on the couch for over three months. I think I told myself that I had to do it to get enough sleep because I had to work all day. Even when I tried to hug her or hold her belly, she pulled away and told me it'd hurt the baby. I know it isn't right, but I felt like killing her and the kid. Now with the separation, I get to see the kids alone and can be with them the way I want. It's working out a lot better.

Similarly, Cal said,

> Jane just decided that at some point in the pregnancy, the baby was hers, and I wasn't going to have anything else to do with the pregnancy or her body. She told me that she had to do all the work of having the baby, and so she was doing it her way. You know, everyone forgets that a kid has a daddy too. I wish I could be the pregnant one. It would be a lot easier. I'm sure that I'd be just as horny with a big tummy as a little one.

Steve agreed that it was a very difficult time, but he and his wife were able to struggle through it:

I was actually shocked when Rosa decided all by herself that it was time to be celibate. No discussion, no argument, just no more sex for five or six months. I was shocked, hurt, angry, and in my typical way, just pulled back and sulked for a few days. When I found myself thinking about my secretary in a nonwork kind of way, I knew that I had to do something. It was very hard to discuss. We never had really talked about sex before. It all worked out for the best though, because when we talked, it turned out that what she didn't want was me on top and vigorous thrusting. We found a lot of ways to be close and make love without intercourse. I'm glad we did do that because now we can do so much more for each other, but I don't want to go through that whole thing again.

The reduction or change in sexual activity itself seems to be less of a problem than the couple's ability to discuss it together. Rarely will a husband want to proceed with intercourse that will cause his wife physical pain. However, if he is simply cut off because of her singular belief that it's bad for the baby, it might have long-term negative effects on the marriage and the way that the father relates to the child.

It is not only the woman who is responsible for reducing sexual activity. Several women reported that they were feeling very passionate but that their partners were unresponsive. There were several reasons given for this, including fears of hurting the baby, feeling unconnected or less attracted to their wives, and overtiredness from the extra work and chores they had assumed.

Some men had psychological reasons to hold back from their partners. Herb put it this way:

When Bev started to get big, I just turned off. I don't know, I kept thinking of her as a mother, and it seemed wrong to be having sex with a mother.

These feelings do not necessarily end during the pregnancy. One father of an eight-year—old child describing his continuing reduced sexual interest in his wife indicated,

You know when I saw something so big (his son) come out of there (his wife's vagina), I felt inadequate in comparison.

The Late-Pregnancy Affair

Most husbands who find themselves feeling sexually rejected by their pregnant wives find ways of discussing and negotiating with their wives to deal with this matter or find alternative outlets for their sexual energy. Sometimes, these husbands become very involved in physical activity or extra work and find themselves "too tired at night to care about sex."

A small but nevertheless alarming number of men attempt to deal with their stress by becoming involved in a sexual affair with another woman. This phenomenon can be particularly devastating to the later relationship of the married couple.

Because couples are usually brought so much closer together during the pregnancy, it is hard to understand how a man might become involved sexually with another woman, yet this is not a completely unique situation. This phenomenon, which has been known for years by psychotherapists and others involved in the pregnancy and birthing process, has most frequently been attributed to the impact of a change in the wife's appearance.

One nurse educator (and mother of three) described it:

> *He just went out and had an affair with another woman. It really galls me to see how as soon as a woman loses her sexy shape, the men are gone to greener pastures.*

It does seem a likely hypothesis that a man might find his pregnant wife less attractive during the last few months of pregnancy, particularly if there was little or no sexual activity for the couple during this time. If so, he might seek sexual expression elsewhere.

The Rest of the Story

In the course of my study of expectant fathers and prior to clinical work with couples, I have been able to interview twenty-seven men who actually had some form of extramarital affair during the latter stages of the pregnancy.[10] While this is a very small number from which to make generalizations, several themes did emerge. Of primary interest is the fact that none of the twenty-seven men reported that their wives were less attractive to them

---

10. After publication of the first edition of *When Men Are Pregnant*, this finding was picked up, misconstrued, and greatly exaggerated by the media. At one point, it was reported that 27 percent of men have affairs during the late pregnancy. In fact, it was 1 to 2 percent of the men studied.

during the pregnancy. Quite the contrary, like most other men surveyed, these fathers found their wives' changing shape even more attractive than ever before. They also indicated that they very much desired affectionate and sexual contact with their wives during this time.

What then could be the reason for their cheating? Several answers to this question emerged.

One particularly interesting common theme was that the person with whom the men had the affair was frequently well known by the spouse. This probably means that the affair had a great deal to do with the marital relationship itself. Was it unconsciously designed to be detected?

In five of the marriages in which the late-pregnancy affair occurred, the marriages did not survive the baby's second birthday. This is not to indicate that the affair *caused* the marriage to go bad. It is just as likely that the affair was a statement of the already-declining course of the marriage. However, it is rare indeed when an extramarital affair might be positive. In each of these marriages, having a child represented a hope of bringing the relationship together. Instead, it was the "straw that broke the camel's back."

In the majority of the pregnancy affairs, several factors were present:

1) The affairs were with a close friend or relative of the wife (in one case her sister and in another her mother).
2) In each case, the men reported being attracted to their wives and "turned on" by her pregnant shape.
3) Interviews with the men all indicated that they felt particularly pushed away by the pregnancy and birth process.
4) Each of the men described a strong need to talk to someone.
5) Most of the men had no previous affairs.

Carlo is a good example. Here is his description of the affair:

> *I really don't know what happened. It all was so sudden. Missy (Nancy's best friend) was over the house, and we were all talking about the baby and all, and then Nancy just sort of disappeared inside with the baby. She gets this fully spaced-out look on her face and doesn't talk or answer questions or anything . . . And then at some point, she just got up and went to bed. I thought she went to the bathroom, but she didn't ever come back . . . Anyhow, Missy and I got to talking and laughing about old times and about how it was hard for both of us to be around Nancy these days . . . We were drinking wine. I know that's no excuse, but we both started to feel real good and close. I know it's hard to believe, but I felt closer to Missy than I did to Nancy, and she was having my baby . . . Well,*

one thing led to another, and we ended up hugging, then kissing and everything else. I felt real bad about it, and so did she. But when we saw each other to talk about what to do, it happened again. I slept with her four times . . . When Nancy found out, she hit the ceiling. She was fit to be tied, and I don't blame her. I'm really ashamed of being so weak now, but when it was happening, I don't know, somehow, it was okay. She won't even talk to Missy anymore. I know this sounds strange, but she was angrier at Missy than at me.

When asked what provoked the affair, Carlo added,

I have thought about that so much and don't have an answer. No excuse. Nothing. I know that I was feeling very lonely and excluded from my wife's life, but that's no reason to have sex with another woman. I know Missy felt the same way. She felt really pushed out of Nancy's life too.

After a year of therapy and lots of pain, anger, sadness, and fear, Carlo and Nancy did come to grips with the affair and moved ahead in their marriage. When I last spoke with them, their daughter was five years old, and they were talking about a second child.

Carlo's story was similar to most of the men who reported having had late-pregnancy affairs. He felt rejected, lonely, and pushed out of the pregnancy. He had a strong need to talk to someone about these feelings. Like most men in our culture, he found it easier to talk about such personal matters to a woman rather than a man.

He chose a person who was close to his wife with the hope that he would be better understood. Unfortunately, the person he confided in also felt abandoned by Nancy. They were either unable or unwilling to deal directly with Nancy about their feelings of abandonment. Neither consciously planned nor wished to hurt Nancy. Both were hurt and angry and may have unconsciously chosen to strike back in this way. That does not minimize the impact on all of them, but it gives us reason to consider the motivation for such unacceptable behavior.

From this modest survey, it seems clear that the late-pregnancy affair is a means for men to seek affection and to counteract the feelings of rejection from their partners. That the affair occurred with a person who was also close to the wife suggests that this other person was also feeling pushed away by the wife and the pregnancy. While other people were available to both of them, their solution to this problem was to draw close together to each other and exclude the pregnant woman. Perhaps the affair was not totally meant to be secret.

From this perspective, we can perceive the need of the expectant father to become closer to his spouse and to try to find other ways to be nourished during the pregnancy. The affair is not an acceptable way in our culture. However, the expectant man must have his needs recognized and must find some acceptable means of resolving them.

It is worth noting that men are not the only partners who had affairs. Several of the men we talked to indicated that they were aware that their wives had had affairs during the pregnancy.

Recent research suggests that it is as likely for a wife to have an extramarital affair as it is for a husband. She is, according to a number of studies, far less likely to talk about it.

An affair, particularly at this time, is almost always detrimental to closeness in a relationship. Very frequently, help from an objective or professional third party is necessary. Marriage counseling with couples who do experience such an affair is most frequently of fairly long duration (a year or longer) and sometimes cannot bridge the gap in trust caused by the affair.

Although the number of men and women who have affairs during pregnancy is clearly a small percentage, there is one additional issue this phenomenon raises: who is really the father?

Paternity Concerns

Almost 60 percent of the men in our sample had at least fleeting questions as to whether the baby was really their own, although a much lower percentage actually thought that their wives might have been sexually involved with another man. Many men apparently do entertain the fantasy or thought that another man was the person responsible for the upcoming birth.

This is not a new concern. As early as the year 330 BC, Aristotle commented about the issue of paternity:

Mothers are more fond of their children than fathers are: for the bringing them forth is more painful and they have more certain knowledge that they are their own.[11]

Interviews on this point were particularly interesting. It was rare when men spontaneously volunteered this information. However, when a specific question was asked, a number of men responded like Fred:

You know it's funny that you should bring that up because I did have just a momentary question. Nothing serious you know. The thought

---

[11.] Ethic: XI 7.

just crossed my mind. I'm really sure that Ali is faithful, but I did think about it.

Jake expressed it a different way, using humor:

I'm sure that it's my baby, but I did joke with her (wife) that "if that kid has blue eyes, I'm gone."

Jake was not alone in discussing expected physical characteristics. One Samoan man who married his Chinese-American wife after discovering that she was pregnant was adamant about his desire to have a child with no "haole" (Caucasian features). This fear was exacerbated by his retroactive jealousy. Prior to meeting him five years ago, she had lived with a Caucasian man for several months.

On the face of it, it is hard to understand why any man would simultaneously question the paternity of his unborn child and be certain of his wife's fidelity. Such doubts are illogical and primarily generated by unconscious fears and concerns.

If you do experience such concerns, it is particularly hard to find solace by confiding in others. For one thing, your public admission of an even fleeting concern seems tantamount to publicly accusing the wife of cheating. Secondly, other men often have such personal fears about such matters that they insensitively joke about it.

Carl described a particularly difficult interchange with his "best friend." He reported telling Jim soon after the birth of his son that he was particularly bothered by a dream of his wife having sex with an old (high school) boyfriend and that resulting in a pregnancy. Jim responded,

Well, that's not too surprising. I mean, she did sleep with the guy before.

Carl answered that they hadn't seen each other for many years and that it mostly came out of the fact that the baby didn't look at all like him.

His "friend" responded, "Well, did you check out the gardener or postman?"

Jim's insensitivity to such a serious matter is probably due to his own anxiety and inability to express empathy without the distancing action of humor. This type of response is not limited to males.

A recent mother, who had lived for some time with an East Indian man prior to her marriage, was told by a woman friend that her blond-haired baby "looked Indian."

What are such illogical fears about? Why should new parents even question the genetic heritage of their baby? Why is such a fear so widespread, even in the face of overwhelming contrary evidence? The answers to these questions are complex and far more involved with spiritual than behavioral concerns.

The birth of one's child brings parents directly into contact with the issue of mortality. In some ways, there is no greater or more basic act possible for humans than the creation of life. Many fathers speculating on the enormity of such an act feel insecure and quite small. Indeed, there was a pervasive sense that, as one recent father put it,

> *I am not good enough, important enough, or powerful enough to create new life. That is not for a man to do. It is a thing that God does. Certainly, it is far greater an accomplishment than I can achieve.*

Furthermore, the beginnings of life also bring with it a deeper knowledge of one's own death. By psychologically denying that the new life might be mine, I can also block from my mind a more imminent sense of my death.

These issues regarding self-identity and concerns regarding sexual inadequacy are important and will be discussed in greater detail later in this chapter.

Your Presence at the Birth.

As recently as your father's and certainly in your grandfather's generation, the clear expectation was that the father would not be in the room observing or participating in the birth of his children. In the 1960s, only about 15 percent of all men were actually present for the birth of their children. In his book *Husband Coached Childbirth*, Dr. Robert Bradley instructed expectant parents how to fight the system to get the dad in.

Because of pioneers like Bradley, this began to change in the 1970s and 1980s; and today, most men expect to be a welcomed participant. In fact, only around 15 percent of expectant fathers now expect to be absent. You will likely not only be present, but you can anticipate taking an active coaching role, with the acknowledgment of the birthing professionals. This reality may either increase or decrease your concerns.

Preparation for the Birth

All of the stresses and tasks unique to this third trimester are leading to one major event: the upcoming birth. This pressure can become quite intense for expectant fathers. The birthing process itself is not well known or understood by most men. As the expected date for birth approaches, expectant fathers become far more aware of the birth and its implications and frequently become more excited and anxious. Because men often reduce anxiety by "doing something" and there is little the expectant can do at this time, it can be very frustrating.

Although some men do not experience these fears because their excitement and joy about the upcoming event is so great and others continue to deny psychologically that anything is extraordinary and thus avoid the experience of anxiety, the majority of expectant fathers do report several concerns that are related to this period, notably performance anxiety, family safety, and financial responsibility.

Performance anxiety. Over 90 percent of the expectant fathers in the survey reported that they were anxious about their performance in the delivery room. While for the most part these men very much wanted to participate in the birth, they often worried that they would become sick or light-headed and/or faint during the delivery. Medical professions do not do a great deal to minimize this anxiety. Indeed, several obstetricians reportedly joked with fathers, "If you faint, try and do it out from underfoot."

One father interviewed three weeks before the birth of his daughter put it this way:

> *I'm hoping I don't get sick because I don't want to miss it. I'm not expecting pretty sights. I just don't want to be surprised.*

Another father indicated that his way of doing things was to figure them out clearly and logically and then to proceed in an appropriate and sensible manner. Thus, in order to "reduce the risk of getting ill during the delivery," he and his wife

> *were very thorough. We checked the whole thing out. We actually went to another birth of our friends' child. That way, we had a real good picture as to what was likely to happen.*

A contrasting approach was represented by a man who had two children and commented that he knew he did not want to be

> *in that (delivery) room . . . I wanted to be down the hall waiting. No*
> *way were they going to get me in there.*

When queried as to the reason, he responded,

> *I want the docs to be doing their thing with my wife. I don't want*
> *them to be reviving me or worrying about me.*

Another father confessed that he had planned to be out of town on urgent business during the period of the due date. When the baby came four weeks early and prior to his planned departure, he was faced with the prospect of "the delivery room ordeal." "Fortunately," he reported, "I got a bad case of the flu, and they wouldn't let me in because of germs."

Several years after the publication of *When Men Are Pregnant,* I was a guest on *The Oprah Winfrey Show.* One of the expectant fathers in the audience expressed his anxiety by repeatedly calling the birth room "the emergency room." It was a powerful reminder of his anticipated worries.

In addition to the fears of queasiness, light-headedness, vomiting, and/ or fainting, many fathers indicated that they were anxious that they might not perform well under pressure. Allen, a man who had spent years as a sportscaster, described his concern that he would be

> *all thumbs. I worry about drawing a blank and not knowing what to*
> *do or coaching my wife wrong and mess her up or something. I want*
> *to be a real help to my wife and the birth team. I don't want to drop*
> *the ball on my way to the winning touchdown.*

Many expectant dads conveyed their desire to be "more of a help than a hindrance" and expressed questions about not knowing "the right thing to do at the right time."

Generally speaking, most of the men who did not report these concerns were fathers who had done it before and medical professionals.

In order to help themselves learn, practice, and retain the important information, most men attended childbirth education classes with their wives.

Childbirth education classes. One very popular feature of the third trimester is enrollment in a childbirth education class at the birthing facility. These classes are frequently run by nurse practitioners or childbirth education specialists. The most popular classes are the Lamaze and Bradley approaches.

Often, hospitals require such a class prior to allowing a partner to participate in the labor and delivery, and all hospitals require classes prior to allowing a husband into a Caesarian section birth. It is advisable that you participate, both as a support for your partner and for your own knowledge and comfort.

Most couples describe these classes as particularly rewarding. They get to be together and work as a team, developing skills for parenting as well as the upcoming birth. The classes provide couples with information about the birthing process and techniques for "natural" childbirth (such as pain control and types of breathing appropriate to each stage of labor and delivery), with the father as a coach and partner. This partnership aspect is not to be minimized. Indeed, many of the fathers in the survey indicated that working together as a team at the classes helped them feel so much more a part of a family than they had before. The time commitment and male involvement in the classes are particularly valuable in helping expectant fathers feel more connected to their wives and to their unborn child.

In addition, it is reassuring to a man to discover that he is not the only one going through the process. The feelings of universality, of seeing other men in the class with the same fears, concerns, problems, and pale faces, can be very comforting. This is especially true for men who have been isolated from the pregnancy through increased workload, psychological avoidance, or feelings of being excluded. It also provides men with a sense that they can participate. Being a labor coach allows us to avoid some of the intense anxiety caused by passivity.

Finally, childbirth education classes provide a valuable opportunity for couples to make new friends who are experiencing similar life events and often share values and interests.

One disadvantage of the classes described by many expectant fathers was a sense that the class was too oriented toward helping their wives and not sufficiently focused on their apprehensions. They did not want to eliminate any of the valuable material presented during the class but wished that they had more opportunity to express and be relieved of many of their own concerns.

To address these concerns, some communities have instituted a few evenings or a weekend retreat for dads only. These group experiences such as Expectant Fathers Only, Daddy Boot Camp, Basic Training for New Dads, or similar classes can be quite valuable.

Coach daddy. Both Bradley and Lamaze childbirth education classes stress the husband's role as labor and delivery coach. During the labor and delivery, he will be the one to drive her to the hospital or alternative birthing place or alert the midwife and other appropriate people if it is to be a home birth. He will also help his wife with her breathing exercises, time the contractions, mop her brow, encourage her to push and rest at the proper times, procure ice chips or the occasional piece of hard candy, and take any abuse that she gives in the throes of pain as good-naturedly as he can.

Safety

Birth in modern Western society is relatively safe. Most children come into the world with little difficulty. Furthermore, women regularly give birth and retain their health. Both hospitals and alternative birth centers have enviable safety records. Most men have faith in their wives' obstetricians and midwives and in the birth methods chosen.

It is therefore very noteworthy that one of the most frequent worries described by the 156 men who responded to an open-ended questionnaire was a fear for the safety of their wives and children.

Many of the expectant fathers had daydreams and nightmares that their wife might perish or become incapacitated during childbirth. These are not the type of overriding fears that would interfere dramatically with the father's role in the birth process or his mental stability, but they are things that most expectant fathers think about and have at least in the back of their minds.

Such thoughts do have some basis in reality. As recently as three to four generations ago, the most frequent cause of death of eighteen—to thirty-five-year-old women was childbirth. Many of the men we interviewed were able to recall stories heard in their childhood of women and infants in their own families perishing in childbirth.

Similarly, a common reaction to any type of stress is to imagine and prepare for the worst and to try and come to grips with that just in case it might occur. The loss of one's spouse was in fact the greatest fear expressed by most of the men in our survey. Many of them had fantasies about being left alone with an infant and no wife or a severely damaged and invalid wife.

Several men commented at length on this fear. Here's Charlie, expecting his fourth child:

> *The one fear I carry is that something will happen to Shereen. The last pregnancy was really hard on her. She didn't even really want another child. I kinda talked her into it. Now I'm worried about her safety. She's scared too because the last delivery was an emergency C-section and the doctor said that this one would have to be a C-section also.*

Bud was a first-timer:

> *If anything happened to Malia, I don't think I could live through it. I keep having dreams that she died and the baby survived. In the dream, I go on and am a great father. But in real life, I just couldn't, no, wouldn't want to, go on.*

The typical man who did not report fears about his wife's safety talked in great length about how young and healthy she was and how careful she had been about her diet and exercise. For these men, the scary thoughts had occurred but were countered by rational argument.

Fred, a father for five days, told the interviewer,

> *I was mostly concerned about her safety. I knew she was healthy and young and strong, but still, I worried. I couldn't tell her that though. I just kept it to myself and hoped for the best. The worst part is that I couldn't tell anyone.*

One interview was done with a man whose wife almost did not survive the birth of their year-old son. The interview was done in their living room, with the baby on his lap, a dish towel over his shoulder, and his wife in a wheelchair next to him. He replied during the interview that he had feared that she would be injured throughout the entire pregnancy.

> *At first, I felt guilty and blamed myself for getting her pregnant in the first place. Then I got very angry at the whole world. You know "why me," and then when the reality hit, I just had to do what it took to keep all of us going. Tracy was in the hospital until three months ago, and there was Kenny to feed, and house to be kept, and a living to be made. I just did it. I don't know how now, but with Tracy getting stronger and the physical therapy, I know that the worst is behind us now.*

> *This might sound nuts to you, but in a strange way, I learned that I had a lot of the right stuff. I never knew before. I managed to be a mother and father and breadwinner, and Kenny turned out okay, and our family survived. I also found out that we had some great friends. They really pitched in. We even talked about having another when Tracy gets on her feet again.*

She smiled when he said that and hastily added,

> *The problems came about because of physician error, and my new doctor said I could have ten kids. It was a miracle that I even survived.*

Two of my former male clients did in fact lose their wives during childbirth or as a result of postpartum complications. For each of these men, adjustment to being a good father and caretaker for their child was immediate. Their personal and social lives were severely debilitated for several years. Both of these men found it especially difficult to form subsequent exclusive intimate relationships with a partner.

Most men tend to restrict their sources of emotional support to a very few people and often rely entirely on their spouses. Because of this, the potential loss of a spouse also can mean the loss of a man's entire emotional support system. There is substantial evidence that males respond to the stress of an actual loss of a spouse far more seriously than women do. They develop far more psychosomatic symptoms and even have a lower likelihood of personal survival.

Wives were not the only object of expectant fathers' fears. Most men described a concern about the health and safety of their infants. They described grave concerns about the baby dying. In fact, not all babies survive childbirth. According to the 2010 data provided by the CIA World Factbook, Population Reference Bureau, there were 5.4 infant deaths for every one thousand live births in the United States. This represents a 50 percent drop from the 1980 figure that was cited in the first edition of *When Men Are Pregnant*.

There were thirty-three countries worldwide with lower infant mortality rates, with Singapore (1.92) being the lowest. The Scandinavian nations (all of which routinely recognize extended paternity leaves) all reported rates of less than 3.0 per thousand births).

Even more frightening to most men surveyed was the thought of their baby being born handicapped or brain damaged.

Seth's response to his fears was pragmatic. He immediately traded in his coupe for an SUV. His approach was not unique. Many of the fathers we talked to described taking steps to make their homes and environments safer for their wives, their children, and themselves. Several couples opted for cars which stressed safety in their advertising. (In Northern California, it seems rare to observe a van, an SUV, or a Volvo without a baby seat firmly tethered into the rear seat.)

Finances

The current custom for pregnant women who work outside the home is to keep working until they become physically unable to do so. When women do stay home during the last few weeks or months, couples often have to adapt to a number of changes. While some women are delighted to quit work and to be home to await the blessed event, many find themselves lonely and bored. There are also financial issues that accompany a woman's taking a maternity leave or quitting work. The two-salary family becomes a one-salary family, often with serious implications. One recent father noted the statistic that a child costs over $245,000 prior to leaving home for college. He opined,

I know where that comes from too. That's the amount my wife would make if she kept working.

He later speculated on how he could make up the difference. As has been described above, the role of financial provider is one that fits most males in our society. Indeed, it is in this role that most males find their entire personal worth judged. Many of the expectant fathers in the study described major changes in their attitudes and behavior around money. As Gene related,

Well, I never thought much about money and stuff until recently. Lisa was taking care of herself before we met and always could, and I did okay. You know, no real savings, but I always could pretty much buy what I wanted. Now I find myself thinking a lot about this baby, and I just don't know. It's different now. I feel like I gotta get the kid all kinds of toys and things, and it's really starting to hit that we have been relying on Lisa's income as well. It's different.

Fred, an engineer at a Silicon Valley computer firm, reported,

It's funny you should ask about that. Actually, I hadn't thought much about it, but I have been putting in more time at the office since about June (the middle of the pregnancy). I had this opportunity to work on a special project night, and I just accepted. It means a lot more money for us. I don't think Carrie minds much. She spends most of the evening online with her mom and friends.

One can't help but notice the reciprocal quality of Fred and Carrie's adjustment. They go from being equals as partners to more shared roles as parenthood approaches. He feels pushed out of the pregnancy and sublimates these feelings into greater work, creativity on the job, and income. She adjusts to his being gone longer hours by focusing more on the baby, her mother, and women friends.

Many men described similar scenarios. This was particularly true for men who were self—employed and whose work somehow began to increase as the pregnancy progressed. In my own case, my private practice, which I always kept at a comfortable level, somehow doubled in size during the last few months of the first pregnancy.

The mythical "typical American family" of the mid-twentieth century with the mom at home caring for the two children and keeping the home presentable and the dad working outside the home for eight hours a day, five days a week, is definitely a phenomenon of the past. Recent surveys indicate that fewer than 14 percent of all American households resemble this pattern. Despite these facts, it is customary in our culture to expect the man to be the breadwinner. Nowhere is this belief more potent than when the woman is in the third trimester of a pregnancy. Almost all of the men that we surveyed talked at length about the increased pressure to make money and work hard at providing for their families. This pressure usually came from the father himself. Bill, a father of five weeks, described it:

> *I never really thought about taking care of anyone but myself. Melody never asked me to take care of her. I think she probably takes care of me in some ways . . . As soon as the pregnancy became a reality though, something changed within me. It was like I became my father. I started to daydream about colleges to send Jason to, and he wasn't even born. I began to worry about money for the first time in my life. Don't get me wrong, I never had much, but I always figured that if I couldn't afford something, I could do without it. But the thought of Jason going without something just brings me to tears. I guess it really started about the sixth month of the pregnancy, and I just had this need to "do what fathers are supposed to do," and that came down to going out in the world and providing for the family. It's strange because Mel doesn't put any extra pressure on me. It's all me and some belief that I have that being a father means being the breadwinner.*

It seems clear from the research that most men face an important role crisis during a pregnancy, particularly the first pregnancy. There are few ways for men to fully experience unique roles in today's society. Financial providing is one of the single most essential male roles that emerge during a pregnancy. It seems natural for men to take on or add to this responsibility at this time.

The possibility of failing as a financial provider did not sit well on the shoulders of our survey fathers. Many men reported dreams and nightmares about being unable to work or becoming destitute. Unemployed fathers in the sample redoubled their efforts to find some source of income.

It is important to note that as a result of the Great Recession of 2009, which began as early as 2006, unemployment doubled and has yet to drop to pre-2008 levels. Many formerly two-income families have become one-income. In addition, according to a 2012 Pew Research report, among married women, over 24 percent make more than their husbands. This can put both a substantial financial and emotional strain on expectant fathers.

A very small percentage of the fathers interviewed took an opposing position. These men expressed a great desire to be home with their infants. For some, this meant amassing some capital during the last trimester. Others made agreements with their wives: she would be the breadwinner as soon as possible, and he would be the primary caregiver. A few expectant fathers attempted to simplify their lives to the point that they could be sufficient on very small amounts of money. These men spoke of bringing up their children "close to the earth."

The Pregnancy Becomes Public

As the pregnancy shows more, larger numbers of people become included in the expectant couple's experience. Baby showers occur at this time. Eager relatives and friends, and even strangers, all show a great deal of interest in the expectant mother. She is often perceived as less capable, physically uncomfortable, and in need of great pampering.

The third-trimester expectant mother gets noticed everywhere she goes. Whether it's to the supermarket, workplace, or social events, the pregnant woman gets acknowledged and approached. She is treated in special ways: doors are opened for her, strangers offer to help her carry bundles, and she gets smiles and other positive reactions. In a sense, she is accorded a special symbolic status of Universal Mother or Temple of Life, representative of the future.

She also simultaneously loses her right to privacy and, to some extent, the opportunity to talk about anything except the pregnancy. It is a common event for strangers to approach a pregnant woman and to comment on the pregnancy.

One father related,

> We couldn't walk down three aisles at the supermarket without some lady coming up and telling my wife that it (the baby) was going to be a girl because of the way she was carrying or a boy because of her coloring or whatnot. At first, it was fun to share the pregnancy with the world. But after a while, buying something at Longs Drugs was like running the gauntlet.

Another expectant father commenting on the intrusiveness of strangers into the pregnancy said,

> I couldn't believe how angry I got at some jerk in the supermarket who put his hand on my wife's belly and smiled. I was ready to kill

the SOB. I mean really, he never would have tried it if she weren't pregnant. Then he starts talking about his two kids and how he and his wife are trying for another. I mean who cares.

Kent commented,

I even got upset when her father and brother went up and felt her belly. I was protective and jealous. Only I'm supposed to do that. But then you feel like a fool because everyone is so happy about the whole thing, and she seems to enjoy it.

Pregnant women do lose their personal space. People walk up and touch them, begin speculating on the sex of the unborn child, or without invitation, talk about their own pregnancies or children. It is usually very friendly contact and often welcomed in our frequently impersonal world. It would probably be welcomed more by expectant fathers if it were not for other important factors.

One of the tasks of the third trimester is for the husband and wife to begin to (re)establish a strong nuclear family into which the infant will be born. Soon after the baby arrives, the family interactions will normally be altered for some time. This means that emotional boundaries within the nuclear family will become unclear, such that it is sometimes hard to tell where the infant ends and the parents begin. Pregnant women experience this physiologically. There is still no distinction between the infant and her since they share one body. At this time, harder boundaries are drawn between the family and the external world. For the third-trimester father who is already developing this enhanced sense of his nuclear family, any intrusion by an "outsider" or a stranger might increase feelings of jealousy, protectiveness, trespass, and fear.

Some fathers not only became upset over the intrusion, they also became uncomfortable over the very fact that *they* were upset by this than their wives. Indeed, many women enjoyed the attention, felt the good will and friendliness of the approaching stranger, and wanted to bask in the celebrity status even while their husbands experienced discomfort.

Some expectant fathers felt particularly isolated and pushed out of the late-pregnancy process, particularly those who felt inhibitions in their own physical contact with their wives.

The Lost Cord

Certainly, a pregnant woman does need extra pampering, attention, special care, and concern. But what is the modern husband's role in these latter stages of the pregnancy? What are his feelings?

A father is, by long tradition, the "protector." He is supposed to support and care for his wife and children. Most men find great comfort in that role and often do a very good job of caring for their partners during this time. They do this without too much question and with pride in the pregnancy. After all, he is going to be a father, yet something is not right. Something is missing. Who will attend to *his* needs as the birth approaches? In fact, he is as emotionally pregnant as she is. He must have multiple needs also.

What happens to him? What can we offer him?

One need that "involved" fathers talked about in depth was the need for some of the attention and credit that comes to their wives. They are emotionally involved in the pregnancy/birth process and at the same time feel very much isolated and pushed out of the limelight. Several authors have speculated that men are not accustomed to being in the assistant, supportive role and that this is difficult for them. Others suggest that there are men that cannot allow their wives to be the center of attention without feeling inadequate. Still others have commented on the need that men have to control their own fate by actively doing something. During this last trimester, men are pretty much there to support their wives and wait for the birth. Even when they are in childbirth education classes, their role as supporter and coach is stressed. For men who only feel good about themselves when they are actively involved, this can be an uneasy time.

Some men deal with this by starting projects at this time (building play or sleeping areas for the new child, taking on new responsibilities at work, changing jobs for one with greater personal demands, getting involved with friends, or coaching youth soccer or Little League). All of these projects can be seen as an antidote to feelings of helplessness, a way of taking active control of some aspect of their environment.

These are important considerations, yet there is something more.

Oftentimes, men have a need to talk about these feelings with others but are reticent to do so. Just as modern culture creates the need by inviting a man into the pregnancy partway than not letting him be completely involved, so does it create a need in him for support and then makes that support fairly unattainable. It is sometimes hard for men to talk about their emotions, especially when there is fear or sadness involved. As a rule, men are not supported for talking about how lonely and helpless they feel during the last stage of pregnancy. For some men, this paradox—being asked to participate, yet having some of their feelings disallowed—is quite devastating.

This cultural double bind plays a role in making a late-pregnancy affair more possible.

If they have no place to talk about this conflict or work it out somehow, expectant fathers may develop symptoms of stress. Normal problems that preexisted the pregnancy might get worse. The couvade (physical pregnancy) symptoms described in the first trimester might reappear or become more intense as the birth approaches. These physical "male pregnancy" symptoms serve a useful purpose. Being sick might entitle him to get some TLC.

There are reports in the psychological literature of emotionally unstable fathers who become more so and behave in antisocial ways. One dad we interviewed confessed,

> *This pregnancy isn't too hard. In fact, I've been pretty good. The first one though . . . I'm embarrassed about this . . . One night, I actually went back to this elementary school I went to and broke about five windows with rocks . . . I couldn't believe that I was doing that, but I did.*

He was asked what that meant for him, and he replied,

> *You mean being a bad boy? Oh, I don't know, maybe a way of getting attention.*

An interesting postscript to this was that he later called and said that the question had got him thinking and he had talked to his parents who told him that he had done the same thing when he was eight years old, a week after his younger brother was born.

Another reaction is escape. Several men found lots of reasons to be out of town a great deal during the pregnancy. One father we interviewed made several business trips during the last trimester which he later realized were unnecessary. One expectant dad went to Europe for a month, and another took a three-week camping trip in the woods during the final stages of the pregnancy. All these forms of avoidance imply to some extent the intensity with which men experience the stress of the impending birth. This does not suggest that any of these is beneficial to the relationship. Indeed, most of them can have far-reaching negative consequences for the couple and familial relationships. Although, it must be added that the fellow who went to Europe did so with his wife's blessing. She didn't "want him moping around underfoot."

Some couples even split up during pregnancy. While this is more prevalent during the earlier trimesters, it is not unheard of that the pressure of the impending birth was the final "straw." This is especially true for couples for whom the pregnancy was an accident or an ill-advised attempt to put a failing marriage together.

Thirteen Tips for the Third Trimester

1. Expect to become more aware that the pregnancy is for real. For most men, the baby becomes much more of a fact during this time. When the awareness develops, find a time to share these feelings with your wife, a close friend, and/or family.

2. Expect to get in touch with a newer sense of your own mortality. When your child is born, you do get pushed back one generation, and so do your parents if they are alive. An upcoming birth is a good reason to (re)connect with your own father and mother in new ways. A religious or spiritual advisor may help, especially if this is the first time that you have ever thought much about life and death.

3. Expect a wide range of sometimes contradictory feelings during this period: feelings of intense closeness to your wife may be interspersed with desires to escape. It is important to let your wife know of these shifting feelings, but be sure that you express your commitment to her and the relationship as you discuss your fears of entrapment.

4. If you do have fleeting thoughts about paternity, share them carefully and nonaccusingly with your partner. *It may help to point out to her that 60 percent of new fathers have such doubts.* Especially find a way to talk about the enormity of creating life.

5. Feelings about pregnancy sometimes appear symbolically. Many men do experience some physical pregnancy symptoms especially weight gain. If you develop any physical problems requiring medical care during the third trimester, don't fail to tell your doctor that your wife is pregnant. Sometimes novel behaviors can be a clue. If you find yourself doing something atypical—one expectant father managed to repeatedly lock his keys in his car—take some time to reflect on what this means to you.

6. Expect some anxiety about the birth and about the future. Spend as much time as possible talking to your partner about your plans, dreams, and fantasies. Think about what "family" and "parenting" mean to you. If the anxiety is strong, consider joining a men's support group or seeing a therapist who specializes in men's life transitions.

7. When you feel concern about your wife's safety or that of the infant, choose a quiet moment and tell her so. In most cases, she will feel more comfortable knowing that you care rather than scared because you are fearful.

8. Spend time talking to your wife about what her needs are for your support during the birth. Tell her also what kinds of anxiety you have. Work out practical procedures so that you both can get as much of what you wish as possible. It is very important that neither of you get

pushed into something that you might resent later. With something as important as the birth of your child, you want to do it your own way. This includes your desire to be or *not* be present.

9. Concerns over queasiness are best reduced by talking to recent fathers who have already gone through the experience. They will remember their own prenatal concerns and will be excellent examples of survivors. Couple-oriented childbirth educators are also excellent for reassurance. There are three groups of experts that are generally best not consulted: other expectant fathers, because they will be just as anxious as you; people who work in the medical field and are prone to "hospital" humor; and women-centered childbirth educators, as they are usually far more concerned with the impact of your concern on your wife than they are with you.

   Remember that *none* of the 227 fathers in our original survey actually did pass out.

10. Discuss any sexual frustration and sexual problems comfortably and without demands with your partner. It is not a problem for you alone, and the two of you need to discuss, explore, and negotiate until you find some solution. If intercourse is uncomfortable, other means of sexual and emotional expression may be crucial. If this is hard for you or your wife to discuss, it is well worth seeing a marriage counselor or therapist for a few sessions to work out the difficulties.

11. If you find yourself leaning toward another woman at this time, stop. Find alternative ways of letting your wife know what you are missing and/or resenting. This is a prime time for marriage counseling: it will be money well spent.

12. Speaking of money, expect the financial pressure of the new family situation to hit. There might be loss of the wife's income (especially if this is a first child) and a surprising number of added expenses that a baby and a pregnancy bring. When you do find yourself more than usually concerned about finances, spend some time with your spouse figuring out your income and expenses. Try to draw up a tentative budget together and try it out. The biggest danger here is trying to do it all yourself. Sometimes overtime and a new or a second job that sidetrack you from long-term goals provide false savings. If trouble persists and a budget cannot be worked out, a financial planner might help.

13. Probably most important of all, do not hesitate or refrain from being romantic with your partner. Your commitment is greater when you have children together, and oftentimes, men feel rushes of warm, loving feelings that they do not share. She really wants to hear that you love her especially now as her shape changes.

Summary

The third trimester is a time of increasing anticipation and stress for expectant fathers. How much stress there is and how to handle it depends on the relationship between the partners and in the man's psychological strength.

A strong pre-pregnancy relationship and a honeymoon-like second trimester will provide a good foundation for this trying time. The anticipation and excitement (at least for a first child) may well moderate any major difficulty for the expectant father. Men in a shaky relationship may experience much greater stress.

The third trimester is marked by a variety of phenomena for fathers. First and foremost, the impending fatherhood becomes much more of a psychological reality. Issues regarding what it is to be a father and an adult male in our society come into focus. As the pregnancy comes to term, men engage in a labor of their own: being providers for their families. They also face many questions about the nature of life and mortality and begin to reflect more on the fathering they received as children. Men also must prepare for the birth itself and for their part in the birthing process. Often, there are classes to attend and new questions to answer. Finally, men need to deal with changes in the sexual relationship with their wives and with the enormous reality that they are a part of the creation of new life.

Each of these third-trimester issues will return and grow as the expectant father becomes a father.

Chapter 8

Get Me to the Birth on Time

'Twas so good to be young then, To be close to the earth.
And to stand by your wife at the moment of birth.
—Traditional

Everyone has seen the *TV* program, cartoon, or film that depicts "the moment."

The couple is sitting in their living room, and the wife utters the fateful words, "I think it's time!" At that moment, her formerly competent, articulate, take-charge-kind-of-guy husband becomes an incompetent, incoherent, bumbling idiot. It is not because his assigned task is so complex. He has only to make a few crucial phone calls and get his wife and suitcase to the planned birthing place.

It is supposed to be funny when he becomes inept. Whether it is Ricky Ricardo, Fred Flintstone, Fonzie, Klinger, or their current counterparts, all of the men are portrayed as helpless and foolish. He is unable to find the car keys, stumbles on the way to the car, *has* trouble starting the engine, and recognizes too late that the gas tank is empty. If he gets past these problems, he is usually pictured driving off alone, leaving his pregnant wife standing in front of their home, looking perplexed. Should they actually reach the hospital in time, the image is usually one of a very pregnant woman pushing a wheelchair containing her undone husband, looking on with a motherly smile, and taking care of everything that her husband cannot do.

While this is only an exaggeration of the general *TV* image of "male as fool, woman as caretaker," it does create some food for thought. Why is it that childbirth is such a generator of humor? Why is the male such an object of ridicule at this time? Is the supposed uselessness of males in pregnancy and childbirth the core of this issue? Are we really just neck albatrosses that our wives must suffer, or is it something else? Perhaps childbirth is such a momentous occasion that we must laugh to protect ourselves from feeling the depth of anxiety and awe. Since we don't dare burden the mother at this point, maybe our anxiety gets directed to the only place possible. Whatever the reason, it is an uncomplimentary representation of expectant fathers and definitely not a model to follow.

Some humor poked at dads underscores the helplessness without being so derisive. In 1984, an Alka-Seltzer commercial showed several men nervously milling around a hospital waiting room. Finally, a nurse comes out and tells each that their child has arrived. The one who has triplets reaches for the sponsor's product. In reality, a new father surprised by the announcement of triplets would likely need something a lot stronger than a fizzy analgesic.

The commercial portrays fatherhood of two decades earlier. Waiting rooms are no longer crowded with nervous expectant fathers. Most expectant fathers today are active participants in bringing their children into the world. As the role men play has become more active, their needs have changed. Everyone involved must begin to understand the new stresses and help incorporate men more fully into the birthing process.

What will the birthday of your child really be like? Probably unlike any day you have previously experienced.

Nine months of preparation, worry, and excitement are coming to fruition. This is the time you have been waiting for. Your child is about to be born. All of the preparation now must come to bear on the next few hours. When your wife tells you that she thinks she is in labor and ready to go to your chosen birthing center, it is time for you to take charge.

The typical sequence. First, you will need to call the obstetrician, hospital, or birthing center and let them know she is coming. If you are with your wife, you will need to get her to the hospital by whatever transportation you have planned. If a taxi is to be the method of conveyance, a call is in order. If you will drive, it is time to get your wife and a suitcase (packed well beforehand with a few belongings) into the car and drive at a safe and comfortable speed to the center. Once you arrive, you will need to see to it that your wife is admitted, examined, and checked into a room. In most cases, you will stay and comfort her during labor and delivery.

You and your wife have entered a most special phase of your partnership, and your joint efforts will soon result in the gift of parenthood.

You may be familiar with the facts of labor and delivery, but this day will be different. All of the emotions and questions that have been emerging during the past several months will be magnified as the big day arrives. Up to now, you have only anticipated worries. Now you must face the reality of your fears, expectancies, and dreams.

Of the many concerns described by fathers as they approach the big day, assisting the delivery and birth is primary at this time.

Get Me to the Birth on Time

How will you respond to your partner's announcement that the moment has arrived?

Sean described his anticipation and reaction:

> *I was ready. Couldn't wait. I had the suitcase packed and by the door, car was filled with gas, doctor's number taped to the phone, and four alternative routes to the hospital mapped out and ready. When Claudia said she was starting labor, I got out the old stopwatch, and we timed the pains. Once they got to the right point, we were galvanized into action like a well-oiled machine, and off we went. Got her there in plenty of time, no hassles with the admitting desk and up to her room. Then she had eighteen more hours of labor before Trent was born.*

Sean was obviously a careful planner. His plans were designed to handle any contingency. Many men described to us their concerns about getting their wife to the hospital in time. Like Sean, several expectant fathers made careful and elaborate strategies to compensate for their worries. Willie noted,

> *I had spent several days planning routes to the hospital and timing the drive. I went out and actually drove the route during the morning rush hour and evening one . . . practiced shortcuts and side roads . . . and timed each way at each time . . . And then just like I thought, we had to go during the morning rush hour . . . I was so glad I was prepared . . . The traffic guy on the radio said a jackknifed big rig had closed off Hospital Curve, so I just took my alternative route through the Mission District and arrived right on schedule. It was good we did that. Cleo came one hour after we walked in the doors.*

Mapping out the routes, being certain that the fuel tank was full, and preparing for contingencies gave many men a feeling of competency and helped reduce the worry that their wives might not make it to the hospital in time. Some comfort could also be found in developing careful strategies for making necessary phone calls, arranging care for the older children, and taking account of weather and road conditions and other "zero hour" details.

Rick excitedly told the interviewer,

I got this great app, phone numbers locked in and programmed, GPS with traffic updates and emergency procedures just in case.

Several men described having thoughts about what would happen if they could not get to the birthing place in time. Others reported dreams of the baby coming early. I had an elaborate and repetitive dream that my infant was being born at a particular Union 76 gas station at the corner of Kalakaua Avenue and Kapiolani Boulevard, roughly two-thirds of the way to the hospital. Toward the end of the third trimester, I was able (in the dream only) to deliver the baby myself and then get to the hospital with everybody safe. Many men reported similar dreams.

Adam had the dream come true. He successfully delivered his baby on the side of the road, a rare and very special fathering experience. Adam had, as a member of the Peace Corps, assisted at several births prior to that of his own child. When Adam related the story, he noted that he and his wife delayed their start to the hospital until the last possible moment. We could not help but wonder if he and his wife had unconsciously planned to deliver this (their fourth) child themselves. Most fathers will be members of the birthing team, but even a father who is an obstetrician will likely not be the person who brings his own baby into the world.

False alarms. Some couples successfully make it to the birthing place only to be told after examination that the pregnant mom is still insufficiently effaced or that the contractions are not close enough together. It is usually recommended that the couple return home and wait until sometime in the near future before returning. The wait could be a matter of a few hours or a few days.

Being sent back home can be a serious disappointment for many. If the travel time is lengthy and anxiety is high, you may want to either check into the hospital early or in a close-by hotel. Those hours of extra waiting will likely pass very slowly.

One mom told us,

> *They told me that I was not effaced enough and that the baby was not coming soon. We were about to leave when I decided to call my grandma on my cell. She said, "No, don't leave. In our family, the babies come real fast." So I told the doc what Grandma had said, and she said, "Okay, let's just check in and wait here." Grandma was so right. My baby arrived in less than three hours.*

A few years ago, my granddaughter seemed very ready to arrive on Christmas Day. As second-time parents, my daughter and son-in-law were attuned to the signals and intervals between contractions. Yet when they got to the hospital, they were told that it was "early labor" and that it'd be a while. They returned home, and they (and four grandparents) had to wait for two days before the birth.

A Few Tips on Packing for Fathers Who Will Be at the Birth

If you will be sharing the birth with your wife, you need also to anticipate contingencies. What do you want to take with you to the hospital?

1. Insurance forms and a hospital admission form filled out in advance, agreements with birthing staff, and any required papers to allow you into the birth
2. Food such as fruit, nuts, crackers, trail mix, or even a sandwich or two. This is for you. You will be at the hospital for some time, and you will need to replenish your own body. You may need to step out briefly to eat. Your partner may not want to see or smell food.
3. A fully charged cell phone and a charger to plug in if you need it. You also will probably want an additional well-charged digital and/ or video camera that is reliable. You want to have fresh batteries and plenty of space on an SD or similar card. Most parents want some special pictures or a recording of the event or at least first pictures of the newborn.

    Be sure you are familiar with your camera equipment. You do not want to be reading instructions on the use of a new DSLR and locating parts spread out on the hospital floor while your wife is in labor. Remember that the photographer is an observer to an event more than an active participant. If you want the extra distance or feel most comfortable taking the pictures yourself, do so, but if you can, try to arrange for someone else to be at least partially responsible for the photography.
4. Lots of loose change. Vending machines and public phones can gobble up lots of change, and many still don't accept credit or debit cards. Bring enough for emergencies.
5. A pad and pencil or an electronic tablet with a useful app for keeping labor diary and records that you already kept at home.
6. A change of clean clothes. Your wife will do most of the sweating during delivery, but you will be active and anxious too. Include also toothbrushes (and contact lens cases) for both of you.
7. Something to pass time. There may be long delays in the early stages of labor. One couple in early 2014 arrived at the hospital right after the mom's water broke. The baby actually arrived (by C-section)

twenty-one hours later. Games (a deck of cards), magazines, a book or an e-book, or an mp3 (iPod) player with favorite tunes or podcasts for you and your wife are often useful. Some modern birthing centers may have Internet access, but I recommend a backup in your suitcase.

What to Expect at the Hospital

Once you get to the birthing center, you will turn your wife over to professional care. This can be a relief or a discomfort. You and your wife should have made a number of advance decisions as to how you wanted the birth to proceed. It is up to you to see that it happens the way you want.

Like all large institutions, hospitals have a host of rules, regulations, and standard procedures that are ostensibly designed to make patient care most effective. However, hospitals are designed primarily to protect and care for individuals who are ill. People with ailments place themselves in the hands of experts, whose job is comfort and cure. Pregnant women are not sick. They may need comfort, but they do not need to be cured. Because of this, some hospital procedures may be unnecessary, needlessly costly, or uncomfortable. These regulations are not designed for the interests of individual patients, but for the efficiency and ease of the staff. They are not always a help to the pregnant mother or expectant father. Many authors have concluded that these regulations actually interfere with the birth process for parents. Dr. Martin Greenberg, psychiatrist and author of *The Birth of a Father*, writes,

> *If the destruction of the family was the hospital's goal, it would be hard to imagine its being accomplished more effectively.*

You will face a number of institutional procedures in any birth setting, and it is well worth your time to study their effectiveness beforehand and decide the extent to which you want to go along. Let's examine some of the common standard procedures, including consent, preparation for the birth, and medication.

Consent forms. Every hospital or alternative birthing center has a set of forms that you will be asked to sign. The forms usually contain an agreement (contract) to pay the hospital, an authorization to bill services to your insurance company, a release in which you give the institution the right to take emergency measures to preserve your partner's life and health, the ubiquitous HIPAA forms regarding confidentiality, and a statement of some specific hospital policies. In the rush to get your laboring wife into a comfortable room, you may sign the forms hurriedly without reading them carefully. Because you are authorizing the hospital to take important steps, it is well worth your while to read the agreements carefully. *The best* time *to do so* is *months before the actual birth.* Ask for the standard admission forms, take them home, read them at your leisure, discuss them, and complete them prior to the big day. You may find that a particular policy is so contrary to your own personal values that you would wish to negotiate in advance or even change hospitals.

For example, you might not agree with an obstetrics policy that insists on trying to save a distressed infant at the expense of the mother's health or life.

When you and your wife make an advance visit to the hospital, get the forms, take the opportunity to tour the obstetrics facility if possible, and familiarize yourselves with the layout and facilities. Often, childbirth education classes do this as a part of their curriculum.

Preparation for the birth. In the next chapter, we'll discuss some of the specific medical procedures your wife will likely encounter at the hospital/birthing center in preparation for the birth, including prep, episiotomies, and various forms of medication.

Rules for father presence. Most hospitals require that fathers have completed a childbirth education class before they can be part of the birthing team. These classes are quite valuable and are recommended for all new fathers. Special additional classes are normally required for fathers who wish to be present for *surgical births.* C-sections are performed in an operating room rather than a delivery room. The rules and procedures are quite different. Even if you have taken the special preparation, you may not be allowed to be present (see chapters 10 and 11).

Presence of others. Husbands (or sometimes the mother of the pregnant woman) may be allowed into nonsurgical births, but others are usually not welcome. Some couples today want to have their older children or other relatives and friends present during the birth. When *The Oprah Winfrey Show* did a program on expectant fathers, cameras were ready in a hospital in nearby Evanston, Illinois, to broadcast the birth of their child. In that situation, millions of viewers were allowed in, at least via their televisions.

Most parents want their older children to visit the hospital after the birth of their new sibling. Many hospitals, however, have clear restrictions and usually will not allow children under the age of eleven to visit their mothers.

Ambience. Many couples want to reduce the trauma and shock of birth and make it as gentle as possible. Several choices can change the ambience of the birth setting. Instead of routinely having the woman in separate rooms for labor, delivery, and recovery, a single room can be requested and used unless there are medical complications. Hospitals also have standard gowns for mothers and restrictions on their movement during labor. Some couples want the mother to wear her own clothes and to be mobile during the early labor. Many midwives have recommended gentle exercises and positioning to make the birth go easier.

Rooming-in. Hospitals are designed for sick people, not their families. Unlike some more family-oriented cultures, relatives of patients in the United States are expected *to* be present only during visiting hours. There are two types of rooming-in: one for the baby and one for the dad. Increasingly, new parents request and birthing centers offer the opportunity for babies to be with their mothers almost full-time for closeness and demand feeding. More and more are also providing a bed in the same room for the husband.

When my grandchildren were born in 2009 and 2011, the birth room seemed more like a hotel room with two beds than a hospital room.

Length of stay. There is often a standard recovery period at hospitals (twenty-four to seventy-two hours) if there are no complications. The release of the mother and child requires approval of the obstetrician and pediatrician. If you want to leave earlier, perhaps hours after the birth, make arrangements in advance.

And Now, the Main Event

The time is drawing nigh. Preparations have been made, forms are filled out, and practiced procedures have been followed. Your wife has indicated she is about to give birth. You have made the requisite phone calls and arranged to get both of you to the planned birthing center. You are now ready to be a major player in a drama that will affect the rest of your life—a drama that cannot be stopped until it runs its full course—the birth of your child.

Chapter 9

A Child Is Born

*No human masterpiece has ever been created
without great labor.*
—Andre Gide, Poetique (1926)

Labor, if you'll pardon the pun, is hard and long work. For a mother having her first child, labor can extend from a few hours to twenty-four or more. The average for primaparas (first child) is approximately fourteen hours. Almost 90 percent of the time is in the first phase, 9 percent in the second phase, and 1 percent in the third. Multiparous women (those having a second or subsequent child) usually have considerably shorter labor. How long it *seems* to you will depend much more on the amount of pain, the pain tolerance of the mother, expectations of both parents, presence and helpfulness of the father, circumstances of the birthing place, nursing care, and a host of other factors.

Childbirth is frequently quite painful. Mothers tell me there is apparently no way to adequately describe it to someone who has not experienced it. (Carol Burnett famously quipped, "If you want to know what it feels like to have a baby, grab hold of your lower lip. Now pull it over the back of your head!")

While labor is ongoing, it often feels that it will never end. Once it is over and has passed for a few months, it is remembered as far more endurable than it seemed at the time. Parents tend to forget much of the pain of labor—undoubtedly an adaptive trait that prompts us to have more children. One mother, after her second child, referred to the phenomenon as God's gift of amnesia.

The Three Phases of Labor

First Phase

Early labor. When a woman's body is ready for the birth, the first phase of labor begins. Muscles in the uterus wall start to tighten around her cervical cavity. These contractions press the child downward and outward and cause the cervix gradually to become thinner and shorter (efface) and begin opening for the baby's passage. In addition, the plug of mucus which remained in the cervical canal throughout the pregnancy as a protection against infection is released and emitted. The passage of this mucous plug is a sign that the labor is true and that the delivery has begun. Sometimes contractions which are not followed by emissions of fluid occur prior to this time. These very common Braxton Hicks contractions—often called false labor—do not get stronger and closer in time. A "bloody show" is often another early sign of the beginning of labor.

As labor progresses, the contractions will get stronger and closer together. As the time between the contractions becomes shorter, preparations need to be made to get your wife to the birthing place. Most doctors want their patients to call them when the contractions are ten minutes apart and to be safely in the hospital by the time they are approximately five minutes apart. Passing of the mucous plug or rupture of the membranes with a slow leak or gush of fluid are other signs that it is time to go. If this happens, your partner will probably feel more comfortable if she's sitting on a towel.

It is important that both you and your partner are comfortable and prepared for this. Contrary to the sitcom portrayal of the expectant father as helpless and hopeless, it is your job to make all necessary arrangements and to give your wife physical and emotional comfort during this time. In addition to getting her to the hospital, you (or someone else who will assist with the birth) should begin to clock and record the time between contractions. At this stage, contractions will last for almost a minute and occur every five minutes or more. You can also encourage and help your wife to rest between the contractions, as they can go on for several hours, and she must keep up her strength for the duration of the labor and delivery. You can rub her back, help her to maintain slow and deep breathing, and encourage her to urinate frequently (at least hourly). You should also get any remaining supplies ready in the suitcase (you packed in the last chapter, remember?).

This early labor is the first stage of the first phase of delivery. It precedes active labor, which should best occur while the woman is already settled into the maternity center.

Hospital preparatory procedures. At the birthing center, after the formal checking-in routine, several steps may be taken to prepare your wife for the birth itself. Some of these procedures are optional. You should have a clear agreement with the staff in advance.

Prep. One standard procedure that meets with disagreement is the slowly diminishing obligatory shaving of pubic hair prior to the birth. This is a moot point, of course, if your partner is already shaven. Women's advocates have been able to effect some changes in these policies such as "partial prep" (only lower pubic hair is shaved) or just clipping the long hairs around the area where suturing may have to be done. If your wife chooses not to have a full shave, you need to clear that with the birthing person. If you will be present while the prep is done, expect the nurse or aide doing it to be somewhat uncomfortable or embarrassed (while using a razor near your wife's private parts). They're still not used to having Dad on the scene and react as if you are unfamiliar with those areas of your wife's anatomy.

Episiotomy. Hospitals who insist on the preparatory shave also often encourage a standard episiotomy. If an episiotomy is not to be done and no stitching is required, the prep is also unnecessary. An episiotomy is a surgical cut in the mother's perineum to facilitate the birth of the baby. Originally, this incision was made only when the birth was particularly difficult or to prevent tearing caused by the baby's passage. A sutured incision will cause less pain and heal better than a tear. However, in recent years, some obstetricians have done episiotomies as standard practice. This also requires pain-killing medication and requires a longer rehabilitation period for the mother than natural childbirth (unless there is a tear). Many women do not like automatic episiotomies because of the pain, because of the increased length of healing before they can be sexually active, and because it is not "natural" childbirth. If you and your wife do not want an episiotomy unless it is essential, it is important to discuss this with the obstetrician. It is also of value to have the doctor give you an estimate of the percentage of births he or she does in which an episiotomy is performed. If the estimate is 80 percent or higher, it can be considered automatic.

Enema. When a woman enters the hospital in early labor, an enema is often standard practice. It is done to reduce discomfort and to clean out the bowel to increase the room available to the descending infant. It is also performed to eliminate any chance of loss of bowel control during the delivery, which can be embarrassing to the mother and unpleasant for the birthing staff. The enema is not safe if the mother's water has broken, if labor is protracted, or if any bleeding occurs.

Some women do not want an enema, and if your wife is one of them, it is important to arrange with the nursing staff. If they insist and your wife wants some control over the procedure, she may consider having an enema at home prior to coming to the hospital.

Fetal monitor. If the birth is to occur at the hospital, a fetal monitor will probably be used. There are two types of monitors: internal and external. The most common internal monitor is a device that that is placed through the cervix and attached to the baby's scalp. A second type may be used to gauge the strength of contractions. This small *intrauterine pressure catheter* (IUPC) is placed in the uterus.

There are also two types of external monitors. One is an ultrasound device that picks up and transmits the baby's heartbeat. It looks like an airplane seat belt with a fancy buckle that is placed on the mother's abdomen. A second device, a *fetoscope*, also measures the baby's heartbeat and can be set to make periodic measurements. The fetoscope replaces and automates stethoscope readings. The advantage of these monitors is that they give an early warning of fetal distress. Many infants who might be oxygen starved or stillborn can be immediately delivered by emergency operations. The difficulty of these monitors is that they produce false positives (indications of distress when there is minimal or correctable danger) which signify a need for emergency surgery that may not be necessary.

The use of a monitor also requires the mother to labor in a prone position. Many birthing experts believe that moving and walking around can speed up the course of labor.

Pitocin (Oxytocin). If a labor is languishing, if the mother has been in labor so long she is "too pooped to push," or if the contractions do not progress as expected, Pitocin may be placed in the mother's IV (intravenous) line. "Pit" is a medication which induces uterine contractions. It is used both to induce or augment labor and also to aid uterine contractions after birth to retain firmness and prevent excess bleeding. Although Pitocin makes the contractions more efficient, it does not diminish the pain, possibly even increases it.

Kate Wolf Pizor, a childbirth educator and family therapist in Northern California, opined,

> *Pitocin intensifies "hard labor" during which there is little respite between contractions. This can tire the mother much more quickly.*

Like all medications, Pitocin has side effects. Some studies indicate that it can mildly affect the baby's chemistry. Some midwives prefer movement such as walking or physical stimulation as an alternative. There is no easy method for deciding whether to use Pitocin. It is probably best left in the hands of the physician after you provide input regarding your personal preferences.

Pain medication. Birth is painful. Women who experience childbirth frequently report that the pain is indescribable to anyone who has not gone through it. Almost every new mother admits that she underestimated the amount of pain she would feel during the birth. Many critics of Lamaze and similar childbirth education classes claim that the exercises, while helpful, are insufficient and lead women to believe that the pain will not be excruciating. Medication is routinely given to help dull the acuteness of the pain. It is also given to mothers who decide during labor and delivery that they need it. No matter how much you plan for natural childbirth, pain might well overcome the will. For couples who are committed to natural childbirth without pain medication, specific Lamaze-type exercises, meditation, or hypnotic techniques can help manage the pain. You need to be clear if you are opposed to the use of anesthesia or analgesics. Hospitals will routinely use them if you do not specify not to.

There are several types of medications:

1. *Intramuscular medication* (IM). These are usually opioid tranquilizers with analgesics. They relax muscle tension and kill some of the experience of pain. Sometimes these are administered in the IV that is attached when she is first admitted. Side effects include drowsiness. This can be a problem because it makes it harder for the woman to push when told to do so and makes her less aware of fluctuations in her contractions. Two other difficulties with IM are the effects of the narcotics on the baby and their impact on the reliability of the fetal monitor. IM procedures tend to falsely indicate a need for emergency surgery.

2. *Local anesthetic blocks.* Anesthesia is often accomplished via injection of a lidocaine-like substance into cervical nerves (paracervical block) or perineal nerves (pudendal block). These anesthetics dull the sensation of pain but do not remove it totally. The paracervical block is used during labor while the cervix is still dilating, and the pudendal block is administered just prior to delivery in the delivery room. These blocks often do not relieve enough of the pain and can deliver high doses of anesthetic to the baby.

3. *Regional anesthetic block.* These are designed to totally eliminate the pain of labor. These methods are considered the safest. Side effects depend on the timing of the medication, the ability to inject it in the proper space, and the amount used. The most common is the *epidural block* in which continuous measured doses of bupivacaine or some similar anesthetic is administered. If the epidural is properly injected during labor, it blocks sensory nerves (pain) without affecting the motor nerves (pushing). It is also not a sedative. However, during delivery, the epidural block will commonly block motor functioning as well. This will cause a loss of feeling in the legs and hips, which

can be disconcerting to the mother. The blocks also might make it difficult for the mother to roll on the bed or to push effectively, thus increasing potential use of forceps and a need for urinary catheterization. Additional side effects include a ringing in the ears, dizziness, spinal headaches, and in rare cases, seizures.

A *saddle block* is given on the delivery table, not to relieve labor pain, but to eliminate the discomfort of pushing the baby down the canal. An injection is made directly into the spinal column which kills all feeling from the waist down. This feeling of paralysis can be unsettling for the mother and makes her role in delivery much less active. Side effects are similar to those for epidural blocks.

4. *General anesthesia.* Today, general anesthesia is primarily used only for emergencies. The two most common exigencies that require that a woman be put to sleep during the birth are "crash (crisis) C-sections" when the situation is life threatening or in cases where the spinal or epidural anesthesia is unsuccessful. General anesthesia usually involves a combination of sodium pentothal, anesthetic gas, nitrous oxide, and valium. The biggest danger is if the woman regurgitates and aspirates food from a full stomach. That can be fatal. Less dangerous but often unpleasant is the fact that the woman misses the subjective experience of giving birth to her child and the child will be born a little drugged and may be listless or suffer fetal depression.

It is important to weigh two factors when deciding about pain medication. First, you must pay attention to your wife's condition and the pain she is enduring. Second, you need to be aware that each intervention technique, like medication, may facilitate delivery but can also increase the likelihood of the necessity of further procedures like forceps or surgery. Some good resources for information about these medications are childbirth educators in your community, literature available at public libraries and birthing centers, and your physician. As with most medical matters, Internet resources need to be taken with a large dose of salt—there are horror stories unsupported by research for any choices.

Active labor. In active labor, the contractions become somewhat more intense, lasting a full minute or so, and occur only about two to four minutes apart. During this stage, the cervix dilates to an opening of two to three inches.

An expectant father who has gone through childbirth education classes will be working with his wife. He will be actively timing the contractions, helping his wife with the breathing and relaxation exercises that they have learned in class and practiced at home, and monitoring her level of comfort. It is a time for back rubs, encouragement, physical and emotional support, massage, mopping her brow, and providing sips of water, ice chips, or a lollipop or similar candy.

You can encourage her to do deep chest breathing, help her change positions, and support her with pillows. If she is lying on her back, she is likely to be far more uncomfortable than if she can sit (and use gravity to help with the child's movement). If she is lying down, it is best (for blood circulation to the infant) if she is on her side rather than on her back. You can also help by holding her or bracing her if she desires certain positions.

You may also do effleurage, a fingertip light massage that helps relax abdominal muscles. This is a technique usually learned in childbirth education classes. Women who are experienced in hypnosis can sometimes be helped to relax by using familiar and practiced hypnotic skills.

Transition. The final stage of the first phase of labor is called transition. Normally, this is a very intense and short stage of labor. The cervix becomes completely dilated (approximately four inches), and contractions are intense, will last for a minute or two, and occur approximately every two minutes. Sometimes they come back-to-back with no respite in between. This is a time when the husband/coach must firmly take charge and instruct his wife as to breathing techniques. The Lamaze system calls for the "pant/blow" method at this time.

It is important that the husband not be put off by his wife's unwillingness to comply with his directions or if she is heaping abuse on him. She is in pain, and your job at this time is to be completely focused on her needs and to rise above your own. This is a period of time when many women opt for anesthesia even though they had previously declined.

In many cases, the interval between transition and delivery is so short that most anesthetics administered at this time have a primarily psychological effect. She may scream expletives at you that would make the guys at the locker room blush. She may say that she's decided that she is not going to have the baby. Fortunately, it is a human trait to forget the extent of the pain *and* the insults that our loved ones can hurl at us. The hospital staff is quite used to this period, and their calm is often a good model for the husband. It is also of value to provide your wife with firm companionship, making eye-to-eye contact and keeping any distractions away (dim the lights and reduce external noise if possible). Reassure her that the pain will not likely get any worse and help her find comfortable positions. Reinforce any instructions from the obstetrician or midwife.

The Second Phase of Labor

Birth. The baby will now pass through the fully dilated cervix and down through the vagina. Contractions will be a minute to ninety seconds in length and will come every two minutes or so apart. It is an incredible time, and it is very important that the woman be kept informed as to the progress that is occurring. Your wife will not be able to clearly see what is happening and might know of the baby's head appearing (crowning) only through your words and descriptions. Provide a running account of what's going on. Your excitement and emotions will help her. Encourage her to push down and forward as per instructions. Provide any physical support possible, such as supporting her head and shoulders as she bears down.

As soon as the baby is born, it should be placed on the mother's abdomen and covered. At this time, the obstetrician or midwife will announce whether you have a son or a daughter and suction any mucous from the baby's mouth. This usually precipitates the awaited first cry, with or without the traditional smack on the bottom. This is the moment for the family to be closest, and it is important that the rush of paternal feelings of love and thankfulness common when the child is born be extended to your partner as well.

A newborn is covered with a thin white substance called vernix. This is a protective layer that covers the infant's skin while in the uterus. There will also be streaks of blood and mucus on the body, especially if there has been an episiotomy. Frequently, the baby's head is elongated and misshapen from the trip through the birth canal. If forceps were used in the delivery, there will be marks or bruises around the head. At birth, the infant will be bluish in color, but it will develop a more pinkish hue as its independent blood flow regulates.

If you have never seen a baby born before, this appearance can be frightening. The bloody appearance and lack of an early cry can lead to a momentary panic that the baby was stillborn. If you have such a frightening feeling, watch the staff. If they have a "business as usual" attitude, everything is probably all right. You can also ask the birth person.

The Third Phase of Labor

The afterbirth. The third phase involves a continuation of lesser contractions that will expel the placenta. Many birthing experts believe that immediate nursing of the infant may also assist in this process. The birthing staff will examine the baby and will call out numbers or "Apgar scores." These indicate the baby's health at birth. Apgar scores are given at one minute and five minutes after the birth. These scores are measures of heart rate, respiration, muscle tone, reflexes/crying, and color. A score of seven to ten is excellent infant health. Normally, the nurse will call out two scores. The first is the one-minute score and the second the five-minute score, which is usually higher. There will be blood and quite a bit of fluid that accompanies the expulsion of the placenta. The doctor may ask the father if he wants to view the placenta (afterbirth) when it does come out. This usually occurs within about five minutes of the birth itself. The umbilical cord will be cut (often by the father) and tied during this period also.

Postpartum

These first moments are very precious. It is important that you and your wife share the intensity of your child's first minutes of life outside the womb. Your wife will want to hold and perhaps try nursing your infant. You may also want to make some physical contact and hold your baby.

Almost immediately after the umbilical cord is cut and clamped, the baby is taken to a warmer, cleaned, weighed, measured, footprinted, given an identification tag, and rewrapped in a blanket. Most hospitals also apply silver nitrate eyedrops at this time, a protection against blindness associated with maternal gonorrhea and frequently required by law. During this time, the physician may begin stitching any episiotomy cut or tear in your wife's perineum which was made during the delivery. If there is excessive bleeding or hemorrhaging, the physician will probably cauterize the wound.

During the first twenty-four hours after the birth, your wife will be carefully observed for any signs of bleeding or infection. As soon as the delivery is complete, she will be moved to the recovery room. Some birthplaces will allow you and your baby to accompany her. She will certainly be physically tired, although she may have quite a bit of excitement energy. During recovery, her heartbeat, temperature, blood pressure, and other vital signs will be monitored until they stabilize. She may be weak from the loss of ten to fifteen pounds of weight and will continue to have some bloody discharge from her vagina. Her uterus will continue to contract as it returns to its former state. Nursing enhances these contractions and speeds the reformation of the uterus.

It is common for all parents to feel somewhat disoriented after the ordeal of birth. Your lives have suddenly been inexorably altered, and the physical exhaustion can be felt. There may be a flood of apparently opposing emotions. If you are able to be together in the recovery room for those first few hours, the closeness and sharing outweighs the content of any verbal exchange. You may also need some time to be alone and reflect or just to rest and recuperate. Both your wife and baby will also need some sleep soon after the birth.

Don't be at all surprised at any very strong emotional reactions. Many dads are brought to tears and simply feel overwhelmed by the experience of seeing their child for the first time. Leon commented,

> *I was most surprised by how much emotion I was overcome with when I finally saw my son for the first time. Uncontrollably, tears came from my eyes. I think it was a mixture of such excitement over my new son, exhaustion from being my wife's biggest cheerleader, and relief that everyone (mom and baby) was healthy and safe.*

The baby will be brought to the nursery soon after the birth for rest and monitoring. You will be able to see your new son or daughter through the glass windows provided for observation.

Some facilities now allow fathers to accompany the baby to the nursery, and some allow the father and baby to remain with the mother. If these options are desirable to you, request them.

In some modern birthing centers, you will be able to go home with your wife and baby the same day as the birth. Most hospitals require a precautionary one—to three-day stay for healthy mothers and infants. It is interesting to recall that in the 1950s, the normal lying-in period was two weeks. The length of stay depends on the health of the mother and the baby and several related factors. For example, during this early time, new mothers are given instructions on how to nurse and to get the baby to suck on the breast.

Some babies take to the breast avidly, and some do not. Some mothers are able to nurse immediately, while others have a delay in the letdown of the milk. Any difficulties with nursing can be very stressful for moms and for dads. It's also a place that a new dad may not feel like he can be helpful. One dad responded,

> *During initial latching for breast-feeding, I felt the need to be supportive but didn't want to seem like I knew what I was doing.*

Problems and Tragedies

Every couple about to have a baby wishes for the perfect birth and the healthy child. They also fear for the health of the baby and the mother. While problem births are rare in modern facilities, it is an unfortunate fact of life that not all babies are born healthy and not all mothers have problem-free births.

Preemies. Premature babies, born before they have been in the womb a full term, are smaller than full-term babies and less capable of survival. "Preemies" are not sufficiently mature to thrive outside of a particularly safe environment. After birth, they are brought directly to the neonatal intensive care unit (NICU) of the hospital, where they are monitored twenty-four hours a day. In these units, the nurse-to-patient ratio is quite high, and emergency care is always available.

Visiting a preemie nursery can be heart wrenching. The babies are so small and often bluish in color and covered with a variety of monitoring devices, making them look more like laboratory specimens than children.

It is a tribute to medical science that these children can live. In times past, most premature infants would perish. We are now blessed with the technology to keep them alive and, in many cases, to allow them to grow up normally. The parents must visit their infant in the nursery and cannot take the infant home with them right away. This can be particularly disappointing and frightening.

If your child is premature, you will have a special responsibility: Immediately after the birth, you will be the link between your wife in her room and your baby in the NICU. You will have to tell her about the infant care in the nursery and the current condition of your child. It is very important that you and your wife spend as much time with the premature infant as allowed. Some hospitals permit mothers to be with their infants most of the day. Breast-feeding is also strongly recommended for the bonding between mother and infant, to keep the milk flow from abating, and for the immunities contained in the mother's milk.

Sometimes the medical technology seems to supersede our emotional and spiritual coping abilities. Some very premature babies can be kept alive, but the cost may be a life with severe handicaps. Even a healthy preemie may have to reside at the hospital for weeks or months. This can place great personal and financial burdens on the parents, who must leave most of the infant's care to the nursing staff and machines. The daily costs for neonatal intensive care can be astronomical.

Down's syndrome and other birth defects. Mongolism, cleft palates, and some other physical and mental defects are immediately apparent at birth. Some of these problems can be rectified. A child with a cleft palate, for example, will require additional hospital stays and operations. However, the problem is usually correctable. Other defects may involve years of testing, special training, and perhaps a child that will never be "normal."

In one family, a Down's syndrome child lived for over two years, requiring twenty-four-hour-a-day care before finally perishing. Five years after his death, I saw the parents for therapy for recurrent problems caused by the tragedy.

When a baby is born with defects, the parents usually need to mourn the "loss" of the perfect child they imagined and come to grips with having a disabled child. Severe defects, however, only occur in approximately 2 percent of babies born in America.

Stillbirth. A very few babies—less than 1 percent—are stillborn. The cause may be undetected infection or an accident during the birth process (such as strangulation by the umbilical cord), but most frequently, the cause is unknown. After nine months of pregnancy, and perhaps years of wanting a child, a loss at birth is deeply painful. Grieving parents often do not encounter the depth of understanding they need. Other people either do not understand the attachment to a person that was never known or are personally threatened by such an immense loss and must maintain psychological distance.

Parents do not soon get over such tragedies. Some try to get pregnant again as quickly as possible, while others cannot face the thought of trying again for some time. Often, memorial services and mourning are appropriate and beneficial. It is helpful if the baby's name is buried with the baby. Using the same name for the next child can be burdensome—the child has to live up to the expectations of two and can feel like a replacement rather than desired for himself/herself.

Should a childbirth tragedy strike you, please seek help from a professional counselor or clergy person. At the very least, it is imperative that you and your partner spend long hours sharing your feelings, thoughts, and other reactions. Parents who suffer loss often feel guilty and blame themselves. They also tend to withdraw and not share the dilemma with loved ones. If you need professional help, get it, but do not neglect your partner. She shares your loss and can best understand your despair and confusion. Support groups are an excellent source of help for survivors of these tragedies and are available in most communities. Contact your church, mental health center, HMO, physician, or a local crisis hotline for referral resources. A few reference sources are also included in the bibliography.

While it is normal to think about potential dangers, it is extremely unlikely that your current pregnancy will end in tragedy. It is reasonable to expect that your son or daughter will be born healthy and strong and that you will be, as Dr. Martin Greenberg calls it, "engrossed" by the birth.

As described by the men surveyed, birth doesn't always go as planned. In retrospect, any regrets were far outweighed by their joy once they saw and held their children. In the process of birth, however, you are probably going to feel every possible emotion, including fear, admiration for your partner's strength, joy, and humility.

Chapter 10

"The Best Thing I Will Ever Do"

It was then that I glimpsed the baby's head
for the first time . . .
It was still a mere dot, but for me, it was a spot *of eternity.*
—Carl Jones

It is at significant junctures in life such as birth that we are reminded so clearly of our ties to all other men and other beings in our universe.

Our heritage as members of the animal kingdom is made most clear at this time. Robert Bradley, MD, a pioneer in the natural childbirth movement, eloquently points out the commonalities in the way that we and our family pets give birth. Family pets and farm animals find places that are free from distractions and that allow for physical comfort. Frequently, animals will create a special "nest" for the birth. They are also careful to find a situation that allows for physical relaxation, controlled breathing, and intense concentration, often with eyes closed to shut out extraneous stimulation. I have a clear memory of having to crawl into a dark space under a house to be with a mother dog to observe the birth of her puppies.

The heritage we share with other animals is worth noting. Our children's birthplaces should also be as quiet and free from distraction as possible. We want our babies to be born in the gentlest way, and we want to provide as much comfort as we can for our wives and our children. This is one of the reasons why couples try so hard during the pregnancy to arrange for the birth to be the way they most want it. As the father, you can influence how your child enters the world and is handled immediately at birth.

Emotional Experiences for Fathers

What emotional experiences do men have at various stages in the birth sequence?

Announcement. The indication from your wife that labor has begun should activate your well-planned moves. You can start timing the contractions, make necessary phone calls, make sure everything is packed in the suitcase, and be with your wife.

Many men react like Otis to the news:

> *Man, when she said the pains were coming closer, I just shifted into high gear. It was a relief that it was finally going to happen. I was all ready. I never even had time to wonder whether I would mess up. I was going to get her to the hospital and do this thing.*

John recalled,

> *I knew it was risky to go to the North Shore so close to the time, but we needed a break from the pressure. We were just sitting up near Sunset (Beach) when her water bag broke. I acted so calm and got her into the car and began the long drive in Sunday traffic back to the hospital. I cursed every slow driver under my breath and made plans of how I could detour to the three hospitals we passed on the way if I had to . . . All the time, I just reassured her and acted like I was in control . . . We made Queens just in time to go to emergency, and she was in the delivery room by the time I parked and got up there. No time for camera, changing clothes, nothing . . . But the baby came out fine, and we were both there.*

Carlos also had some travelling to do:

> *I didn't want to go in to work that day because I thought it was the day, but Lena just said I was too nervous and pacing around the house, so I went in. There was bad traffic, and it took almost an hour to arrive. When I got there, the lady in the front office says, "Call home. Your wife's been calling. I think the baby's coming." So I call, and she says, "Meet me at the hospital," and I say, "Try and wait for me. I'm coming now." Anyhow, when I got home, she says, "The pain stopped," so I waited. Then three hours later, it was the real time. By the time I got to the hospital, I was already worn out and hungry. Then she has twenty hours of labor. We were both*

wasted when the baby came . . . but never so happy in my life as when I see his head and know my son is okay.

While many men reported anxiety, none suffered the comic pratfalls often portrayed in the media. Most recognized the importance of being in charge and taking care of their wives.

Labor. There are some rewards for your efforts to support and comfort her labor. You and your wife will feel more like a team, and the basis for your work as a family unit will be enhanced.

Dr. Martin Greenberg recalled,

As the labor progressed, *I experienced a powerful sense of intimacy with my wife . . . I enjoyed coaching Claudia. In a way, I found it to be fun.*

Dr. Greenberg and many other men felt quite good as the protector of a vulnerable wife.

Chris proudly reported,

Lois is always so organized and strong. I'm usually the family klutz. Now she was tossing and screaming, and I was the one to calm her down and take care of her. Afterwards, she told me I was perfect and that my reassurance really got through.

Not every man saw his wife as weak. One new father reported,

I have a new respect for Terri. She was so strong. She handled all the pain and showed me such courage. I don't think I'll ever look at her again without some admiration and a sense of closeness.

Many recent fathers indicated that the biggest and most trying surprise during the pregnancy and birth of their child was the difficulty of seeing their wives in such intense pain. Several said that they gained new respect for the strength of their partner by being with her during labor and delivery. Others reported that they would "give anything to take the pain away from her and take it" onto themselves. Some men had so much difficulty seeing their wives in such distress that they encouraged the hospital staff to administer painkillers despite prior agreements and desires to have the birth naturally.

Transition. As labor progresses, women become tired, irritable, discouraged, even depressed. Transition is a very short part of the labor, but it is a time that many women feel the greatest physical pain. They are often unable to respond to their husbands or focus on anything outside of themselves. The pain and discouragement are frequently projected outward onto the members of the birth team, especially the husband, and expressed as anger.

As her husband, you might share her feelings of fear, discouragement, and helplessness. You may also experience some guilt for "putting her through such an ordeal." Perhaps you're feeling rejected too: she's ignoring your well-intentioned help. This is not a time to indulge those feelings. Focus your attention on your wife. There will be time to express your own feelings later.

Delivery. During delivery, your wife is going through intense physical exercise and will frequently be in acute and prolonged pain. Yours is a voice she may hear, and your reassurance and assistance will be very valuable, at least in retrospect. It will be up to you to keep her informed as to what is happening. Her pain, or anesthesia-produced lack of feeling, requires you to be the one to translate.

Few experiences in your life have the potential for joy that the delivery of your child presents.

Dr. Martin Greenberg again recalled,

> *I heard a loud cry even before the baby was completely delivered, and the next thing I knew, there was this beautiful baby boy before my eyes. I couldn't believe it, and for a brief instant, I felt stunned by his size. When I saw him, I began to laugh. I laughed and laughed almost uncontrollably, as if some unseen floodgates had suddenly been released. It was a laugh of joy and happiness, and I hugged my wife and kept kissing her as I repeated, "Look! Look! We have a baby. We have a baby boy. We produced a boy!"* (Birth of a Father, p. 16)

Postpartum. The moments after a healthy baby is born are intense and unique. If you are present for the birth, your infant is truly born into a family. Fathers' reactions ran from stunned and speechless to shouts of joy, or "I just couldn't stop crying. She was crying, I was crying, the baby was crying. For all I know, the nurses and doctor were crying."

Most men reported feelings of awe at being part of what author Carl Jones (*Mind over Labor*) calls the birth miracle. If your wife tries to hold or nurse the baby, try to hold her and the baby too. Physical contact helps make the whole experience feel more real.

Because my own daughter was born by C-section, I got to hold her first. What an amazing experience! She was so small, fragile, and light, I was afraid I might break her. Yet I was flooded with new feelings of paternal pride and protectiveness.

Parental Control over the Birth

As you have gone through the pregnancy and educated yourself about childbirth, you have probably developed some specific desires about how you would ideally like the birth of your child to progress. Childbirth education classes frequently encourage couples to have as much control and comfort as possible during the birth. Many couples develop an intense desire to have the experience their way.

If, after considering the options, you have made choices about how you want the birth to proceed, you will probably have quite an emotional investment in those choices. The expectant father must bear the responsibility to try to achieve the birth as chosen. It is a rare birth that is as perfect as the new parents have planned. Many arrangements are altered at the last minute. As the expectant father, you must be the judge of whether to allow or contest a change.

Father's Presence

One of the plans that often changes suddenly is the father's decision to participate in the birth. Fathers who have been ambiguous about being at the birth have to make spontaneous decisions at the last moment. The greatest number of these men opt to be present.

"Well, I hadn't really planned to be there, but . . ." Irving was clear that he was not going to be present for the actual birth. He was helpful in supporting his wife, getting her settled into her room while the labor started, and providing her with any comfort possible. It was his intention to leave when the doctor came. He was so certain of his plan that he had not even attended the childbirth education classes. Thus, it came as a surprise to him

> when Dr. B. asked if I was coming into the delivery room. I somehow found myself in there . . . gown, mask, and in the middle of this swirl of activity. When Gina saw me, she just smiled. In retrospect, don't know how I could have considered missing it. It was terrific. Dr. B. told me I did a great job. I know it was Gina and him, but I was there.

Phil was also certain that he would be absent. He hadn't even considered the possibility of trying to be present, because as a navy submariner, he was supposed to be on deployment during the expected arrival date. He was therefore surprised when the baby arrived early while his ship was docked for extra repairs:

There we were. Debbie said she thinks she's in labor. I told her it couldn't be . . . It was too early. An hour later, we were at the doctor's office and two hours into the hospital. I really don't know what all happened. The next thing I knew, the nurse asked me to help prop Debbie up, and then I was in the delivery room. It was hard. For a while I thought I was going to pass out seeing her in such pain, but I couldn't leave her either. I regret I didn't know more. I didn't learn how to be a good coach because I wasn't expecting to be there. I could have been a better help to her. Afterwards, she told me she was glad I was there. That made me happy. I'm not sure if I would have chosen to do it for me, but I would for her and Kimmy.

"You know, I think I've changed my mind." A few fathers decided at the last minute that they would not be present. Each of these men had been relatively uninvolved in the pregnancy and had been ambivalent about being present up to the last moment. In opting to be absent, they usually reasoned that they'd be a hindrance to their wives. Tom described his feelings:

I know I couldn't help and I'd be in the way. I'm just not good in these situations. Besides, I pass out every time they [draw] my blood for a test.

Melinda, his wife, agreed:

I didn't really care if he was there or not. We're very traditional. I didn't want to be distracted from the doctor and kinda discouraged him from coming along. It's fine. We all came through it fine, and he was waiting for me when I was back in the room.

"It can't be over. I just got here." Even if you plan to be at the birth, you may not be able to be present. This is likely to occur if the baby comes so quickly that you cannot reach the hospital in time. Ted described his disappointment:

She called at ten-thirty at the office, said the pains were six minutes apart, and the doctor said to go to the hospital right away. We planned to meet there, but by the time I arrived, so had Danielle. Amazing, two hours of labor for a first-time mother. They say the first takes the longest. Next time, I don't leave home without her.

Another father, an anesthesiologist, was working in a lengthy surgery; and by the time he emerged, his daughter had been born in another hospital across town.

No admittance. Fathers need not apply. The most frequent cause for men's absence at the actual birth is intervention from some external source. Many men told of circumstances where it was determined that an emergency Caesarian section needed to be done and found themselves in the waiting room while their wives were wheeled to an operating room.

One recent father bitterly recounted,

> *I couldn't believe the way the hospital staff took over when they decided to do a Caesarian. They asked us, and as soon as I agreed (as if they gave me a choice), I was literally pushed out of the room with no explanation, nothing, and they were wheeling her down the hall. Nobody even came out to tell me it was okay until thirty minutes after Sophia was born.*

Other fathers were confronted with unanticipated hospital policies or changes in procedure at the critical moment and denied admittance to the delivery. Jim was furious when he remembered the treatment he and his wife received at the HMO at which his son was born:

> *First of all, we got a new obstetrician. The woman doctor we had talked to for six months was not on duty that day. Then this new guy asks me if I had some special course he requires for all expectant fathers. I never even heard of it. So he says I can't stay with Rosa. I didn't dare argue with him because she is in pain and if I delay, I don't know what could happen. I was stuck in the waiting room for two hours. Then afterwards, he comes out and says it was a hard birth and wasn't I glad he didn't let me in. If I wasn't so worried about my wife and baby, I would have dropped him right there.*

As unfair and horrible as these stories sound, they are still not uncommon. In the 1987 CBS television movie *Warm Hearts, Cold Feet*, the fetal monitor measured distress as the second of a pair of twins was being born. The obstetrician responded, "We're going to have an emergency C-section," and ordered the husband to leave over his objections. As the husband is crying alone in the corridor, his son is born vaginally. Dramatic emphasis aside, it was clearly portrayed as permissible for the doctor to force the husband out of the delivery room if a C-section was possible.

At least one new dad took it in stride:

*I think what surprised me most was how much we can plan/dream/
worry about how the birth will go, but ultimately, our baby had his
its own way of coming into the world. I'm grateful that my wife
and I were both willing to go with the flow and just be grateful for
a healthy result. Otherwise, it could've seen been very emotional
or disappointing when they took her away to do an emergency
C-section . . . This was very different from the way our daughter
came into the world.*

The OB-GYN Establishment

Almost every couple tells about how the birth did not go as they had
planned or wished. To some extent, that is inevitable. Every couple wants
to have the perfect birth (following the perfect pregnancy and preceding the
perfect child). Nobody can have that, but some of the complaints about the
treatment of people becoming parents were astounding.

It is one thing for the expectant father to feel helpless in the presence of
the inexorable progress of nature in childbirth. It is yet another when he feels
that he must do battle with the professionals who are supposed to be helping.

Hospital policies, designed ostensibly for the best interests of patients,
commonly diminish choice and place responsibility for care in the hands
of the trained professionals. Hospitals provide medical advantages at the
expense of social costs. They are more convenient than homes for physician
scheduling, they are prepared for emergencies, they always have staff
available, but they are run according to policies which are designed for
patients who are relatively helpless, unknowledgeable, and devoid of choices
or rights to make changes.

An expectant father, already ambivalent about his role, fearful for the
health and safety of his child, and unsure of himself in an alien setting, can
be readily convinced that what he and his wife have planned is impractical
or unwise. Many men reported a feeling of being out of control, as well as out
of place.

Men who talked to hospital personnel about their fear of queasiness were
less frequently reassured than encouraged to be absent. Bart told a nurse
half-jokingly,

*I was worried about losing the contents of my stomach or passing
out during the delivery, so I ordered an immaculate delivery. I told
my wife that the baby could come out clean just as well as it could
come out bloody. She agreed, and we spoke to the kid through her
belly last night. It's all set.*

The nurse's response was not joking at all:

> *I recommend that you wait in the waiting room. I can promise you that it will be very bloody.*

Bart rejoined,

> *Well, I want to be in there. I'll just look at her face the whole time.*

And she countered,

> *You know, if you get sick in there, your wife could be in jeopardy. Besides, the doctor doesn't like interference. He could be more uncomfortable if you are watching over his shoulder. You really would be more comfortable in the waiting room.*

Contrast this with Jamal's experience in 2013. His jokes with the nurses were met with understanding that he was anxious, and one of the nurses responded with a hearty laugh, "No problem, I'll catch you with one arm and your baby with the other!" Jamal said at that moment he knew it would all be fine.

Deception and Failure to Disclose

Couples who wanted to have control over the birth frequently became quite angry and frustrated at the apparent interference of the hospital staff. One dad complained,

> *They were better at advertising than at follow-through. After the whole thing was over, I felt like I had when I bought a used car. Lots of promises, lots of lies.*

In the course of research for this book, I discovered that some hospitals that claimed to have special birthing rooms with low lights, birthing bed, and decor that simulated closely a "home" environment often did not have such rooms available when the time came for the birth. One Honolulu hospital which advertised both "living in" and a birthing room confronted couples about to give birth with the "unfortunate" fact that the room was nonfunctional because "the bed was broken." An investigation by maternal-child nursing graduate students indicated that the bed had been nonfunctional for over six months.

My own experience as an expectant father during the day of my daughter's birth was particularly disconcerting. Although the ordeal created by the hospital did not overcome the joy my wife and I experienced, it certainly caused me a great deal of unnecessary distress. The following excerpt comes from a letter I wrote to the consumer advocate at the hospital in which my daughter was born. It is of note that the hospital never responded to the letter but did discuss the letter in a staff meeting in an attempt to discover if the father was "a weirdo."

> *By far the grossest incompetence took place on the day of the C-section birth of our child. On that day, dishonesty, stupidity, insensitivity and outright poor medical practice were rampant.*

1. *The operation was four hours later than we were told, with no consistent explanation or reason for the delay.*
2. *My wife was prepped and left on a gurney in the cold hallway for over one hour, while I was kept in the waiting room. There is no reason why she had to be alone and uncomfortable, when I could have been with her, providing care and comfort.*
3. *Despite multiple discussions and agreements that I was to be with my wife throughout the operation, I was allowed in only after the operation had begun, and then only after I insisted, and my wife complained several times that I was not with her.*
4. *I was dressed in a scrub outfit for sterile conditions during the operation, and then was sent back to the waiting room, which I shared with two smokers and seven other people including five children. In short, I was routed from the waiting room in my street clothes to the dressing room where I put on a scrub suit, then back to the waiting room, and then directly into the operating room. If the hospital staff were seriously concerned about breaking a sterile field, this method is somewhat inadequate.*
5. *Prior to the operation, my wife requested the opportunity to observe the proceedings [a spinal anesthesia was used] and was informed that mirrors were unavailable. When she arrived in the Operating Room, she was able to view the proceedings through a reflection in the glass cabinet. She expressed her pleasure at this, and in response, a nurse covered the glass to prevent this. Since my wife is a Registered Nurse and has assisted at many births and other operations, she knew what the procedure looked like and would not have been upset. However, without explanation, that choice was arbitrarily removed.*
6. *During the operation, once I was present, I informed my wife that the cutting had begun, and that Dr. Y. had already gone through two*

layers of tissue. At that moment, the staff member who was standing in the anesthesiologist's position told us both that _the operation had not begun, and that the skin was intact. Perhaps she told this outright lie in a bizarre and misguided attempt to assuage some of her own projected fears. Whatever the reason, this unconscionable action was worse than distasteful, and expanded fears of incompetence. We also requested that we be told when the uterus had been reached. She refused, and it was only the willingness of Dr. Y. to keep us informed that limited the impact of this staff member's absurd behavior.

Frankly, this was the most upsetting component of the process for me.

7. *After our daughter was born, we were offered the choice of my staying with my wife, or "accompanying [my] daughter to the nursery." Having been told that my wife would be on the operating table for just a few more minutes, we decided that I would accompany the baby to the nursery. However, as soon as I was out of the operating room, the baby was taken from me and I was informed that I could not go to the nursery, nor even be in the same elevator. Furthermore, I was not allowed back in the operating room to assist my wife for reasons of contamination [see #4 above]. She was in the OR for almost 45 more minutes.*

8. *My wife specifically asked that no post-operative medication be administered unless she specifically requested it, yet she had to interrupt the OR nurse from surreptitiously placing a narcotic in her IV. Were she not a nurse and knew what was happening, she would have been specifically denied her requested rights.*

9. *Despite an allergy to Percodan noted in the chart, Percodan was ordered as PRN Medication.*

At the time when this letter was written, I was a professor in the school of nursing at the University of Hawaii. Since the hospital did not think my letter deserved a response, I shared the contents with several obstetricians, maternal-child nurse practitioners, and instructors at the school of nursing. Nobody expressed surprise or outrage, but each of them responded by guessing the name of the hospital at which these events occurred. Most of the area hospitals were guessed. Many talked about their own similar or more horrifying experiences. This suggests that the number of inappropriate and medically potentially dangerous events were not unique and often part of what makes the birth day somewhat more of an ordeal than is necessary.

What You Can Do

If it is important to you to personalize your birth experience, you need to take several precautionary steps:

1. During the second and third trimesters, investigate all options available. Be careful to talk to recent parents and check out their experiences.
2. Visit and walk through any special birthing rooms and facilities. Find out how many such rooms are available and whether you can be assured of one for your labor and delivery. Ask if reservations are allowed. If a birthing room is unavailable, ask if the birth can occur in the labor room. Many hospitals now have special birth facilities in which all of the rooms meet your criteria, not just a few that may be occupied.
3. If your obstetrician will not be available for the birth of your child, who will be? Meet the other alternative physicians/partners who might substitute and be sure to go over with each of them what you want for the birth. You cannot rely on them pre-reading the chart, even when it is computerized.
4. Take childbirth education classes together, even if you do not plan to be present for the birth. If you change your mind at the last minute, you will be better prepared.
5. Find out the hospital policy on (and percentage of) Caesarian sections. If you want to be present for an emergency surgical birth, be sure that you have taken any required classes and made advance agreements for your presence.
6. Give yourself plenty of time to deal with hospital policies. One of the ways that administrators can frustrate you is by delaying responses to your questions. If the birth is only two weeks away, a three-month delay will not be very helpful.
7. Be assertive about what you want, but don't become so argumentative that your wife and baby suffer. Remember, unless you live in a rural area or military base or are locked into a single location by an HMO or PPO, you can shop around and take your business to someone who will give you what you want.

Dealing with bureaucracies is always difficult, time-consuming, and trying. It is worth a battle only if you can win something that your family wants. It sometimes seems that fighting off the ob-gyn version of Nurse Ratched (*One Flew Over the Cuckoo's Nest*) also serves as the modern-day equivalent of slaying a saber-toothed tiger in order to celebrate a new birth.

In these ways, the struggle might be valuable. However, obstacles presented by institutions are minor compared to fears for the safety of your wife and child.

The Miracle

The birthday of your child is potentially the most important and wonderful day in your life. Being present at the births of their children was the clear highlight in these men's lives.

Jed spoke excitedly,

The birth . . . seeing her little head squeeze through . . . hearing the cry . . . being with my wife at that moment . . . *There are no words to describe the thrill.*

Ahmed had similar reactions:

A gift from God . . . It's the richest experience possible. I am just now coming to grips with the mystery and rhythm of life and death. I became a full human when my son was born.

Maurice remembered the moment this way:

The baby wasn't breathing at birth. The labor was almost forty hours, and it was scary the way the doctors handled it. I was shocked, and then the cry came. What joy! When I held him, I lifted him up to face level and saw the life in his eyes. Pain to death to life in an instant. The look made it all worthwhile.

Wing focused on the relationship with his wife:

When Amanda was born . . . the moment she was born . . . my connection to Wendy was forever. Our bodies had merged and created a new being.

Bonnie described her husband at the birth of their first child:

Ryan just bawled and bawled. That minute was the happiest we've ever been.

On January 1, 2014, Jose reflected on the New Year's gift when his son was born at two o'clock in the morning:

> *I was ready for the change in my life. I wasn't even partway prepared for that much love and joy.*

Soon after the birth of Tasha, my own daughter, I wrote in my journal,

> *This is the best thing I will ever do. Her birth and being reaffirms all that gives meaning to human life.*

It's still true thirty-two years later, and I got to reexperience the moment when my son was born six years later.

Chapter 11

Caesarian Section: The 40 Percent Solution

Things which you do not hope happen more frequently than things which you do hope.
—Titus Plautus (circa 210 BC)

It was devastating to me. I wanted this to be the perfect birth. Everything perfect! Now the baby is breech, and it's not close to perfect or anything . . . I'm worried about Jean and the anesthesia and watching the operation. It's so frustrating. We went to the [Lamaze] classes and had everything so well planned. Now we have to rely on others and surgery.
—From an interview with an expectant father three days before the birth of his son

Guilty, guilty, guilty, that's how I felt. I was the cause. She got herpes from me when we were first dating, and she got it so bad, there was no way we could risk having Jennifer right. I think she'll always be angry with me. She says the only important thing is that Jennifer is healthy, but I know she resents me . . . and the scar.
—From an interview with a young father six weeks after his daughter was born

I know this sounds terrible, but I was relieved. I never did feel comfortable with the responsibility of "coach," and now it's out of my hands. I couldn't do anything even if I wanted.
—A common reaction expressed on a radio call-in show

All parents want the births of their children to go normally, naturally, and without complications. Prenatal education classes promote the value of natural childbirth, and the increasing social pressure on pregnant couples to have a "perfect" birth creates a situation that may ill-prepare couples for complicated deliveries and births.

The Caesarian section is an increasingly common procedure in modern births performed for a lot of reasons:

- excessively long labor with loss of strength by the woman
- active or potentially active cases of certain diseases or viruses that could harm the baby, like genital herpes
- anatomical problems of disproportion, such as a mother's pelvis which is too small or too bony for the size of the infant
- certain types of breech positions for the infant
- complications during the birth process that would threaten the viability of life for the child, such as a strangulating cord
- the advantage to physicians of scheduling the birth and avoiding long waiting through protracted labor
- the relative ease of the operation (In fact, many obstetricians consider it a lot easier and safer than vaginal birth.)
- because it is surgery carried out by a medical team, it may be more comfortable for physicians who cling to traditional roles

For all these reasons and several more, the number of C-sections in the US is on the rise. According to a 2013 study by the US Centers for Disease Control and Prevention, the national average was approximately one-third of all births are surgical rather than vaginal. The percentage varies broadly, reaching above 40 percent of live births in some hospitals. However, Caesarian birth is unquestionably less preferred by parents since it is a major surgery, the recovery is slower, and there is a greater probability of complications such as hemorrhage and infection.

Caesarian Section: A Definition

The C-Section is properly defined as a surgical procedure. It is a major surgery. Anesthesia is used, either general (in which the woman is put to sleep for the duration of the operation) or regional. The two most common types of regional anesthetics are epidural and spinal. Both of these block the transmission of pain during the operation but do not affect the woman's level of consciousness. For prospective parents who have attended classes and believe in natural, husband-coached childbirth, the spinal block or epidural is a logical choice. In this way, the couple can still be together (unless the hospital forbids the husband access) and consciously observe and experience the emergence of their infant into the world, even if physical sensation for the mother is limited.

The Caesarian operation allows the child to be born through the abdomen of the mother rather than via the vaginal canal. This is done by means of an operation in which an incision is made in the abdomen of the mother. The incision—often called a bikini cut because it would be hidden by a bikini bathing suit—is usually made at or about the top of the pubic hair line and passes through several layers of skin, muscle, and fat tissue and finally ends at the wall of the uterus. A small incision, approximately the size of a fully dilated cervix (five inches), is made in the uterine wall, and the surgeon places a hand under the infant and lifts it out. Once the child and placenta are out of the uterus, the normal procedures for infant care and cutting of the umbilical cord are followed. However, the procedure is quite different for the mother and the obstetrician.

Implications of Caesarian Births

In some ways, C-sections are a miracle of modern science: women do not often die in childbirth as they once did, and infants are not as frequently stillborn or brain damaged. They also tend to look a lot cuter than infants whose heads have been molded and squished by traveling down the birth canal. But *it is also major* surgery, and the mother's recovery from it is slower. The effects of anesthesia and other surgical by-products can also delay early bonding between mother and infant.

Following a surgical birth, hospitals often restrict privileges like the husband's presence during birth or rooming-in. The mother and child will be delayed in coming home due to postsurgical care. In addition, hospitals frequently limit visiting hours on surgical floors, so fathers may have far less opportunity to be with their new families during the first week after the birth.

The father's role in the childbirth itself is dramatically limited by the occurrence of a birth by C-section. He may lose the opportunity of even supportive participation in a birth by surgery. Some hospitals do not allow fathers into the operating room at all. Hospital policies vary, and more hospitals today are open to the father's presence during a surgical birth, but this is by no means guaranteed. For a new dad who has practiced childbirth exercises with his wife and wants to be present for the birth, this can be a terrible letdown.

If the Caesarian is an emergency, he loses the opportunity of sharing this time of birth with his family and giving real support to his wife during the operation itself (presuming that she is not given general anesthesia).

One father described the events of his daughter's birth in the following manner:

> *She was so tired. Labor went on for hours, and there was no push left when the doctor began to worry about oxygen getting to the baby. In like ten seconds, everyone was going fifty miles an hour. They gave her gas, wheeled her into the operating room, and pushed me into this waiting room with four chain-smokers. I was so worried about both of them. I couldn't stand being in that room, but I also couldn't leave. It seemed like an eternity until a nurse came out and told me that both wife and baby were fine, but she left before I could think to ask when I could see either of them. It was almost five hours before I saw Sandy, and Alisha was behind glass in the nursery until Sandy was awake enough to nurse her. I didn't even get to hold her until the next day. Maybe it's me. I mean I'm mostly grateful that they're both okay, but I wanted to be much more a part of her birth.*

The hospital procedure and policy of exclusion hurt and disappointed this father. In his mind, all of his preparation, study, and training for the birth of his daughter were for naught. The C-section caused him to miss one of the most significant moments of his life. He would have chosen to be present even for a surgical birth. The general anesthesia used for his wife also meant that she was similarly unable to experience Alisha's entrance into the world.

This is not the only perspective, however. Some men have greater problems if they are allowed to be in the surgical delivery room. Very few people look forward to watching an operation, especially on a loved one. Most men truly fear becoming queasy in that setting. Indeed, most men worry about being uncomfortable during a *normal* birth with its outpouring of blood and other fluids. As one recent father put it,

> *All that "gooey" stuff is supposed to stay under the skin, not go all over the place.*

It is one thing to be prepared for the blood and other fluids that accompany natural childbirth. It is quite another to be prepared for the advent of surgery and the cutting of skin.

Most people in our culture are uncomfortable with these things, but the man becoming a father has few ways to deal with his concern. It seems selfish and unmanly to be worried about the sight of blood when his wife is the person getting cut and doing the bleeding. Talking about it would help a great deal, but with whom does he discuss such concerns? He certainly does not want to add his discomfort to his wife's fears about surgery. The only other people present are normally doctors and nurses, who are experienced in such matters but are often the worst people to try to tell such concerns to—they do not have a loved one on the table and tend to see the operation as a set of "procedures." As professionals, they have devised ways of looking at the surgical patient as a health problem that they will correct. In short, they do not feel queasy and probably went into a medical profession because, in part, they do not experience such feelings as strongly as others. They will have practical suggestions (i.e., "Don't look at the first incision") or jokes, but not a lot of empathy. One man described his experience by saying,

> *I asked the doctor what I should do if I felt faint. By the time he was done lecturing me on the way medicine was going to the dogs with all these outsiders around, I was afraid that he would get so distracted he'd forget about my wife.*

Another man was "jokingly" told by the obstetrician (his brother-in-law) on the way into the operating room,

> *Hey, Bill, if you pass out, try to roll away from the table. Don't want you getting underfoot.*

Very few people would choose to spend an afternoon in an operating room with a member of their family on the table. For many men, being at a birth is difficult enough. The advent of being at a birth by surgery is beyond what they can comfortably do, and it is important that they have the option not to attend. One father said,

> *Look, man, there's no way they're gonna get me in there. The closest I want to get to that surgery room is giving the boy his name.*

Another father called a radio talk show and described his feelings on air,

> *I was there for all three of my kids . . . each born by section . . . I hated the first one, and it was worse each time. I love my wife and kids and didn't have the heart to say no, but it was the three worst experiences of my life . . . I wish I was in the military like my friend . . . He was out on patrol whenever his wife was in the hospital.*

Disappointment and disgust are not the only reactions expectant fathers have about Caesarian births. Many are substantially relieved to have the burden of responsibility removed. In fact, several dads indicated that they were quite happy to be ordered out of the operating room and into the waiting room. The tension of assisting the wife was now gone, as was the fear of not holding up under the pressure and the concern about becoming faint or queasy. There was no recourse—nobody could blame him for not being present. Katharyn May's research is instructive here. In one study, she and Deanna Sollid found that 52 percent of fathers were more relieved than disappointed at handing the birth back over to the doctors.

The Frequency of Caesarian Section Births

There is great disagreement among experts regarding the exact rates of C-sections. In 1974, Robert Bradley (*Husband Coached Childbirth*) estimated that 3 percent of all births were by C-section. A much higher figure—20 percent—is given for 1980 by the American College of Obstetrics and Gynecology and Grad et al. (*The Father Book*, 1981). An informal survey of San Francisco area obstetricians yielded a 1981 "guesstimate" of 40-50 percent. Research by graduate maternal-child nurses at Honolulu hospitals produced rates between 40 and 59 percent for C-sections during 1980-1982. The figure in 2012 for the past four years provided by the US Center for Disease Control and Prevention was 34 percent.

Whatever the actual figures, there is complete agreement that the frequency of surgical births has increased dramatically since the early 1960s. This seems almost paradoxical. At a time when the medical establishment was yielding to pressure from feminist and family movements in terms of accessibility to the birth for the father and (medically) nontraditional birth arrangements, the number of C-sections increased by 150-500 percent. There are several reasons for this, primarily related to the times in which we're living.

Technological advances have allowed for earlier detection of potential problems and have indicated the use of surgical instead of vaginal delivery for the safety of mother and child. Sonograms, amniocentesis, and the controversial fetal monitor have all played a part in increasing the number of sections ordered.

The fetal monitor measures potential or developing problems for the fetus during labor and delivery, providing a readout of the baby's heart rate and the mother's contractions. When distress is indicated on the monitor, surgical procedures are prescribed to protect the life of the mother and the baby. Critics of the monitor argue that it is unreliable and that it creates a large number of false positives (indicating surgery when it is not mandatory). Because monitor readings are based on deviations from statistical curves, many infants showing temporary distress may never get the opportunity to stabilize and be born vaginally. Physicians are unlikely to ignore the distress signal, both because of their honest desire to save their patients and because of potential lawsuits if they delay once the fetal monitor registers a distress call.

The increasing number of lawsuits for malpractice and the inevitable rise in malpractice insurance rates have made many doctors too frightened to deviate from the most conservative course. In fact, obstetricians generally pay exceptionally high insurance premiums since any errors that they make might involve support payments over the entire life span of the victim. It has been justifiably claimed that these considerations have greatly increased the number of Caesarian births. Another cause for the increased number of surgical births emerges from the discomfort some obstetricians have in performing their work in front of the husband and/or other family members and friends. It is easy to understand why physicians, who are used to working with the discipline of the medical team, might not be as comfortable in a different atmosphere. They might be more attuned to those factors which indicate the need for surgery. Feminist leaders have aptly called this phenomenon as passive aggressive (non)compliance.

In some ways, sections are easier for the obstetrician. The procedure is sometimes scheduled in advance and thus comes on doctor's time rather than nature's time. But even in an emergency, many of the problems and complications of vaginal births (especially if labor is protracted, the baby needs to be turned, or forceps are used) are eliminated. Thus, the procedure is easier for the physician (and possibly for both parents).

If herpes simplex (a disease that has reached epidemic proportions in America today) or similar viruses are present during the infant's progress down the birth canal, severe damage (i.e., encephalitis) is possible. Thus, if there is any possibility of an active case of herpes, sound medical practice demands a choice of the safer surgical delivery.

Also, with advances in safer surgical technology, recently graduated ob-gyns simply have less training and practice with forceps deliveries and with delivering or turning breech babies. No doubt new ob-gyns choose the procedures with which they have greater training: a new style is popularized; an older art is lost.

Finally, several members of OB teams indicated their cynical suspicions that the increases in numbers of Caesarian births are somewhat a function of the fact that there is often more money in surgery than in vaginal childbirth. While the vast majority of obstetricians are exemplary in terms of professional ethics, a small number might choose the more expensive procedure because of greed and/or pressure from increasingly profit-oriented hospital administrations.

Implications for the Expectant Father

According to a recent Gallup Poll, four out of five men today expect to be present at the birth of their children. Since between 20 and 40 percent of these births will be surgical, it is important that men have adequate preparation for this possibility.

Interviews of men who have experienced a surgical birth suggest that preparations in three general categories might be of particular value to new expectant fathers: *information*, *support*, and *courage*.

Information. Prior to the birth of their own children, few men have any contact with or knowledge about Caesarian births. What they do know is often shrouded in myths, fears, and misinformation. Prenatal classes and OB team members could help allay such fears and misinformation by careful attention to education regarding nonvaginal births, especially since the incidence of surgical births has grown.

By the time the labor is protracted and the obstetrician decides to do a section, it is too late for you to ask for information. The question of a section must be discussed during the pregnancy with your spouse and the childbirth experts and not during the crisis. Your role in the event of a section must also be carefully planned. It is not sufficient for involved expectant fathers to be passive and wait for this information. You have to go out and ask the childbirth educators and the physician (or midwife) for the input you require.

If you want more information on Caesarian births, there are several excellent resources recommended in the bibliography and online.

Support. Many expectant fathers need an opportunity to discuss their concerns with someone who has recently experienced a section birth. It is also important that the husband discuss the surgical birth option with his wife prior to any need for a decision. The father who feels more a part of the decision will feel more connected to the birth. This is not to suggest that he have veto power over any decision, only that he be included.

Many hospitals and obstetricians today restrict the access of third parties to the operating room. Others put extreme pressure on fathers to be present. *I believe expectant fathers have the right to make that decision* and need to receive some emotional support for their choice. It is absolutely right for some fathers to be present at the surgical births of their children and equally right for others to be absent. This decision is best made by the couple prior to the birth, with the father having 50 percent of the decision power and 50 percent of the support.

It must also be acknowledged that many men do change their minds at the last minute. Twelve fathers in the original survey and three in the 2013 survey indicated that despite a prior decision to be absent in the case of a Caesarian birth, they actually remained with their wives during the operation. Three fathers made the opposite decision, and two expectant fathers were denied access to the operating room by hospital staff after planning to be present. Modern family-friendly hospitals in 2014 usually allow one person in the operating room, most often the partner, but some require signing special waivers or taking a class in advance.

Some fathers-to-be arrange to have a friend present after the birth during the new mother's recovery time. Shortly after the birth, the infant will be moved to the nursery and the mother to the recovery room. This is a time when some men want to be busy (i.e., make all the phone calls), others want to be alone and reflect, and many want to have someone to talk to about the recent birth. Don't neglect this type of planning for your own well-being.

Courage. It is not easy to stand up to an expert and state your own needs clearly, especially when that expert is a physician or hospital administrator who is engaged in caring for your wife and child. Yet if the expectant father does not ask the questions that are important to him and insist on answers and options, the birth of his child may not go the way he and his partner want it to. For example, except in rare emergency circumstances, it need not be the hospital's decision whether a general or regional anesthesia will be used. This decision can be made prior to labor by the pregnant parents and discussed in advance with the obstetrics staff. The parents can also decide on such issues as rooming-in, being together in the recovery room, the type of feeding (scheduled or demand) that the infant receives in the hospital, whether pain control medications (which can affect nursing) will be administered, and of course, the extent of husband participation in a Caesarian birth.

It is the right and duty of the expectant father to question, cajole, negotiate, and even struggle with the hospital to procure the best possible birth for his wife and child. Instructive on this point were the responses to our survey question "Do you have any regrets about the whole pregnancy process?" Sixty-six of the 227 men in the original survey and twelve of forty-nine in the 2013 survey reported that they wished that they had been more courageous in dealing with the hospital. Alan, a thirty-year-old first-time father, who was excluded from the Caesarian birth, put it this way:

> *I guess the biggest regret is that I let the hospital push me around. Every time I asked for something that Diana and I wanted, they told me "no" because of hospital policy. I know now that I never should have missed the birth and never will let anyone keep me out again. I just didn't feel like I could fight them. Diana and I were so*

scared about her and the baby's safety that neither of us demanded our rights. I'm sure now that I was wrong. Diana was in no shape to fight. I'm embarrassed that I didn't either.

In a sense, unless you have arranged for a doula, the expectant father is the only person who can ensure that the couple's desires are fulfilled as completely as practicable. He will often have to be very courageous to fight the system at the time of greatest concern for his family. It will be helpful to him if he decides in advance on which issues he is willing to compromise and which are most important for him and his spouse. After all, a child is only born once. Anything that is lost from that moment is not recapturable.

A Personal Note

My daughter was born through a scheduled C-section procedure. She was in a "footling breech presentation," and medical advice was clear: there was a higher probability of danger to her oxygen supply and hence increased danger of brain damage in a vaginal birth. The obstetrician (who told us that she was a breech delivery) strongly recommended a C-section, and my wife and I felt that any potential for additional danger for our baby was too much. Thus, the hours of planning, preparing, and practicing breathing were for naught, and the new fears and problems of a surgical delivery had to be confronted. This choice was not without a great deal of anxiety for Susan and me. One thing was clear to us both: I was to be present for the birth. The hospital was only marginally cooperative, but I was allowed to be present for the operation.

Five things stand out as a particular help to me in being able to endure the surgical birth. They are, in order of importance to us, as follows:

1. Because we knew in advance of the breech position, the surgery was scheduled two weeks prior to the birth. This allowed Susan (my wife) and me to talk about the C-section and all of our considerations and fears. Being able to share these fears and to support each other made the event itself less threatening. As we talked about it, we became even closer, something I had thought impossible.
2. I discussed my feelings with a male friend who had recently had the same experience. He was exceptionally supportive and able to understand my concerns about becoming queasy at the sight of blood and cutting of the person I hold most dear. I remember one thing he said after a particularly tough racquetball game as he recalled his reaction to his wife's C-section,

I thought I'd pass out or lose my cookies or something, but you know, when I was there, I was so tuned into (my wife) and what we were doing and my kid being born, I was just excited and never even came close to any disaster.

He made this statement in an athletic club locker room, and to our surprise, another man, who had overheard our conversation, volunteered information on his own recent experience and agreed. I can only speculate on the impact that unusual conversation might have had on other men within earshot.

3. I was able to view a film of three Caesarian births during our Lamaze class. This film was very discomforting to watch, but when the time for our daughter's birth came, that film had replayed in my head fifty times. I was far less fearful because I had a great deal of information and didn't believe anything would surprise me.

4. The nursing staff and administration of the hospital were constantly presenting barriers to my participation. I was so determined to fight them and be with my wife and baby through the operation that any fears I might have had were diminished in the battle. They were simply not going to keep the three of us apart on the most important day in our lives.

5. Perhaps most important of all was the joy of the moment. Being present at my daughter's entrance into the world and being a family together at the beginning of a new life easily overwhelmed any queasiness that I might have had.

I discovered one additional advantage to fathers at a section birth. I got to hold Tasha first!

A Final Controversy: Vaginal Birth after C-Section (VBAC)

One medical rule of thumb in obstetrics has shifted in both directions over time. One view is "Once a section, always a section." This notion held by many obstetricians means that for all practical purposes, once a woman has had a baby via Caesarian section, she must have all subsequent children surgically also. Mandated repeat Caesarians are, of course, one of the reasons for the high rate of surgical births mentioned earlier. In fact, the American College of Obstetrics and Gynecology (ACOG) estimated that in 1980, 25 to 30 percent of the C-sections performed were repeat sections. Today, ACOG holds the official position that VBACs are relatively safe, and many obstetricians now recommend at least a trial labor, especially if the mother is younger than thirty-five years of age, if the prior surgery was due to a breech or feet-down position of the fetus rather than for stalled labor, if labor and dilation occur naturally, and if there was a prior successful vaginal birth.

The VBAC controversy still exists, with many parents, midwives, and some obstetricians and maternal-child nurses arguing that the automatic repeat Caesarian is both unnecessary and excessive.

ACOG recommends certain safeguards be in place prior to a VBAC. The first is that that expectant parents need to know in advance of the first C-section and plan with their obstetrician prior to the first birth. Thus, for elective VBAC, it is essential that the initial section be a "low transverse segment uterine incision" to minimize future complications. Similarly, VBAC requires that there be no complications, continuous fetal monitoring, and an anesthesiologist and pediatrician available if a section becomes necessary.

The major bind here is that while statistics indicate that vaginal birth after a Caesarian birth is as safe and has the same probability as vaginal births in general, it may be difficult to find an obstetrician who is willing to do them. One of the reasons for advance planning for section births is to find the proper birthing expert.

For parents, discussions about such matters may be new, complex, and very trying. It is important for new mothers and fathers to be aware of all possibilities and fully understand their own preferences prior to any surgical birth. Since these births often take place without planning, it is essential that the parents-to-be discuss the matter prior to delivery and that expectant fathers have the opportunity to be a part of the decisions.

This is another example that was very personal. My son was born vaginally in 1988, six years after his older sister arrived via C-section: an uncomplicated VBAC.

Some Steps to Increasing Odds of a Vaginal Birth

If you and your partner truly want to have a "natural" vaginal birth if at all possible, there are some steps to take beforehand. Of course, if the health and safety of the woman or baby are in jeopardy, you should go with medical advice.

1. Be sure to take a childbirth education class.
2. Consider having a doula, a birth helper who is knowledgeable about births, present. She can often help keep the labor manageable and also mediate with the medical staff.

3. Ob-gyns are surgeons. They are trained and comfortable in surgical births. By contrast, qualified, licensed midwives are not surgeons. They are far less likely to call for C-section births.

4. Check out the C-section rates for potential obstetricians and hospitals. In my local area, one hospital has rates 50 percent lower than another. If your medical group is reticent to provide you with information, the website www.caesarianrates.com has a wealth of data.

5. Similarly, inquire about the policy on VBACs. A hospital that bans them routinely against ACOG recommendations might be a poor choice. Such a hospital will automatically have more surgical births.

6. Walking and moving around can keep labor progressing in ways that lying down doesn't. Find positions, such as on all fours, and move as much as possible. Hospitals that insist on fetal monitors restrict such movement.

7. Try to labor at home until it's time to go to a hospital. You likely want your partner to be in the safe hospital for the birth, but she may be better at home for much of the early labor.

8. Be in a birth environment that is most comfortable for you and especially for your pregnant partner. A baby delivered by a midwife at home has more comfort, but in case of an emergency, it is less convenient than a hospital. The newer hospital-attached birth wings may be a nice compromise.

9. Of course, if there is any reason to expect infant distress, closeness to a NICU is essential.

Chapter 12

The First Six Weeks

All couples were well prepared for labor and delivery;
few for parenting.
—Fein (1976)

The birth of your child launches a metamorphosis in your life. If you are like many new parents, you may only now begin to reflect on what has happened. Your reactions to the inevitable changes may well surprise you. Many men experienced new emotional realizations soon after they became a father.

Mark remembered driving home from the hospital after visiting his wife and infant,

All of a sudden, it struck me that they were really going to send this baby home with me.

Victor, a father of five days, recalled,

Last night, Jolie and I sat on the couch and looked at each other. Then we said almost in unison, "What do we do now?"

The First Few days

The ordeal is over. Your child is born, and your partner is resting comfortably and recovering from the birth. You are a parent (perhaps again). If your wife and baby are still at the hospital, your first few days will be spent preparing the home for the baby's arrival, doing necessary things to assure that your wife and child are recovering from the birth ordeal, and caring for yourself. There may be older children to care for, travel arrangements to make for a visiting mother—or sister-in-law, or a dozen other details to keep you running, not to mention your regular job.

Until your family returns home, responsibility for the care of your loved ones remains in the hands of the institution. They will decide what the baby is fed, when it is fed, who will be allowed to visit your wife and infant, and what kind of privileges the parents can have.

Some new parents welcome this interlude between the delivery and the need to be twenty-four—hour-a-day caretakers as a time to learn infant care and become adjusted to their new status. Others strongly resent the intrusiveness and control over their own lives. Mothers and their infants may be kept separate for significant portions of every day. Fathers may be allowed in only at certain times, and other visitors may be quite restricted. Often, grandparents and siblings of the new baby are kept out of direct contact.

Most often today, your partner and baby will be able to return home within a day of the birth unless there are complications or particular health needs for the baby or new mother. In the twenty-first century, most of the adjustment period has been moved from the hospital to the home. This is quite a shift. Just a generation or two ago, a five—to seven-day stay was common. If there is some extra time in the hospital, you might have some strong feelings about how you and your partner want the first days of your child's life to proceed. Some new dads may be frustrated and angered by hospital policies.

Marshall told me,

> *I just got fed up with the gestapo tactics and checked us out. I knew she wasn't fully recovered, but we wanted to breast-feed on demand and have lots of tactile contact with the baby, and they brought him out for fifteen minutes every three hours or so . . . And when the baby was in the room, I was shoved out.*

My own experience was similar. Despite being promised rooming-in and demand feeding, the nursing staff brought Tasha from the nursery to Susan for feeding exactly at twelve, three, six, and nine o'clock. When we complained about it, we were told that all the babies demanded food all the time "and you can't tell which one is crying in the nursery," a very insensitive thing to tell new parents. For this hospital, "demand feeding" referred to the convenience and demand of the nurses—not the infants. Susan had to keep her overflowing breasts in a towel while they were bottle-feeding our child contrary to our wishes.

Maternity wards do this to provide rest for the mother and care for the infant. While these procedures probably do accomplish their goal in physical terms, they can create significant emotional stress that could be worse for the parents and the baby. Most proponents of natural childbirth, nonhospital birth centers, and of breast-feeding insist on rooming-in and encourage parents to go home as soon as possible after the birth to avoid these conflicts.

Pediatricians can be of great help in shortcutting the system and helping you achieve the amount and type of contact you desire. If you have consulted with your baby's doctor during the pregnancy and agreed on postnatal care, he/she can write orders in the baby's chart that will conform to your wishes at least to the extent that your baby's health is not compromised.

Father's Work

The day after his first child was born, Rafael mused,

Well, now I've done everything I was prepared for. Now I have eighteen years of flying by the seat of my pants.

What is there for a father to do? First of all, you can begin by getting used to that word. *You are a father!* Your actions, your attitudes, your values, all will be passed on to another generation. You have new financial, emotional, and social responsibilities.

Most men want to clean up any outstanding obstacles during this early-postpartum period. If the nursery is incomplete, this is a time to get it done. There are baby things to buy, including a safety seat for your infant's first ride in a car.

Getting the baby from the birth center to home. The car seat, mandated by law, is essential to bring your new baby home. In the US, children up to seven years old must be properly restrained. It is wise to check the current safety standards in your state of residence. The standards for crash and fire are upgraded regularly. In California in 2012, car seats in the backseat are required for children under the age of eight or less than four feet nine inches in height. If you buy a new car and safety seat, it will be up to standards. Be careful with used car seats, they may be out of date. Also, it's wise to stay away from any car seat that has been in an accident.

There are three basic types of car seats: infant-only car seats with listed weight limits usually up to thirty-five pounds (that always should be rear-facing), infant-toddler car seats designed for a child of up to forty pounds rear-facing and up to seventy pounds forward-facing, and belt-positioning booster seats for children who are four or older and at least forty pounds. The

American Academy of Pediatrics (AAP) recommends that the child be in a rear-facing car seat until the age of two.[12]

Soak in and share the new experience. You want to be with your wife and baby and also need a chance to be alone and have some reflective moments. Like the iconic image of the African father who held his infant up to the sky in the TV adaptation of Alex Haley's *Roots*, you want to give yourself the opportunity to experience the depth of feeling and awe fatherhood brings.

There are also some (pleasant) duties to accomplish, like letting others know of the birth and making arrangements for assistance when your wife and child come home.

Telling family and friends. In a day with instant communication, you may prefer a short text, an e-mail, or a Twitter or other social network announcement to let most people know of the birth. That may be a good idea for a general initial announcement (to be followed by an official birth announcement later), especially if you want the information out and prefer not to talk with people directly. However, you may want to reserve more interactive comments for close family and friends. This is ideally done from the hospital once mother and child are resting and recuperating after the birth ordeal or in the evening when you are home alone. It is almost always a good idea to contact family prior to sending out a social media blast—your parents don't want to get the news from a neighbor or a social media site.

> *Hey, Dad, you're a grandpa.*

> *Hello, Mom, Dad, congratulations, you are grandparents. You have a granddaughter. Yeah, that's right, a little girl. Beth is fine. She's resting now. The baby came at 5:35 this morning, and everything is fine. Seven pounds! Yeah, I'm real happy, and I'm tired. You can see her tomorrow morning at the hospital, or we'll be home Wednesday. Love you, bye.*

Jason, guess what? You have a little sister. You will have prepared your older children months ahead for the arrival of a sibling. They certainly have been very aware of mom's growing belly over the past few months. Now that the big day has arrived, they will need to know how their mother is, that you

---

[12.] In addition to your state motor vehicle information, two good Web sites for car seat safety are the American Academy of Pediatrics' shopping guide to car seats (http://www.healthychildren.org/English/safety-prevention/on-the-go/Pages/Car-Safety-Seats-Information-for-Families.aspx) and the National Highway Traffic Safety Administration child passenger safety (http://www.safercar.gov/parents/index.htm).

love them still, that there will be a new brother/sister, when the baby will be home, where the baby will sleep, and when they can see and play with their brother or sister. If they were at the birth, there will be some explanations and lots of questions to answer. If possible, they should be taken to see the baby in the nursery.

Hey, Joe, have a cigar. Telling friends and associates is normally secondary to family, but quite important. Men need to celebrate the birth with their peers. I remember a friend bringing a bottle of vodka to the university when we were both graduate students. We drank together and felt a felt great closeness reveling in the thrill of his son's birth. Because several others also shared the experience, he had to be driven home to sleep off some of his celebration.

The reaction of coworkers and friends is very important as Darnell recalled,

> *You know Alison's birth really hit home. When I was telling Rick how proud I was and we both began to get moist eyes. No words were necessary. I knew he understood.*

Oftentimes, new fathers are disappointed that their friends do not get as excited as they are. They also become aware that the questions about the wife so common in pregnancy once again supersede any interest in themselves.

Some family members and "friends" can be especially callous in discussing the gender of your child. Many men found themselves shocked that their own parents or friends would offer condolences if they had a girl instead of a boy, for example. Assuming that the father shared their prejudices, they would then push to have the new dad admit he was dissatisfied with his new infant. Most new fathers felt distanced and disillusioned by such experiences.

I was lucky. Two of my close friends were particularly understanding to my feelings about the birth. After displaying excitement at my announcement of Tasha's arrival, they asked about Susan, then paused and asked with evident interest, "So how are you? What's it like to be a daddy?" What was particularly gratifying was that their enthusiasm did not flag during my lengthy rambling response.

Help for the Early Adjustment

Giving birth and caring for an infant takes a great deal out of anyone. The first few days at home will be exhausting and difficult. If your wife had a surgical birth, the recuperation period will be more painful and lengthy than for a vaginal birth. Often, new mothers are best served by having help with early childcare. Arrangements will have been made in advance for a relative, a friend, or a nurse to stay for the first few days. You will have to confirm plans, call and arrange to get the person to your home, and perhaps entertain them. It is important that your wife comes home to the kind of help she needs and the kind of household that will support her. Discuss with the helper exactly what help you desire. Most couples want help who will care for the home and mother's needs so the parents can care for the baby.

After the Birth: Getting Everybody Home Safely

Last-minute details at the hospital. Hospitals are designed for sick people. Before you can exit with your wife and baby, you have to be released from the doctor's care. You also have to attend to hospital fiscal procedures, sign forms, perhaps make payments, and keep your cool at delays in your departure.

One father who waited in lines for almost two hours at a large metropolitan hospital just to check his wife out declared,

> *Now I know what prisoners must experience after hearing of their release but still being held in captivity precious yards from freedom.*

When I tried to leave the hospital with my wife and baby, I was informed that my wife had to be in a wheelchair and that a nurse would carry the baby. For the expressed rationale of insurance coverage, we as parents were viewed as incapable of the task until our infant was outside the hospital sliding glass doors. I was prohibited for the second time in three days from being in the same elevator as my baby, and only the threat of a major scene allowed Susan (the mother) to share the elevator ride.

Meanwhile, I was dispatched to the hospital fiscal office where I attempted to pay the remaining $28 of the bill. While I was standing at the window, anxiously watching down the corridor for Susan and Tasha, two profoundly inept and passive aggressive clerks gossiped with each other and failed to locate my account file for almost twenty minutes. Once the business was completed, I received my "pass" and faced the absurd situation of presenting the slip from the hospital fiscal office in trade for my child.

No wonder men like Willy exclaimed,

> *I just didn't feel safe until we were out of there and into my own car. I couldn't believe that I was actually going to get my family to freedom while they were in that place.*

Jordan, a man who shared those concerns, actually went so far as to draft a comprehensive plan to smuggle his wife and child out of the hospital if there was any attempt to keep them. These men were not designing an escape from Alcatraz. They were just checking their wife and infant out of the birthplace. Perhaps it is the combination of a new father's runaway feelings of protectiveness and insensitive institutional policies that create an environment that mobilizes such dramatic responses in some men.

Not every new father reacts with distrust. Some men truly appreciate the respite between the birth and full responsibility for the infant. Randy described the birth of his son as

> *perfect. The doctor, nurses, everybody was so right on. I was so happy, and they were there when we needed them but allowed us a feeling of privacy. We were back home within twenty-four hours, and everyone was healthy.*

Hal was also grateful for the obstetrician when

> *Ann hemorrhaged after the birth and they had to take care of her. I never saw a team work so efficiently. I really felt like we were in good hands.*

I had a similar experience when my wife began hemorrhaging after the birth of our son. The obstetrician was prepared to cauterize. I asked if he could hold off for just a few minutes while we used hypnosis to stop the blood. Within two minutes, Susan was able to implement the suggestion to stop the bleeding. The doctor was full of praise and quite comfortable with the intervention on his turf.

Each couple has their own reaction to the early-postpartum care. If you are unhappy with some procedures, it is best to be prepared and to try and get the institution to respond to your desires. Discovering that I was writing a book for expectant fathers, one longtime father commented,

> *Be sure you tell them that if they don't like what is going on at the hospital, they can always just up and leave. The hospital has no legal right to keep you there unless it's truly dangerous for your wife and child to go.*

I know that I breathed a sigh of relief when I drove out of the hospital parking lot and headed home with my wife and newborn. Susan told me that I seemed tense until I was driving up the hill to our home.

The drive home is of interest. The day you take your infant home for the first time, you will feel more protective and drive more defensively than ever before.

What do you do once your family is home? A major period of adjustment begins.

Older Children

If this is your first child, the shift to a family life from a couple's life is massive, but there is no easy way to integrate newer children into an ongoing family either. As one childbirth educator put it,

> For the first baby, you know you don't know anything. When the second one comes, you're fooled by the illusion that you know what is going on.

Children who are home will have been quite involved and curious about the pregnancy or at least in the changes in their mommy. If they are two or older, they will probably have a great interest in babies. Older children will also have concerns about the impact the new sibling will have on them. The normal amount of attention paid to a new infant may cause other children to feel left out. Oftentimes, these children regress in their behaviors (i.e., bed-wetting) as a way of indicating their own neediness. You and your wife will have to reassure them that you still love them and that the new child will not supplant them. Let the new mom hand the new baby to dad and greet the older child(ren) on arriving home.

Another approach suggested by childbirth educator and marriage and family therapist Kate Wolf Pizor is to take older children to prepared sibling classes to help them with self-esteem and adjustment to their new status as a big brother or sister. A child-planned birthday party for the newest family member, replete with balloons, cake, and presents for all the children, can also speed adjustment.

Older children also respond well to being included in caring for the baby. When mom is nursing for example, they can bring her a glass of water.

Attending to a newborn and older children can leave both parents quite depleted and incapable of giving much to each other. Many fathers become closer to their older children as a way of meeting their own needs for affection and closeness to family at this time. Affectionate expression, which returns to normal after the postpartum period, can help smooth the early adjustment for everyone. If the husband-wife relationship does not regain its former primacy, however, problems could develop for all members of the family.

"That's What Mothers Are For!"

Your wife may require or desire extra assistance for the first few weeks after the baby is born. Remember that only a few decades ago, she would have remained in the hospital for two weeks, regaining her strength and having few responsibilities. For example, when Clint and Justine were offered two extra days in the hospital while waiting for the lactation specialist, they eagerly accepted. Clint commented,

> *Dylan was our second, and Justine was so wiped out with the first baby, I just figured it was a blessing to have us both pampered for two days. I was in the room with her, and the grandparents were with Lindsey. It was a good break before reality had to set in.*

Many women want to have a relative, frequently their own mother, do the helping, if possible. Having an experienced baby bearer and homemaker around to do some pampering, cooking, cleaning, and laundry can be quite a significant help. It is reassuring to have someone who is personally invested in the new child, such as the grandmother. She can also care for her older grandchildren during a period when the parents are quite busy and exhausted.

Having your mother-in-law at home is sometimes a mixed blessing. She will naturally reconnect with her daughter and begin a relationship with her grandchild, and you might again feel like you are being pushed out of the family or that you must compete with your mother-in-law for your wife's affection.

Keenan recalled,

> *Having Mary (mother-in-law) there was great for Eileen, and I guess for me too. She cooked and cleaned, ran loads of wash, and held the baby while Eileen slept. But she was did some weird stuff with me, like constantly taking the baby from me when I held him, telling Eileen that I was too rough with him, and hinting that I was in the way and should go to work and leave them alone in the house.*

Mark had an even stronger reaction:

> *Well, it's her mother see, so like I couldn't just get rid of her, but she was worse than the damn nurse at the hospital. I couldn't get near my wife or the kid without her buttin' in. Every time we started to talk, there she was dominatin' the whole discussion. Then she started to hint about stayin' longer. I thought I'd flip out. She told*

my wife that I should sleep in the spare bedroom so she could get some sleep. It was easy to remember why I never wanted to visit her.

Beverly, Mark's wife, concurred with him but added,

Mom is like he said and worse. I know she was bitchy to him, and I felt bad, but I also needed my mom at this time. Mark took it pretty well, considering that she tried to get him out of our bedroom. I knew when she said she'd stay longer, it was too much, but I wanted her to take care of me like when I was a baby, and she did. It was worth the trouble until I could get on my feet.

Jonathon recalled the days as a "honeymoon period":

Carolyn's parents were always the perfect in-laws. I always felt closer to them than I did to my own folks. Her mom was just perfect. She came, cooked us great meals, cleaned the house, put up with Carolyn's and the baby's constant demands with a smile, and generally took over. But she didn't get in the way either . . . just low key . . . My father-in-law is a trip too. He just played with his grandson and held him for hours . . . no diapering though. That, he claimed, was women's work. He's the older generation. The best thing was that they knew when to come and when to leave. I wish they could have stayed longer, but it was time for us to take over.

If you do envision difficulties with in-laws, it is important for you to be able to talk about your concerns with your wife. Perhaps you and she together can set it up so an intrusive mother-in-law cannot be divisive. It may be possible to turn the situation positive by being prepared to use the expected problems to your advantage. Bob and Sheila managed to work as a team in finding ways to support and express appreciation for each other, so much that the only way Sheila's mother could be involved was to join them in a loving and helpful way. Thus, she obtained no benefit from her normal hypercritical way of getting personal attention. Instead, she was rewarded for helping and giving them the opportunity to be alone and share their reactions to the baby.

Another technique favored by many men is to get their mothers-in-law reflecting on their own pregnancies, especially the birth of the daughter who has now become a mother herself. In that way, grandma becomes a respected expert and much more appreciative of her son-in-law

Whatever the early arrangements for care, the first few days and weeks of parenthood are exciting, anxiety provoking, and exhausting. The family must adjust, responsibilities must be reexamined, and constant rearrangements must be made. Most families take these weeks to focus inward. Personal differences diminish as the family establishes its new identity and system for functioning. As attention is turned inward toward the nuclear family, there is a corresponding lack of interest in matters outside the family system. In this way, the family can accommodate the new family members and begin to adjust to the changes. Later, the family must resume contact with the world at large and begin to define itself socially.

Your Baby Is Home: The Journey Continues

Your reactions to your infant will depend on many factors, including your readiness for parenthood, the nature and strength of your relationship with your partner, other concurrent life stresses, and the characteristics of the baby. Babies and parents come in all shapes, sizes, and types. Your normal infant is not the same as all other normal infants and is born with certain traits that will impact on the type of care you need to provide.

Infant temperament. At a recent baby and parent class, one woman sat comfortably with her nine-month-old child. The child sat contentedly beside his mom, quietly looking around, playing with a rattle, and generally looking alert and thoughtful. His mother talked about how easy he was and how she and her husband planned to have another baby soon. In the same class was a mother with a nine-month-old daughter. The daughter demanded the breast, lost interest when it was proffered, and climbed around and over the mother and the other mothers and children. At irregular intervals, she cried and made a shrieking sound that could potentially shatter teeth. The mother had to pay constant attention and was distracted from the group. She seemed harried and in need of relief.

Both of these babies were behaving "normally." They are just different.

Like adults, infants can be moody. They may adapt to new experiences either with interest and delight or with fear and demands. They can sleep through the night or waken every couple of hours. Some babies seem happy no matter what happens, and others seem impossible to please. Pediatricians and nurses say that about 10 percent of all babies are truly "difficult." They are poor sleepers, constant criers, impossible to please, and unable to be comforted. These babies are particularly perplexing for new parents, and the added stress often shows. Such babies are also more frequently at risk for abuse and neglect by parents who come to their wits' end and do not have sufficient social and psychological support.

New parents have to develop techniques for caring for these children and for themselves.

Activity levels. While all infants are unique, it is possible to group them according to their general level of activity. Even casual observers of babies in a nursery can see that some infants are far more active than others. *Active* children usually demand more parental attention than passive ones. There is no way to predict whether you will have an active, medium, or passive child. There is no reason to believe that one type is more intelligent or destined for a more difficult life. Parents who have active babies simply have more to do and need to be on call more.

Keep in mind that babies in different families will be born with different activity levels, but so will babies born to the same parents. If you have an "easy" first child, there is no assurance of a second "easy" one. Similarly, a very active first child is no guarantee of another. One father of four suggested that whatever you are prepared for will be the opposite of what you will receive. It has been commonly observed that when parents have a second child, they become firm believers in the nature side of the nature—nurture continuum.

Related to activity is the *natural sleep pattern* of your child. Almost all babies sleep quite a bit during the first few days after birth. After this period, infants show natural patterns of waking and sleep that may or may not coincide with society's notion that days are for waking and nights for sleep. Some babies naturally adapt to their parents' rhythm, and others do just the opposite. A nursing baby will be awake several times during the night. Feedings at 2:00 a.m. can be a special time for parents to be close with a new child. They can also be a painful reminder that you haven't had enough sleep to function properly. The exhaustion common to new parents is probably related to the interrupted sleep over an extended period. Nobody can prepare you in advance for the impact of interrupted sleep on both your mood and ability to think. Celeste, a new mom, described, "My pregnancy brain turned into postpartum brain with a fury!"

Colic. Some babies have stomach pain starting in the first few weeks of their lives. Colic is not a disease. It is digestive pain due to immature development of the colon. Babies with colic are in almost-constant discomfort and cry almost without stop during the first few months of their lives. Parents with a colicky child usually suffer substantial sleep deficits and tend to be irritable and disillusioned. The fantasy of the perfect family gives way quickly to a sense of servitude and unrelenting stress. Most colic mercifully disappears in the third or fourth month. While it is going on, it is quite difficult for the parents to have the time or energy for a life together. Preexisting marital problems can become worse. Many mental health and childcare professionals strongly encourage stressed parents to seek relief through childcare, trading-off duties, support groups, and finding time alone together as a couple.

Preemies. If your child was premature, you may well have to go home and leave the baby in the care of the hospital professionals. Adjustment to a child who can be visited but not brought home is particularly confusing and problematic. Assimilating such an infant into the family involves overcoming the physical reality of its absence and psychological reminders of an empty crib and nursery and the feelings of being "on hold."

Try to stay at the hospital with your infant as much as possible and support your wife to do so. If your wife wants eventually to nurse this baby, you can help her learn to express and store milk which the nurses can feed to your child.

Handicaps. If your infant is handicapped in some ways, you will have to deal with the extra physical help the baby needs and the emotional needs you might have. You may, for example, feel that you have to mourn the loss of your fantasy "perfect infant." You may have to begin to let go of dreams for the child. You may need to become prepared for multiple doctor and specialist visits and an almost-constant fear for the health and safety of your child.

It would probably be wise to get some professional help and support for yourselves, should you face this additional challenge as new parents.

The ever-changing infant. One thing that will be true no matter what your infant is like is that the demands that you have to accommodate will be ever changing. Comic strips such as *Marvin* and *Baby Blues* are designed completely around the unpredictability of a new child's behavior. Your flexibility and patience in adapting to your infant's changing behavior will serve you well at each subsequent stage of your child's development. A great deal of practice in the early years will be necessary to survive your offspring's adolescence later on. Each age brings new behaviors, new miracles, and new dilemmas for parents. For example, by the time your infant is six to twelve months old and is mobile, he/she will be able to get into everything. You'll have to adjust by a careful balance of constant attention and childproofing your home—"living three feet above the ground."

Exhaustion

One of the things that amaze almost all new parents is the pure physical exhaustion that follows the birth of a child. This exhaustion is undoubtedly caused by a multitude of factors, including interrupted sleep, physical tiredness from the birth experience, a delayed release of all the stored-up tension that preceded the birth, stress, and adjustment to the new family situation.

You can expect most of your pre-pregnancy energy levels to return sometimes in the first two years following the birth unless there are additional stressors or pregnancies during that time. The length and depth of the feeling of constant tiredness is something that cannot be fully appreciated until you personally experience it. Often, activities which seemed like a good idea at the time they were planned will have to be cancelled by the physical and emotional limitations that come with being a new parent.

Try to avoid accepting any other new commitments during this time.

Paternity Leave

In America today, it is customary for a man to be able to get off work for actual day of his child's birth. He may also get a second-day "sick leave" after the baby is born. However, extended paternity leaves for deeper bonding and substantial contact with newborns are rare. Many men try to arrange at least a few days to be home with the family, especially if there is no additional helper at home. Some find ways of taking vacation time or sick leaves to be with their new baby. For many, this is insufficient. Jeremy said,

> I was out only five days after Sammy was born when the boss started calling. She was adamant that I come back in because they "needed" me at the office. I regret that I folded and went to work. When I was home, I worried that I'd lose my job; and when I was there (office), I missed Sammy and Shonda.

Recent fathers who did arrange to be with the child the first few days and weeks and who were intimately involved in feeding, diapering, and holding the infant developed a much stronger early bond. I was able to take a full month off when both my children were born (Tasha came conveniently at the university's semester break, and Gabe arrived when I was on leave). Decades later, I still treasure those early times.

Because the first days at home with a newborn are likely to be hectic, you can also bond better as a family by being with your wife and child and starting to build a working alliance for subsequent child and house care.

Maternity Leave

When will your partner go back to work? Will it be days, weeks, months, or years, if ever? Who will do what and when? What are the financial implications of her being out of paid work? Compensated maternity leaves in this country normally extend only two to six weeks. More typically, the job is preserved for a certain length of time (up to six months) without pay.

What will determine how long your wife will stay home with your child? Will she follow the oft-cited example of Asian peasant women who work in the fields, have their babies, and return to the rice paddies in a matter of hours? This is hardly an approach consistent with the life and health concerns of modern-day women in industrialized countries. Asian peasant women would no doubt relinquish it if they were given any choice. What factors will influence the decision? Will it be finances? Career demands? Values about the importance of mothers being at home? The availability of good childcare?

It is important to discuss these questions prior to the birth, but expect a change of mind after the baby is home. Many career-oriented resolutions disappear when it means the loss of contact with one's baby.

Many couples will be forced to have short maternity leaves because of *financial pressure*. If a woman truly desires being with her baby but feels compelled to return to work after a few short weeks, she is liable to be sad, resentful, and ill at ease while she is on the job. Many couples prefer to struggle financially, do without anything but the basics, and get by marginally rather than have a mother separated from her infant. Of course some women do not have husbands who will support them or have partners who are unable to work because of disability or the job market. These women often have to work to support the family. In increasing, yet still small numbers, men become the primary caregivers for their infants. Kyle Pruitt's *Nurturing Father* provides an excellent account of such men.

Career pressures also can influence the timing of a woman's return to work. Cliff described the dilemma he and his wife faced when the pressures built for an early return to her work as an attorney,

> *Willa wanted to stay home, but she was also very into being a partner at the firm. Well, three weeks after Jimmy was born, she had the opportunity of a major corporate client and could bill close to half a million dollars in the next two years. If she turned it down, it could mean no partnership, or at least a loss in the competition with the males in her office. I was against it, but she went back and got the account. It meant giving up nursing, getting childcare, and a lot of ambivalence for her. She's still not sure she did the right thing. It was a hard choice. I went along because I know if she wants to stay with (the law firm), she had to be better than the men. I think they were testing her loyalty. The lawyers can be that sick. It's like they were saying she has to be more loyal to us than her baby.*

Cliff and Willa were not forced by finances to give up her being home with the baby. It was more of a professional decision. Willa was ambivalent.

She wanted to stay home with her child, but she did not want to give up her potential advancement. Many couples face these decisions today. Is it fair for a woman to have to lose ground in a competitive field or in her schooling to stay home with her infant? There is no simple answer to such a question. It depends on the values you and your wife hold. Some women expect to stay home and be full-time moms and homemakers for some period of time. Others expect to hire childcare or *au pair* help and wouldn't consider being home full-time. Most new mothers have both feelings and ride a seesaw of ambivalence and guilt for years.

Deciding that you want to get some *childcare* provides no guarantee that it will be readily available. In some areas, couples simply cannot find satisfactory care for their infants, or the costs can be prohibitive. Cal related,

> *When Lynn decided to go back to work, we looked for someone who would come in every day. The only one we liked was* (over) *$200 a week. That was more than Lynn's take-home pay.*

Many couples spend weeks interviewing for childcare and remain unsatisfied. Qualified people are few and far between, and stories of physical and sexual abuse of children make parents rightfully very cautious.

Some opt for a live-in person. That way, they can offer room and board in place of a high salary—obviously a trade-off in privacy. Those seeking such positions are usually young women who have not yet decided what they will do with their own lives and cannot or choose not to live at home. They usually stay only a short term, are relatively inexperienced in childcare, and are in the word of one father, "like having another kid in the house." Some parents choose an *au pair*, a girl from a foreign country who wants to spend a year or so in America as a way of experiencing a new culture and is willing to take a job that offers room and board and a small salary.

A small number of parents have had the experience of hiring someone who stayed with the family for many years almost as part of the family. Roger reported that Elena

> *came to live with us when she was just twenty and new to the US when Ty was born. She is still with us and the children, and he is in college now. She is very much one of us after more than twenty years.*

Other parents prefer to take their baby to childcare. One common setting is a home with a woman who cares for a small number of youngsters, often including her own. If the number of infants is small and the provider is competent and loving, this may be the least expensive and best care for your infant. Many states regulate both the qualifications of childcare providers and the number of infants and older children that can be present.

Childcare centers offer a possibility for parents, but fewer take infants. Most childcare centers are primarily set up for babies over six months of age.

Finally, there are people in our culture who live in communal or extended-family settings and have relatives or members of their own household community for childcare. A trusted relative is usually superior to a stranger. For one thing, the grandparents, aunt, godparents, or other relatives will have a personal relationship with the baby. In addition, they might well be available at odd times for spontaneous scheduling. Most couples who have such a person available do choose this option and feel good about it. Those who complained often reported some "mother-in-law intrusion" and a sense that this other person was critical about the way they were raising the baby.

As parents, you must be alert to difficulties with anyone who cares for your child. It is a sad fact of modern life that young children are abused and molested. Any signs of abuse or fear shown by your child toward a caretaker must be taken seriously. The Adams and Fay book *No More Secrets* gives excellent guidelines for selecting safe childcare.

Male Involvement in Maternity Leaves

You may have strong feelings about what your wife will do after the baby comes. Will she stay at home to care for your child, or will she be out at work supporting the family financially?

Keith was surprised by the rush of protectiveness he experienced when his daughter was born:

> *During the whole pregnancy, we agreed that Lani would go back to the bank when Maile was six weeks. But as the weeks passed, I had second thoughts. I knew that she would be fine with my mother, but all of a sudden, I felt strongly that a baby should be with her mother. I know that Lani was also having doubts, but each time we talked, it was . . . does the baby really need her mom all day vs. losing a good easy job. In the end, emotions won out. I know I seem hard line about it, but it was important to me that the mother stay home.*

Ryan had different feelings:

> *I know Myra wanted to stay home with Kali, but she would start to vegetate in no time. She's a smart woman and needs the competitiveness of the business world . . . She also expects me to*

listen to her for hours when I come home. She needs more adult contact, or it's a real problem for me.

It is important for you to become aware of just what values and beliefs you have about the mother-infant bond. Talk about these issues with your wife prior to the birth. You may have to reassess the decision after your child arrives. The most common misgiving new parents reported was going back to full-time work prematurely.

Many men are ego involved in the maternity leave decision. A number of fathers felt shame at being unable to be the sole financial provider for their families. Fern and Howard had such a conflict. Fern believed that she could be the supermom: maintain her career and nurse her baby during the day and be a mom and homemaker after working hours. Howard was proud that he earned a good-enough living to allow Fern to be home with their infant. In marital therapy, they examined their myths about "real men" and "real women" and learned to let go of the "shoulds" of "supermom" and "macho man" without losing self-esteem.

As a rule of thumb, if your partner's maternity leave is causing relationship problems, examine your personal motives and psychological needs. The issues are of importance to all expectant fathers, but the need to do it "your way" is *your* problem. Don't let it sabotage your relationship.

Chapter 13

A Couple Becomes a Family

Perhaps the greatest social service that can be rendered
by anybody to this country and to mankind is to
bring up a family
—George Bernard Shaw

The change in status from couple to family is one of the most difficult adjustments people can make. You move quite suddenly from an adult-oriented home to one of service and almost-constant distraction. The addition of a helpless, needy infant to a couple's life limits freedom of movement, changes role expectancies, places physical demands on parents, and restricts spontaneity. Formerly simple acts like going out for a movie and pizza on the spur of the moment turn into major productions. Many adjustments and accommodations must be made by new parents who are physically fatigued and emotionally depleted. It should come as no surprise that this is a fertile environment for new mothers and fathers to grow resentful and feel uniquely burdened and neglected. Often, both parents feel that they are making most or all of the concessions to the change in lifestyle. Sociologist Jesse Bernard describes these discrepancies in adjustment as "his" marriage and "her" marriage.

Men and women do experience the family genesis transition somewhat differently. Unfortunately, this particular transition has been neglected in theories of the family life cycle.

It should come as no surprise to expectant and recent fathers that most of the research to date has been with women. Because of this, our understanding of your wife's adjustment difficulties is more complete. There is a feminine bias in advice commonly given to new parents trying to cope. Expect and anticipate certain changes in your wife because she will have to make a greater adjustment.

Changes for the Mother

Since the late 1950s, researchers have reported that mothers experience significantly greater crises than fathers. Fathers, on the other hand, have often described their marriages as "better" following the birth of the first child. There are several reasons for these two findings:

- Mothers experience a more profound shift in identity.
- A woman's sources of stimulation and gratification often contract, becoming more limited to the baby and spouse.
- New mothers often report a decline in marital cohesiveness.
- Mom has to change more, be more attuned to the needs of an infant, and accept less fulfilment of her own needs, especially if she is nursing.
- By contrast, her working husband typically retains his vocational and social contacts.

The new mother's daily life pattern is dramatically changed. Her infant's frequent distraction prevents or delays completion of normal tasks. "The constant strain of being alert" adds stress to the estimated fifteen plus hours per day which household/infant activity may require. The repetitive, unstimulating, and unsatisfying tasks which new mothers abruptly encounter can create a redefinition of the physical environment, leading women to feel isolated, cramped, and inconvenienced. Several women in one study reported, "When you stay home all day, you feel different, duller." Another researcher reported that women often feel "welded" to the home. Added to this are constant fatigue and changes in her physical appearance which may result in frustration, loss of self-esteem, and an identity crisis. New mothers report that they feel less energetic and attractive than they were before they bore children.

The antidotes to such feelings are the joys and fulfillment of motherhood, right? Not always. "Natural mother's love" may not provide all the direction, training, and confidence required for coping with an infant's needs. A new mother may blame herself or her husband for the unhappiness she experiences and fail to appreciate the complex social factors which contribute to her frustration. The very belief that motherhood is "so natural" deters new mothers from acquiring some rudimentary training in childcare.

Baby blues. About 50 percent of all women suffer a low emotional period in the first few weeks after birth. Symptoms include a lack of energy, irritability, crying episodes, mental confusion, insomnia, headaches, inability to think clearly, and depression. Several theories are proffered as the cause. Many obstetricians believe that the birth process so powerfully upsets a woman's chemical balance that hormonal fluctuations create the despondency. Others believe that the reaction is similar to "battle fatigue," a delayed reaction to the physical and emotional stress of labor and delivery and a deficit of deep sleep.

Psychologists point to the feelings of loss of the pregnancy and the status that accompanied it. Many women feel "an emptiness" when they lose intimate internal connection with the fetus. Women also commonly report feeling defenseless and vulnerable, conditions which have both psychological and physiological roots. The reality of the baby and the attendant dramatic changes in life, responsibility, and protectiveness can also be factors in this depression. Frequently, women experience a sudden anxiety and a feeling of inadequacy about caring for the baby. Finally, some feel guilt about sexual matters as "what caused the baby" and the specifics of the birth.

For the most part, these problems are temporary and respond well to understanding and tender loving care. Rest and a balanced diet often help a great deal. In a small percentage of women, however, a serious depression can ensue and psychiatric care may be necessary. You need to be very careful about the kind of treatment your wife receives under these conditions. A few psychiatric facilities still use electroconvulsive shock as a treatment for this "postpartum depression." Such "treatment" can actually make some of the temporary problems more permanent. Careful diagnosis, psychotherapy, temporary use of antidepressant medication if needed, and your understanding and assistance with the baby are sufficient to resolve the difficulties in most cases.

Changes for the Father

It is not unusual for men to have similar feelings to a lesser degree. However, no serious research has addressed men's "baby blues." Despite an expanding literature on the quantity and quality of changes that women undergo, there is a typical dearth of corresponding information on the male. Precious few empirical studies of average expectant and recent fathers have appeared in professional literature. Most existing knowledge about fatherhood concerns men who are atypical in some respect, men for whom fatherhood precipitated mental illness or who were in prison or the military. There is also a psychiatric literature which highlights those rare fathers who exhibited extreme reactions such as psychosis, sexual acting out, and unusual couvade symptoms.

Even studies which have focused on the average father have emphasized the new father's stress only insofar as it affected his wife's or his child's well-being.

One reviewer commenting on the status of fathers in childbirth education concluded that fatherhood has never truly been seen as valuable. Another described the father's role in contemporary society as being vague, indefinite, and poorly informed. Studies that attend to fathers are often restricted to the impact of early father-infant relationship on child development and the effects of father absence on children. None of these relates directly to the needs of fathers. In a classic confirmation of this cultural trend, a 1975 investigation of birth in American culture examined 269 births but failed to include any fathers' reactions. To date, twenty-first century studies are similarly limited.

Some of this bias is due to the common belief that men's lives are less changed than those of their wives. Most men still commonly go to the same job, see the same colleagues and associates, and come home at the same time. While their time at home changes, the overall alteration in their lives is less than for their wives.

If modern-day fathers followed the similar paths of their predecessors, this assessment of their needs might be sufficient. However, firsthand accounts by new fathers who actively prepare for and participate in labor and delivery show that *fathers of today are indeed quite involved emotionally and physically in the early days of their children's lives.* Felipe described his typical day:

> I get up with the baby before work and bring her to Shelly for feeding, then I change her and play with her until I have to go to work. I call through the day to check in on them both. I really miss them when I'm at work. Then after my shift, I come home and take over the childcare while Shelly gets her shower and makes us dinner. I usually put the baby to sleep around seven, and then I change my clothes and take care of the dishes and maybe watch thirty minutes of TV before crashing. Then on the weekends, I try to take care of the baby as much as I can to give Shelly a break.

Being actively involved in pregnancy, labor, and birth affects the father's early bonding and closeness to his newborn as well as his feelings toward his wife. Fathers who were present at childbirth often have a very strong early emotional bond to their infants. Dr. Martin Greenberg uses the term "engrossment" to define a father like Felipe, who is involved with his thoughts and feelings for his wife and child even while he is on the job. You may not be overwhelmed by the constant demands of infant care and being on call, but you may be absorbed by your relationship with your baby and be frustrated by the interference created by having to work away from home.

Involved fathers deeply feel the absence of their children and will not want to miss the baby's first words (especially "da da"), steps, or independent rollover. They may feel cheated out of these singular pleasures.

Lew described a particular conflict between monetary and emotional needs:

> *I know if I do a little overtime, Carol doesn't have to work outside the home and can take care of Barry, which is great. The problem is that if I go in at 7:00 a.m. and come home at 8:00 p.m., I only get to see him asleep or cranky. I never get to hold him and play with him. I don't know what is best. Do I take my kid's mother away or his father? And what do I do with my feelings?*

Several men described becoming closer to their babies as an antidote to the feelings of alienation. Changing diapers, feeding, and 3:00 a.m. strolls around the living room to quiet a crying baby can be times of intense closeness and intimacy. Men often complain about the disruption in their lives and at the same time love the moments.

Brad described one special pleasure:

> *You know what, the best thing was when I could come out and take the baby away from*

> *Sandi and be the one who quieted him. I take a great deal of satisfaction from that.*

In a strange way, men can be more affected by the emotional changes because they have few models or expectancies about how to act. There is little support for men who want to spend more time at home with their infants, little understanding from bosses and coworkers for men whose minds are more focused on their new babies than their committee meetings, and few places where they can reveal the pleasure of holding, smelling, and talking to their babies.

New fathers who actively get involved in caring for the basic needs of their infants commonly are the object of jokes. One man who was expertly changing his new daughter's diaper at a family gathering was chided by his uncle,

Well, there it is. The official record of the one diaper Lee will change.

Mr. Mom

All of the above is of course predicated on the typical cultural pattern of man as the financial provider and woman as the caretaker. If the roles are reversed, so are the typical reactions. If the man is the primary caregiver, he will feel the normal mothering dilemma, and his partner will experience the characteristic fatherly frustrations.

Most couples today try to split both career and home responsibilities. These nontraditional arrangements have some true benefits in terms of fairness, equality, and balance for both parents and child. Some developmental psychologists consider such arrangements as particularly helpful for young children's personality development. Unfortunately, such egalitarian arrangements frequently end up with both parents doing more than they can sustain, both inside and outside of the home. It is well known that most "half-time" jobs become full-time jobs with half the pay.

Couples Issues

When the baby arrives, the number of tasks that need to be performed multiply. As you might guess, there needs to be a certain amount of negotiation to determine who will do what jobs and how you will decide the allocation of new duties. Caring for your infant requires a great deal of mandatory service. This can cause conflicts for people who previously had enough time and altruism to divide household tasks without either feeling burdened. Unless you are careful, these conflicts can interfere with your spousal relationship in many areas, not just childcare.

If you have a modern egalitarian relationship rather than traditional sex roles, you are likely to experience greater difficulty. Several authors have noted that less time for shared activity, sex, and intimacy may transform a once-egalitarian marriage into a more traditional arrangement.

If you and your partner agree on the changes in roles and career adjustments, there are likely to be fewer problems. Gary described it this way:

> *Marty and I both wanted her to stay at home for the first few months. She was tired of work anyhow and was excited about being a full-time mother. I also think it's best for the baby and for me.*

She concurred,

> *I just wouldn't want it any other way. I can't imagine anyone else taking care of my baby. My career can wait. This is what is important.*

Jim and Talia had no such agreement. He expected her to put her career on hold and care for their infant son. Her reaction was equally clear:

Why should I be the one to lose ground? Is my career less important that his? I am sick of this patriarchal society telling me how I should feel as a mother. There is no reason why we can't use childcare or why he can't work half-time so I can continue my job. Who says it's the woman whose work is unimportant? The hell with that! If he wants the kid to have a parent at home all the time, let him be home.

Current research suggests that the amount of agreement between husband and wife on how they wanted to raise the children significantly affects marital satisfaction. The greater the disagreement, the higher the likelihood for dissatisfaction, particularly for the mother.

Generally, marital satisfaction is more related to the act of coming to an agreement than to the specific arrangements. Couples who agree about who does what and how they do it are far more comfortable about the arrangements even if the particular agreement seemed unfair objectively.

Generally, mothers report more dissatisfaction than dads. Career-oriented women were more likely to be discontent with their pregnancies and early mothering than more traditional women. The younger mother and those with lower family income were more likely to be comfortable staying at home with their infants.

Often, the more someone expects a choice, the more need there is for negotiation. It has been frequently noted that for many women, there are three choices: continue working, stay at home, or work part-time outside the home. For most men, there is no choice except to remain working. These differing expectations may play a part in the different level of dissatisfaction reported by men and women.

It would be well worth your time and effort to explore these values and beliefs with your partner prior to conception or early in the pregnancy long before the baby arrives.

Social Support

In times past, new parents leaned heavily on extended family for support during the early days after pregnancy. Families tended to be closer geographically, and there were traditionally several experienced caretakers and homemakers available. New mothers were able to apprentice themselves to their mothers, sisters, relatives, and neighbors as they learned the craft of child-rearing. Many contemporary nuclear couples do not have these resources available. They must singularly bear the burdens of the family genesis transition. They need to be sudden experts and provide support for each other, even while they are individually needy and emotionally depleted.

One reason it is so hard to seek help is the natural orientation that new families develop. As the couple becomes a family, primary concerns are bonding and attachment to the infant and each other. There is little initial interest in the outside world until the family constellation has crystallized. Many men reported that this shift in emphasis created some feelings of isolation and stressful restriction of adult activity. In addition, both partners were bothered by interrupted sleep, suggestions and intrusions from in-laws, increased financial burdens, additional work caused by the baby, and necessary changes of plans.

Sex

A couple's sex life is highly likely to be altered with the birth of a baby. Among the changes is a reduction of privacy. After all, a third person will be present for the next eighteen years or so!

Physical changes occur in the woman's appearance and her energy level, and there is soreness in her reproductive organs. This is especially true if there was any tearing or an episiotomy during the delivery.

Under normal circumstances, women begin to be physically ready for intercourse between three and six weeks following a vaginal birth. Complications can make that period much longer.

Emotions play an even greater role in affecting sexual arousal and responsiveness following the birth of your child.

For women. Many new mothers have a major hormonal unbalance for weeks following the birth. (Recall the discussion of "postpartum depression" earlier in this chapter.) Their emotions during this period are quite unstable. Even after they have healed physically, unpredictable emotional swings can leave them feeling particularly vulnerable during sexual contact. Many remember too well the pain of childbirth and associate sexual intercourse with that pain.

Other factors which inhibit sexual feelings include fear of another immediate pregnancy, breast-feeding, tiredness, fear of a loss of boundary and control, feelings of suffocation from too much physical contact, and tendency to focus more on her infant than on her husband.

Kenny related that when he started to fondle his wife's breasts, she startled them both by responding with anger, "Leave those alone, that's for the baby!" It took some time before they could joke about their feelings of surprise.

Some women feel that sexuality should only serve procreative goals. One mother of three told the interviewer that she thought that her husband was sexually disturbed because he had no change in his sexual drive before or after the birth of the children. She further suggested that once procreation was taken care of, it was unseemly of her to desire any additional sexuality unless she wanted more children.

For men. Childbirth can also dramatically affect a man's sexual impulses. Some men are particularly aroused by the enhanced closeness and love they feel for their wife and baby after having gone through the birth together. These men desire physical contact and sexual intercourse as soon as the wife's physical state allows. They feel rejected if there are additional delays in their intimate relating. Like most men, however, they are very aware of birth control. Prior to the conception and pregnancy, birth control is a concept believed in only theoretically. It is only after a pregnancy that couples become fully aware of how easy it is to get pregnant.

Male disinterest. Not all men show an interest in immediate sexual contact with their wives. Often, new fathers are worried about injuring their wives soon after the birth.

Some men who were present at the birth reported that they have some emotional difficulty being sexual with the part of their wives that produced their children.

I know this is terrible to say, but I was really disgusted by the birth of my daughter. I was so turned off by my wife after that.

Another man commented,

After seeing something so large coming out of her vagina, I didn't have the feeling of wanting to put anything in there. I just was turned off. I didn't mind at all that she wasn't interested in sex for a while.

When I was a guest on *The Oprah Winfrey Show*, one of the audience members said that he was progressively getting closer to feeling sexual, but he still was somewhat traumatized by the birth experience.

One man described a repetitive fear of castration brought about by seeing the plentiful supply of blood that accompanied the birth of his first son. Somehow, the location of the reproductive organs and the blood allowed him to project himself and his own sexual organs into the situation, and the blood could only indicate a significant loss.

Similar sentiments were expressed by other men who were affected by the previously discussed Madonna-whore complex: *mothers are not sex objects.*

Some women may make the same association. Many men reported that their wives seemed to be totally uninterested in being sexual because that is not an appropriate thing for mothers to do. Once they became mothers themselves, they began to emulate their images of their own mothers into their behavior—pictures devoid of sexuality.

Delays in resuming normal (for the couple) sexual frequency are typical. If the disinterest persists beyond three months or so and there are no physical complications, it would be wise to seek help from a therapist.

The Role of Parenting Education and Preparedness

Particularly frustrating for many young parents is the fact that prior experience and proficiency in other arenas are of little value in being a competent parent. Childbirth educators and researchers commonly report that many parents were surprised by the amount of work required to care for a baby and their emotional responses to the demands of parenting.

Some childbirth educators have attempted to provide information about the postnatal period as part of prenatal instruction. Several recent studies indicate that couples who received such information adjusted more quickly to the conflicting demands of marriage, career, and parenting. They also reported less anxiety with the emotional changes and greater understanding of the stresses of early parenthood. Guidance on anticipated problems and specific suggestions about coping strategies were most useful for new parents.

Such education only blunts the impact of the shift from couple to family: new parents have to be on duty twenty-four hours a day, during which a great deal will occur for which they are less than totally prepared. New baby classes are often quite helpful in obtaining information and helpful hints and garnering emotional support. Usually, these are for mothers who bring their newborns to meetings. Men who are primary caregivers do not seem to partake of these opportunities. Whether they feel different, macho, or unwelcome, they do not avail themselves of the opportunity to share their concerns.

There is a great deal of information and support for new parents online. Of course, each new parent needs to be a cautious consumer, especially on the Internet where many opinions are presented as factual. Two Internet sites that I have found generally helpful are www.babycenter.com and www.parenting101.com, but you are best advised to follow the advice of your pediatrician and others in your support network.

Social support systems which do exist typically fail to provide new parents with sufficient opportunities for adaptation and/or relief from the multiple changes of the transition. Programs which have been developed to address some of those needs of new parents are seldom individualized enough to be useful except in the most basic ways. Mothers are the primary recipients of some social support, while fathers rarely receive acknowledgment for their newly evident needs. The social support available to men from their work settings come in the form of good wishes rather than in the form of flextime or other measures of institutional aid. Those few fathers who did receive more flexibility and control over their working hours reported better personal adjustment to the parenting role.

The two things that most surprise parents that cannot be effectively conveyed in classes or others' experiences are the impact of long-term interrupted sleep and the incredible amount of love you will likely feel for your new baby.

Men's Emotional Reactions to Fatherhood

Margaret Mead is widely quoted as saying,

There's a taboo against men handling or touching their newborns. For it is known somewhere that if they did, the new fathers would become so hooked that they would not get out and do their thing (for society) properly.

Emerging from the closeness and bonding at birth or soon thereafter is the surprising realization that infants have an amazing ability to make contact.

I wrote in my journal at 3:00 a.m. ten days after Tasha's birth,

The biggest surprise is how much she gives me. I thought there'd be no real giving contact until she was three or four.

I had an amazing reminder of this far more recently when my two-day-old granddaughter fell asleep on my chest while I was holding her. The feeling was of absolute bliss.

Michael put it poignantly,

It's like falling in love like I never did before.

Charlie commented,

When I held Jennifer in my hands at the instant after her birth, I felt an immediate attraction. We were linked forever.

Breast-feeding

Actually, I had never even thought about breast vs. bottle myself. When Tammy said she was going to nurse, I thought "far out." I never really figured I could or should have much input into the decision. It's her body, and I think it's something very special to women. I know I'd want to try it if I was a woman.

What feelings do men have about their wives nursing their babies? It's quite a range. Some men felt proud; others embarrassed if their wives were nursing in a public place. Some resented being left out of the feeding process, while others truly appreciated their own inability and nonresponsibility to take care of a hungry baby at midnight.

Several men favored breast-feeding because of the health advantages to their infants. They strongly encouraged their wives to try to breast-feed.

The initial decision to breast-feed was not the only important determination. How long a woman nurses may be consequential also. It is not unusual for a woman to nurse for a year or even two until the baby weans itself or she makes a decision to stop. Some men were like Larry:

> *I was all for the nursing in the beginning, but now it's going on six months, and I get uncomfortable with her breast being out in public with a bigger kid. He's always pulling at her clothes too. Maybe I'm just jealous. Her nipples are so sensitive, and she thinks of her breasts as the baby's food, not something I should be messin' with . . . But then I feel guilty about depriving my kid and think I'm being selfish.*

Like Larry, many men who were bothered by extended nursing had concerns about the sexual relationship with their wives. Some men are turned off by large full breasts that frequently leak or squirt during intercourse; others find the same experience exciting and erotic.

Curtis added one additional consideration:

> *I kind of like the feeling of the baby being fed by Penny's body. There is one thing though. He wants to suck my nipples too. It's okay, but I feel embarrassed, and I worry if I let him, will he turn out wrong, or will he get frustrated by getting nothing and turn away from me or both of us?*

It seems important for a new father to personally explore his own feelings about nursing and talk to his wife without trying to dictate her decision. This is especially important because nursing mothers are often ambivalent themselves. Remember that a temporary decision to stop nursing is irreversible. The milk will dry up.

When Nursing Is Problematic

It would seem that nursing a baby would be the most natural thing in the world. For many new mothers, the letdown reflex kicks in soon after birth; and within a short time, the milk is flowing. We know that nursing helps prevent diseases and provides intense bonding and attachment between mother and infant. Some estimates are that three out of five women now nurse their infants—a number almost triple the estimate of forty years ago.

Yet sometimes, it just doesn't work well or at all. Many women report a number of problems: insufficient amounts of milk, breasts that do not sufficiently fill, inverted or flat nipples, sore or cracked nipples making nursing painful, babies who seem uninterested in or refuse the breast, babies that cannot latch on successfully, mastitis (infection), and breasts leaking through their nursing bras and clothing.

Lactation specialists, present at almost all birth centers, have helpful solutions for most of these problems; and usually, with their help, the nursing can become more comfortable and effective. Ordinarily, if a new mom plans to nurse, there is a scheduled meeting with a lactation specialist prior to leaving the birthing facility for the first time.

If you are like most men, lactation is alien territory, and your best efforts can be in supporting and encouraging your partner. There are, however, two areas where more active help may be advised. Some women feel very much like failures if they cannot nurse or it takes a great deal of intervention and work to get what "should be natural" going at all. If your partner is suffering such problems with self-esteem, your support, even if apparently rebuffed initially, will be quite valuable. This is not a time to problem-solve. That is for her and the lactation expert. The most important thing you can do is to be empathic with her and express love and support.

Secondly, some lactation specialists and groups may be quite militant, trying to pressure your wife into nursing regardless of her own difficulty. In such an instance, your role as protector is useful. If the troubles are not readily resolved, you may need to help her stand up to unreasonable ordeals or feelings of guilt. Although nursing is a best choice for many, it is not the only choice. If it is more problematic and deeply impacts your partner's self-perception, you may need to help her stand up to someone else's pressure and standards of "what is correct" for your family.

Permanence and Commitment

Many men talked in great depth about the change in their commitment to their spouse once the baby arrived. John's reaction was typical:

> When Junior came along, I felt something quite different for me . . .
> something enduring . . . permanent . . . deeper in ways I hadn't

allowed myself to feel before. My love for Judith expanded. I knew
when he was born . . . I mean really knew . . . this was for life.

It is true that the fathering of a child is a lifelong emotional commitment. You cannot divorce a child. Men who leave a child often report a hole in their heart that never quite departs. Sharing biology with another person and creating a living being provides a living testament to your connection. Establishment of such an emotional commitment is not always easy to handle. For some men, the enforced sense of permanence generates a crisis. Men who are particularly fearful of entrapment or suffocation can develop a desire to flee from the situation. Some actually do run away.

An expectant father who feels the loss of freedom when his child is born has to face unresolved conflicts from his past and probably needs to deal with feelings about his own parents. Psychotherapy is a real help when men are ready to do this type of introspection.

That's How Daddies Are

Despite nine months of lead time (and possibly years of planning), men cease being expectant fathers and become actual fathers rather suddenly and find themselves faced with many important life adjustments.

The couple relationship changes inexorably. Fathers' fears and concerns that were emerging during the pregnancy seem to expand. Once again, men report a heightened sense of their own and their family members' mortality. A second, closely related concern is a need expressed by many new fathers to reexamine their relationship to spiritual matters. Family finances and work habits take on a new salience. Finally, there is a renewed sense of connectedness to other men, especially one's own father.

There are multiple roles for today's fathers. It is no longer sufficient to be solely a financial provider. We expect that we will also be great parents, marvelous lovers, part-time homemakers, and someday experts on school homework we couldn't do when we were boys. The fact that nobody could fulfil all these roles successfully does little to diminish the pressure to be *superdad*. After all, you are probably married to someone striving with the same urgency to be *supermom*. Modern fathers frequently feel helpless and responsible at the same time. The existence of your son or daughter is clear evidence of your potency and powerlessness. As a parent, you can be expected to get little credit for achievements but notoriety for errors.

Yet with all this, it's still the best game in town. The love you share with your child is inestimable. As a modern-day father, you have a definite advantage over your own dad. You can be unabashedly absorbed and involved with your children and share a more complete (if far more complex) life with your family.

Adoption

If adjustment is sudden for men who have a nine-month preparation period, imagine how precipitous it is for adoptive fathers. These fathers must experience the entire phenomenon after the baby arrives. Furthermore, while they do avoid the fears for the safety of their wives in childbirth, they must face daily the fear that the baby could be taken away after they have become attached.

Sometimes adoptive fathers have to wait until the adoption is final before beginning to fully attach and face the reality of emotional parenthood. This period of being in limbo can be quite trying.

Fourteen Tips for New Fathers

The following advice was culled from a group of recent fathers.

1. Get to know your baby. Recognize how perfect he/she is. Cuddle and learn to care for your baby. You probably don't have much experience holding or even dreaming about infants. It's an opportunity for you to begin fresh and learn along with and from your baby.
2. Take some time alone with the infant. Change diapers and get the hang of it. Your child's screaming and apparent fragility can be a potential deterrent, but don't let it get the better of you. It's a dirty job, but you can do it. (I recommend disposable diapers!)
3. Find some time alone without the baby. You will need time to reflect on your changed life and new perspectives. It is important to give yourself that time. In some ways, it is as important to get to know yourself in this new phase of life as it is to get to know your infant.
4. Find some time alone with your wife without the baby. The couple is the core of the family. You need time to talk, plan, and replenish each other. Discuss the division of labor and role expectancies you have. Become involved and negotiate for the kind of childcare you prefer.
5. Hold your baby in a way that is comfortable for you. Men usually carry babies so that the baby looks out to the world that the father sees. Mothers tend to fold babies into themselves. It's perfectly fine to be somewhat playful with your infant. The "football" carry is actually comfortable for most men. Once the baby reaches toddler stage, you

will have to find different positions to carry him/her than your wife. You probably lack a natural baby seat (hip) that your spouse got as standard equipment. Many men opt for a backpack or front pack, which also allows their babies a different perspective on the world.

6. Find some way to be involved in the feeding of your baby. It's a special time. Even if your wife is nursing, arrange to give the baby some expressed milk from a bottle.

7. Do your best to respond to your baby. Infants cannot be spoiled. It is never a good idea to let them "cry it out." They cry because they are needy. The baby is not willfully trying to drive you crazy. If you find yourself at your wit's end, get some relief, but don't take it out on the child.

8. Be as safety conscious as possible. Kiddie car seats may be inconvenient and a challenge getting them properly tethered, but safety is a must. If you run into greater difficulties, your local fire station is often a good resource. Make your home and auto more secure. Wear seat belts and pay attention to your own as well as your family's health.

9. If you haven't already, get a washer and dryer for home and learn how to use them. You cannot imagine the number of washes per week a baby creates. If you have counted on your wife for fresh clean clothes, be sure you have at least a week to ten-day supply when the baby comes.

10. Lay in an extra supply of bottles, diapers, nursing pads, wet wipes, nipples, and pacifiers. You will need them. Keep frozen food available and locate some good take-out or delivery places.

11. If there are communication and/or sexual problems after the baby arrives, get some help with them. Early marital counseling can be an excellent preventative measure.

12. If you are distressed by the early-postpartum care at the birthing center, do what you can to procure the kind of consideration you desire for your family.

13. Make the kind of paternity leave arrangements that best suit you within the possibilities offered by your workplace.

14. Revel in being a father. There are few accomplishments in life that outrank being called "daddy."

Chapter 14

Advice for a Pregnant Woman

My husband is expecting.
What's a pregnant woman to do?

Throughout this book, I have been describing what it's like for men to be expecting a child. This is in no way meant to minimize the importance of a woman's needs during this time. There is no question that the woman is the one who is pregnant, who experiences the labor, who delivers the baby, and who has had the life growing in her body for nine months. Carl Whitaker, an eminent family therapist, suggested that the emotional umbilical cord between a mother and her child is never truly cut.

You are probably well aware of the host of material available to you on pregnancy, childbirth and motherhood. (I have included a list of resources for mothers in the bibliography of this book as well.) The unique aspect of this book is that it is about your male partner. If you bought this for him, and have read parts of it yourself, you have a great deal of information about what men typically go through.

Now that you know this, what can you do to help your husband with his concerns? How can this information help you and the baby?

This chapter is for you.

How much do you want your partner to be involved? Some women want total participation, some want to be the central attraction with their husbands by their sides for support, and others want the partner to play a very minimal role.

Two wives of men in the study volunteered opposing feelings about this.

Jenny, a twenty-nine-year-old, described her feelings about her prior marriage and pregnancy:

When I was pregnant with my first, I didn't want anything to do with him. I didn't want him in the room when she was born. I didn't want him in the classes. This was my baby, and I didn't want him to be the star again.

Kate's reaction was quite different:

As soon as I found out, I knew that I wanted Bill to be as pregnant as I was. I wanted him to feel the feelings, have the excitement. If I could, I would have had him have half the labor and delivery.

It is crucial that you make this determination about your pregnancy and then negotiate with your partner to try to achieve your mutual desires as much as possible within the limits of the relationship. If you want greater involvement from your husband, there are several things that you can do to make it easier for him to participate more fully.

As a general rule, the *most important thing you can do is to include him in the excitement and anticipation you feel about the pregnancy and about having a family.* This may include both positive and negative feelings.

If you are excited about your pregnancy and your baby, it will be harder for your husband to share in the excitement unless he knows that it is his pregnancy also. It is an interesting and telling point that women normally describe their children as *"my* son," *"my* daughter," or *"my* children." Men normally refer to the children as *"our* son" or *"our* daughter." If you invite your partner into the pregnancy, you must share it with him.

There are a number of specific things you can do to help your man get involved.

1. Help him get more familiar with your body and changing shape. Help him explore your physical self as a way of becoming close to you and the child. Touching your body will be valuable to him, to you, and to the baby. Remember, you are aware of the child partially because of the biological reality. In order for your husband to bond with the child before it is born, he must do it through you. Help him explore the changes in your abdomen, feel the baby's movement, and talk to the baby within you. Whether or not the baby can actually hear his father's voice is less important than the bonding that will occur for your husband and for the two of you.

2. If your husband has difficulty expressing how he feels, you can really help him by providing the labels for his feelings. Questions like the following can particularly help him figure out what his own needs and feelings are:

Are you worried about this pregnancy?

What do you think it will be like having a third (fourth, fifth, and so on) person around the house?
What are your concerns about the actual delivery?

I know I'll need help the first few weeks after the baby comes home. I really want my mother (sister) to come. How do you feel about that? Will you be able to take off a week or two when the baby arrives so we can be together?

Do you want to do that?

3. Keep the lines of communication open. Allow time for both of you to share your ideas and feelings. Try to talk about the things that are important, but be careful not to do it all on your own timeline. Because of social and physiological factors, men are generally much slower than women to fully appreciate the reality of the pregnancy. You can ask him whether the pregnancy feels real yet. Give him the encouragement and the space to gradually increase his awareness of the reality of the baby.

    One of the most important factors is the setting in which such important conversations take place. Talking about your child is not something that you want to do during a quick and harried phone call to him at work or the moment he gets home.

    Remember that it is always easier to share important emotions in a safe, comfortable setting and during a quiet time rather than a time of stress. Choose times that are comfortable and lengthy enough that he can ease into a discussion. Talking over a nice dinner at a restaurant or during a walk in the park or a leisurely drive is far superior to trying to get his attention while he is involved in something else like watching his favorite TV program, fixing the house or stereo wiring, paying the monthly bills, or during the ninth inning or fourth quarter *of the* game. Take your husband out to a nice meal or arrange a special evening at home alone. Talk about your own excitement and fears and then ask him how he feels about it. If he is comfortable and knows that you truly want to know what he's experiencing, it will be easier for him to express his concerns.

    It is important to note that most men talk and listen more comfortably with a shoulder-to-shoulder rather than a face-to-face conversation. It may be easier for you to engage him if these important discussions occur when you are side by side.

This book or other written materials or films might be an excellent lead-in to such a conversation.

She: *I read that "pregnant" men often have lots of extra concerns when their wives quit work and they have to support the new family. Have you been thinking about that?*

He: *You don't need to worry. I'll handle the finances.*

She: *I don't really worry. I know that we'll find a way, but I am concerned that you will feel too much of a burden, and I want you to know that I do want to help, even if we decide that I won't work for a while.*

He: *I don't want you to have to work. I want the baby to have his mother.*

She: *We agree on that. I just am interested in what kind of thoughts you've been having. The book said that sometimes men think about doing overtime or getting another job.*

He: *I have had thoughts about how I could pick up some extra work.*

She: *You know I'd rather have less and have you home more if we can work it out.*

He: *I'd prefer that too . . . I read in a magazine that a girl costs $250,000, and that doesn't even include college or a wedding!*

She: *No wonder it's a concern for so many people. I think I know of one kid who better not cost that much!*

Although the financial problems are not resolved so easily, the couple does get to work on the problem together. She allows her husband to talk about his concerns *at his speed and in his way* and lets him know that *he* doesn't have to bear the financial burden alone.

4. Maintain a close sexual relationship, even though your body and comfort may dictate changing positions. For many men, sexuality is the pathway to intimacy, while often, for women, it is the result of intimate feelings. When your husband is feeling insecure, he may well need to be reassured by greater physical contact. Actually, many couples report that their sex lives are the absolute best during the second trimester. At any rate, pregnancy is a good time for lots of physical contact for both of you. If your husband shies away because

he feels that you, as a pregnant mother, are too fragile, he needs you to let him know what, how much, and where is pleasurable for you.

5. Invite couples with children and arrange for the men and kids to be alone (best during daytime when kids are not irritable). Let your husband be around other male diaper changers. Let him talk to other fathers and share with them. (This is my wife's idea. It sure worked for us!) The impact of the chaos will likely recede in the face of another guy's competence and comfort.

6. Initiate family contacts. Discuss your nuclear family relationship in a threesome (foursome). Try to anticipate and discuss adjustments to your lifestyle once the baby comes. If you assume none, rethink it. What new sleeping arrangements will have to be made? Which areas of your home will be reserved for adults and which for children? What will you have to do to maintain the primacy of your marital relationship? Many couples try to formally arrange a "date" night. Get a babysitter and go out together for a few hours. A date night is different from a "business" meeting. In the latter, you can talk about the kids and what has to be done. While on a date night, try to be as romantic and have as much fun as possible.

    Try to bring extended family into your lives to the extent you and your husband desire. Making contact with your family and your in-laws can help you deal with any unfinished business from your past. The advent of grandchildren sometimes opens clogged communication lines and fosters reconnections.

7. Indulge your husband and encourage him to pamper you. Pay attention to each other's creature comforts. As he nurtures you and experiences you nurturing him during the pregnancy, he'll become more familiar with caretaking and better prepared to care for an infant.

8. If you find this book before he does, give it to him and talk about the chapters together.

In addition to these general guidelines, you can also address some of the following apprehensions that seem to be shared by most expectant fathers: financial, physical, relationship, and performance.

Financial Concerns

What can a woman do to help her mate with the financial responsibility issues?

First and foremost, recognize that the concerns about finances are not simple balance-sheet matters. There are at least two equally important components: fiscal and emotional.

Fiscal ingredients. The first task is to track the money. Whoever is in charge of checkbook balancing, bill paying, and investments should present a summary of current income and expenses and go over it carefully with the spouse.

Where does the money go normally? What are the financial realities? To what extent does the birth and potential loss of income really affect lifestyle? What couple measures can be taken to adjust to the changes?

This is the easy part.

Emotional ingredients. Financial planning has as much to do with emotional planning and values as it does with money or numbers. With the beginnings or additions to the family, allocations of resources and budgeting may become important for the first time.

What kind of patterns do you each have? What is of value? There are huge differences between people in terms of how they spend money. The following values were common for fathers in the survey:

- Anything for the child is money well spent.
- Children need to understand that money doesn't grow on trees, and the earlier, the better.
- If it's for education, it's always worth it.
- The most important thing is that the child is happy and has a better life than I did.
- I was always embarrassed by my poor clothes as a kid. My son will not have to experience that.
- Save a certain percentage of what we have and teach the children to save.
- Live for now and spend while you have it. You never know what the future will bring.

If you and your husband agree on the way money should be spent and what it means emotionally to have a "nest egg" or to live within your means, there should be little problem. By contrast, if there's a disagreement, a lot of talk and negotiation is of great value.

How can you go about it?

Explore his concerns that are about money. Most men assume that their salaries will have to make the difference because they really don't believe that their partner will add significantly to the family financial status after the baby is born.

Above all, listen carefully to the concerns he mentions. Do not try and find a solution to the problem until you clearly understand the emotional components. A simple monetary solution may work for the short run, but if you haven't reached some basic agreement on gut-level issues, you may be in trouble before long.

Paul and Reggie made enough money to keep the bill payers far away. In fact, Paul's salary at a Silicon Valley engineering firm surpassed all of their budget needs. From a purely monetary viewpoint, adding a child should not have been anything more than a minor financial inconvenience. Despite this, Paul was excessively concerned about the state of their finances. When Reggie mentioned staying out of work for six months after their child was born, it took several hours of listening (without trying to solve the problem) to realize that the reassurance Paul needed was not about money matters, but about being partners. The resolution came when she began pointing out all the things they would have to do together as a family. Instead of trying to take away responsibility, she found that by adding things they would have to do *together*, he calmed down.

Paul came from a family in which his father was nowhere to be seen or heard. He was a "shadowy figure" who served as a disciplinarian and always seemed to be working alone on a project in the garage. For Paul, even a fight about money was helpful because it indicated that they were in this together.

John's concern about finances began the day Sara left her job during the fifth month of the pregnancy. They had agreed that she would take it easy and make all the arrangements to get the new house together before the baby came. However, the agreements were not helpful in reducing his concern and obsession with money matters. Sara felt unfairly blamed and struck back with logic and reminders that the agreement was as much his idea as hers. He responded to this with greater defensiveness, accusations that she didn't listen to what he said, and reminders that she had to rely on him financially. The escalations ceased when Sara began to realize, with the help of marital counseling, that the issue was not money or agreements. John was emotionally reacting to some other factor in his past.

When I asked John what it was like for him to make money, the following interaction occurred:

John: *I had to go to work when I was fourteen and have worked every day since then.*

JLS: *So what about now is different?*

John: *When she stopped working, it all kind of hit me that I could never stop.*

JLS: *That may be true, but something about having this child and supporting him or her is very crucial.*

John: *Her! We had the amniocentesis. It's a girl . . . It's just that I always swore that my kids would never have to go through what I went through as a kid.*

JLS: *So Sara's quitting her job is less crucial than how you feel about how you want your daughter to live and to help her live better than you did.*

When John nodded affirmatively, I asked him to share with his wife his desires for a better life for their daughter. Sara was much better equipped to deal with that issue than she was to try and make money and quit at the same time. His concern that he will "never" be able to stop work remains a future consideration.

Financial Security

One aspect of planning that couples often consider for the first time when their family is beginning is the value of life or disability insurance. This is a difficult subject to broach for most people on both emotional and consumer grounds. First-time buyers are confronted with a confusing array of products, salesmen who represent their own best interests (often their commissions are higher with certain products), and no-easy comparability between policies. If you are a couple who does need the extra security that is represented by some kind of insurance, it is best to shop around, gear the policies and premiums to your individual needs and resources, and ask for advice from trusted friends and family. *Consumer Reports* regularly publishes excellent comparative reviews of life insurance.

Most financial planners recommend that young couples get as much protection as possible at the lowest possible cost. That generally means buying *term* insurance.

Encourage your husband to explore the need for insurance without making it seem that you are trying to figure out how much you could profit from his death. The topic should be part of your financial discussions.

Wills, trusts, estates. Only about two-thirds of all Americans have wills, but it is of value for couples with children to consider how they want their children to be protected financially and who would be the caretaker in case of a mutual disaster. Drawing up a simple will need not generate expensive attorney fees. Internet sites, software programs, bookstores, and the public library provide basic do-it-yourself plans. Making out a will is an emotional experience and often frightening. It is also something the two of you can do together, and it will likely open up many important discussions.

Physical Concerns

The pregnancy within you. Like most men, your husband probably knows little more than the basic fundamentals of female anatomy and reproductive biology. It would be helpful for him to learn more in a way that he isn't made to feel embarrassed for his prior lack of knowledge. There are several books and websites on birth and development of the fetus which include pictures. A few that I have found particularly useful are listed in the bibliography.

As you become more intimately involved with your changing body and the child growing inside, you can serve as a guide to your husband. Having him gently touch your changing shape to feel kicks, movement, and changes can bring him into the pregnancy in a very personal way that will stimulate his bonding with the infant and your bonding as a family.

His physical changes. Women are not the only ones to change during pregnancy. Sympathetic pregnancy symptoms (couvade) are often experienced by many men. These are often the occasion for jokes about uterus jealousy and reproductive envy. It is particularly important for you to recognize that these symptoms—weight gain, nausea, emotional sensitivity, and even cravings—represent an unconscious attempt by husbands to be a greater part of the birth and to be closer to you. While the humorous side is present (and tempting), responding to his need to be closer and more a part of the pregnancy is of special importance. Cherishing his cravings is as important as his cherishing your own. I still remember my disappointment about being unable to find a restaurant in all of Honolulu that would not serve us cream of asparagus soup for lunch. The fact that it was my wife's craving and not my own made it no less important.

Health and safety: His. During pregnancy, men often become more aware and concerned about their own health and body. It is important for a woman to encourage him to have a physical exam and to keep fit. Often, it is his concern for her health that makes his own suddenly important, or perhaps the added responsibility makes him aware that he can't afford to be ill.

Sometimes a man's way of dealing with this is by trying to improve the entire physical environment through fixing up parts of the home as well as himself. You might be very understanding of his "nesting" if you have also had urges to clean out that cupboard or reorganize the kitchen drawers.

Health and safety: Yours. Once the reality of the pregnancy has set in, you can expect your husband to become protective of you and of the baby you are carrying. He may well overdo it and treat you as if you were an invalid. Enjoy any pampering that comes your way during this time, but also set limits on his overprotectiveness. Continue to be competent in areas that do not involve excess physical strain. Engage him in discussion of his fears that something might happen to you and/or the baby and share your similar concerns with him. Support him in having and expressing his concerns for your safety. Then support each other in recognizing that millions of healthy babies are born each year to exhausted but quite-healthy parents.

Daddy's trip to the gynecologist. Closely related to the physical issues are the reactions men have to the ob-gyn aspects of medicine. This is seriously no man's land. Offices and examining rooms are not set up for male clients or observers. Every part of the environment is alien, from the stirrups to the attitudes of the staff. A woman who wants her husband to participate actively with the birth may well need also to be his guide through this new jungle. Being prepared is more than half the battle, and nobody is better able to help men be prepared for the pelvic exam than his partner.

Relationship Concerns

When a couple becomes a family, their relationship changes. It can stretch, grow, flower, and expand; or it can narrow, wither, and deteriorate. Family genesis demands change. The changes begin with the decision to have a child and continue with the pregnancy and birth. Your husband will probably have worries about the changes that will take place. He may well be concerned that you will no longer consider him number 1. He may fear that your affection and sexual relationship will decline. When you turn inward during the pregnancy to communicate with your baby, he may feel left out.

The most important thing you can give him is reassurance that the relationship is important to you also. You might also confide in him any fears that you have of his being less interested in you as your pregnancy begins to show. Most of the 326 men in the surveys found their wives increasingly attractive (and sexy) as the pregnancy progressed at least until the final month or so.

Sex. It is an uncomfortable reality that sexual contact often serves different purposes for men and women. Recognizing that no generalization is ever universally true, it is commonly accepted in American culture that sexual contact is the path to intimacy for men, whereas for women, it is often the result of intimacy. If this is true of you and your husband, it is important to recognize his goal in approaching (or neglecting to approach) you in a sexual way while you are pregnant.

For men, one of the discomforts of pregnancy is their expectation of or actual loss of sexual contact with their partners. During the nine months of pregnancy, sexual desire and contact change. Sometimes for a woman, hormonal and physical alterations make any kind of sexuality unthinkable and undesirable. At other times, just the reverse is true. Similarly, a man's sexual feelings often change as his partner progresses through pregnancy. Each couple must work out a comfortable level and type of sexual contact during the pregnancy. The woman can best involve the man by being open about her desires and feelings. If she is desirous of more touching, she needs to say so. If certain types of contact make the morning sickness worse or better, it is important to share the information with her husband. Although I have never met your partner, I am confident stating that he is a terrible mind reader.

For a man who is bursting with love for his enlarging wife and thrilled with the excitement of the impending infant, sexuality may be his only way to express these feelings. This doesn't mean that a woman should sacrifice her own needs. Indeed, it is a time for her to be particularly verbal about what she might want. This is especially true in the later stages of pregnancy where usual positions for sexual intercourse might be less favored, and new ways of gratification may be found.

Do mothers have sex? Aligned with these considerations are his concerns, fantasies, and expectations about what sex will be like during the pregnancy and after the child is born. Once a woman is a mother, does she change in his eyes as a sexual object? The couple needs to talk about both of their concerns about the changes that will occur after the baby is home, especially a first child.

Fears of being replaced. It is very important for women to assure their husbands that the baby will not replace them in their affections. It is sometimes easy for mothers (or fathers) to lavish attention on their infant and to expect that their spouse will know that they are still loved in a different yet powerful way. Sexual intimacy is one means of assurance. Others include affection, attention, comradeship, and verbalization.

Your husband will be going through as many psychological changes as you will during these precious nine months. It is important to share with him your feelings and listen carefully for his. You should pay attention to what he is doing and express true interest in his way of preparing for the child. It will be quite valuable for him to know that the two of you are in this together . . . and for the long haul.

If he is feeling trapped by the pregnancy, help him explore some ways that he can have more freedom *within* the relationship. If he is feeling rejected or abandoned, help him by finding ways of including him in your world and joining him in his.

Performance Concerns

Any new endeavor brings with it a certain amount of performance anxiety. When the life and safety of those you hold most dear are in any perceived danger, this anxiety can become very intense.

Your husband may very much want to be the coach and assistant at the birth of your child, and he may also be very frightened by the prospect of being there. Almost every man in our survey who had not previously been present at a birth was at least somewhat concerned about feeling queasy or faint at the delivery. It may be hard for you to have much empathy for him when you will be experiencing all the pain and stress of labor and delivery, but you may want to consider the strain he will face and help him plan for it.

Many of the men surveyed expressed the particular pain of helplessness in the face of pain to a loved one.

Mark, a thirty-six-year-old first-time father, said,

> *The labor lasted almost twenty-two hours, and Sylvia was in such pain. I tried everything. The breathing. Joking. Yelling. I would do anything to take that pain away from her. I even prayed that I could have it instead of her. That would have been easier than helplessness . . . I was wounded in Nam, and it hurt a lot, but it was nothing like the pain I felt in my heart for her. I'd have gladly taken that (shrapnel) again to get her out of the labor. It was such a relief when Jason finally came.*

The helplessness he felt was a terrible burden, and perhaps it was his subconscious way of sharing in the pain of labor.

The best preparation for most men is to observe films of births, attend an actual birth, and talk over their concerns and fears that they won't perform well under pressure.

A few husbands did not know until the last moment that they would actually go through with it. A choice you don't have! But at the critical time, most men found themselves there with their wives unless they were blocked by the hospital or the wife herself.

Joe confessed,

> *Well, I carefully planned my trip out of town to coincide with the due date. Business, you know. Then I had my Guard commitment during the classes . . . so missed two of those. I really had it set up to avoid the whole scene. Then the little sneak came three and a half weeks early, and as they were wheelin' my lady into that room, I figured, "Hey, I gotta be in there." Then when the nurse tried to block me, it was the last straw. Man, nobody was gonna keep me out . . . It was good. I wasn't gonna let her know how scared I was . . . It was real good seein' my son come out too. Glad he tricked me into being around . . . You know, it was funny. It wasn't until the whole scene was over that I remembered that my old man delivered me in the backseat of the station wagon. I didn't wait around either.*

Chapter 15

FAQs: Dear Jerry

Old people liked to give good advice, as solace for no longer being
able to provide bad examples.
—Francois, Duc de las Rochefoucald
Reflections (1665)

Having a child is a major life event which will change your life in significant ways. You may not experience many of the feelings that other men have described, but you will be influenced by being an expectant father. The timing of your own feelings about the pregnancy and fatherhood may depend on factors such as your sensitivity, your desire for the child, the nature of the relationship with your partner, how the decision to have the child was made, and a host of other personal considerations.

The most important message I can give you is pay attention to your own reactions and feelings. Once you are aware of these feelings, find someone with whom you can share them. Assume that your concerns are normal and talk to others who have similar feelings and thoughts.

Four major areas of concern are likely to be of concern: financial, physical, relationship, and performance.

Financial Concerns

Recognize the importance of your questions about finances, even if they appear illogical. Monetary concerns always contain both fiscal and emotional components. You will probably need to discuss these separately with your partner. If you fear that spending is exceeding the projected income, you need to make a plan that both of you will follow. A budget is hard work, but it gives security by providing a true picture of where the money goes.

Talk about your feelings about money, responsibility, spending, and saving. Explore the meaning money had in the family in which each of you grew up. How does this impact what you each want for your children? What are the implications of being certain that your children all go to college or make their own way or don't live the way you did?

If you disagree about spending, explain to your wife how important it is that she hears and understands your concerns. Try to avoid blaming or being blamed. Instead, try to clarify the values you both have regarding money and negotiate agreements you both can live with. If these agreements are hard to come by, get help from a marital counselor. Usually, the emotional side of the money problem causes the most difficulty.

Physical Concerns

Learn about female anatomy. Most men have little notion about the specific details in a birth and nobody expects you to be an expert in female reproductive anatomy. A list of good books and websites are found in the bibliography. Also, childbirth education classes are a must if you plan to participate. These classes come in all types, but nearly all do a good job of explaining the woman's experience, her expectations for your help, and the biology of the birth process. If you come from a community large enough to offer a choice, you may be able to find a class which also focuses on the relationship between husband and wife with some knowledge of the male perspective. Some communities have weekend retreats for expectant dads alone. My son-in-law and nephew both went to Daddy Boot Camp in the Denver area. In those workshops, expectant fathers meet recent dads and their infants. Most men find it quite reassuring.

Her body. Gently and carefully explore your wife's changing body with her. Think about the baby inside her, ask her about her feelings, and join with her in naming the child (joke names are normal during the months leading up to birth) and in communicating with the infant. You can expect that discussions about the real name chosen may be very emotional and sometimes conflictual.

Some fathers sing to their babies or talk to them. Dr. Kyle Pruitt writes in *The Nurturing Father* of a father who sang to the baby every night while he was in the womb, and when the infant was born and the father spoke to him, there was an almost-transfixed eye contact between them even moments after birth. Take pictures to record, remember, and preserve the stages of the pregnancy.

Discuss with your partner your concerns for her health and safety and that of the baby. While such a conversation might initially worry her a bit, they will resonate with her own and ultimately allow for a closer partnership.

Your body. Be aware of your own physical condition and concerns. Almost half of all expectant fathers in our survey had some kinds of symptoms psychologically related to the pregnancy. Common couvade symptoms include weight gain, nausea, greater emotionality, tearfulness at sentimental movies (especially if they involve young children), stomach and urinary tract problems, and forgetfulness. If you do have physical symptoms, be sure to tell any physician that examines you that your wife is pregnant.

Talk to your wife about your own concerns for your health and the added stress of your role as provider.

Relationship Concerns

Having a baby creates a new intimate triangle, and being intimate with more than one other person inevitably creates problems. In groups of three, there is almost always a pairing of two members, with the third person on the periphery.

During a pregnancy, a primary relationship develops between the mother and the baby, with the father as the outsider. If you are feeling left out, it is important that you let your partner know. Explain that you love her and the baby, but you need affection too, especially when she seems preoccupied for extended lengths of time.

Don't expect your needs to be met at the expense of the baby's, however. And keep in mind that you can get a great deal of emotional satisfaction by paying lots of attention to the baby yourself before and after birth.

If you feel jealous of the attention she gives the fetus, talk to her about it in a nonblaming way. Ask for something for yourself rather than request she give less to your child. Many men fear being replaced by their infant children. You may even remember having replaced your own father as your mother's primary object of affection.

Your partner may not be aware that you are feeling left out. If you openly share your concerns with her, she may be able to include you more, and she may well appreciate how desirable you find her. She certainly cannot remedy the situation until you let her know. Don't expect her to read your mind. If you fail to talk with her about your apprehensions, they are likely to grow into far greater marital discord. Don't hesitate to seek help from a marital counselor, a clergyperson, or close friends who are experienced parents.

Sex. Your sex life, of course, will change during and after the pregnancy. During the latter phases of the pregnancy, it is important that you approach your partner with the same level of effort and romance that went into courting her. For some men, the thought of the baby that you are making together serves as a strong aphrodisiac. Be sensitive to your partner, but if you feel ardent, express it.

If you find that the pregnancy serves only to turn you off sexually, you may want to talk to a professional. There are some psychological reasons for this that could be important to resolve for your later benefit and enjoyment.

There will be a one—to three-month (on average) hiatus for sexual intercourse near the birthdate. This does not mean an end to sexuality. Many couples find alternative means of expressing sexuality and affection during this time. After the birth of the infant, your wife will need time to heal, time to allay the unbelievable exhaustion most new mothers feel, and time for her hormones to reestablish their balance. You may also have an infant who knows how to cry for attention at any moment you and your wife get together.

After she comes home from the hospital, get her a sexy nightgown. She'll be reassured that you find her sexually attractive.

Performance Concerns

As a male in modern America, you have been taught that you will be evaluated on almost everything you do. It is difficult to go through an experience as complex and demanding as becoming a father without feeling like you are constantly being tested. If this is the first child, it is a very unfair test. There are no ground rules, no practice sessions, and no sense that if you blow it the first time, you just try harder the next. There are some ways to get help.

- Get all the information you need from books, online, and from childbirth educators and experienced fathers.
- Talk to your wife and try to go through the experience together as much as possible.
- Go to childbirth education classes and childcare classes. Choose those that will answer your questions.

Queasiness. Almost every man in the survey was concerned about getting queasy in the delivery room, perhaps even becoming faint or passing out. There are some things you can do to help prepare yourself. See the birth films that are available in classes or at public libraries and replay them in your mind. Plan a strategy for dealing with the situation if you find it hard to watch any particular aspect of the birth. It is always okay, for example, to look at your wife's face at critical times. It may also be reassuring that, although most of the men in the survey feared passing out, *none of them did*. There is just too much excitement going on to think about it at the actual time.

Will I be a good father? Among the questions men express are concerns about being good as fathers. Some of these questions include the following:

Will I be able to provide financially for my family?
Will I be the emotionally strong kind of father I hope to be?
What traits will I pass on? Do I feel ugly, dumb, or thoughtless?
What will my child inherit that will be my fault?

These are all good questions. How can you answer them positively? Can you anticipate any physical, intellectual, emotional, or psychological issues that will influence your fathering?

In my book *The Measure of a Man: Becoming the Father You Wish Your Father Had Been*, I reveal the important fact from many studies that the most important factor for both father and child is the *quantity of time together*. Your presence may be more important than any traits or specific behaviors. Similarly, in a study of empathy in young boys, Dr. Susan Bernadett-Shapiro (my wife) showed that the most significant factor increasing boys' empathy was time with dad.

Expectancy is a natural time for reflection. It is a time to confront yourself and to discover those qualities you might want to change. It is also a time to acknowledge those qualities in yourself that are admirable. If you need to work through some issues, this is the time. Psychotherapy can be helpful if you get stuck or wish to move through the issues faster or in greater depth. This is a good time to take stock and begin the alterations which will enhance your own life as well as those of your wife and child.

Questions and Answers (FAQs)

What do men and women want to know about expectant fatherhood?

In the course of the research upon which this book is built, many fathers indicated that their questions frequently pass unnoticed, unheard, and most often unspoken. As I was becoming a father to Tasha, I too found that I had many questions that I wanted to have answered—questions that I had not previously considered. The remainder of this chapter answers some of the most frequently asked questions over the past thirty-three years.

I don't know if I'm selfish or what, but like when I'm at work, everyone always asks me how my wife is. Nobody asks how I'm doing.

You are describing the experience of most of the men in the original and subsequent surveys. In prior generations, it was not expected that our fathers be involved at all in the pregnancy or birth of the children, except to provide food, shelter, and a safe life. Since the early 1970s, a major shift has taken place. Fathers like yourself are now expected to be involved and usually enjoy the experience and closeness to their wives and children. However, with increasing involvement in the process, men have discovered that they are not yet fully invited into this previous female sanctum. Our culture remains insufficiently prepared for fathers to be so involved as to have feelings of their own. I have found some amazing reactions from the men when I asked them how the pregnancy was going for *them* before asking about how their wives were faring.

> Bob: *You know, you're the first one to ask me that. I'll tell ya, it has been a roller-coaster ride for me. Sometimes I feel so proud I think my chest will burst through my shirt. Sometimes I get so scared of the responsibility and all, I feel like saying, "Hey, I changed my mind, let's have the baby in two years."*

> Will: *Me? How am I? Jeez, I'm not sure I know how I am these days. I just spent lunch with three guys who thought it was funny to joke about Barbara's ex being the father of the child. You know people are so* (insensitive) *about the whole thing. The other day some lady comes up in the supermarket and puts her hand on Barbara . . . didn't even ask or nothin'. I tell you. Mostly, I'm on guard ever since she told me six months ago.*

In this final example, notice how hard it was for the expectant father to switch to his own feelings. It was much easier for him to talk about his wife.

Sam: *Well, Sue is having a rough time with the morning sickness. She feels nauseous all the time, and she is worried about the baby being healthy. Someone told her that lots of morning sickness means that a miscarriage is less likely. So she's not so upset about that.*

JLS: *How has that been for you?*

Sam: *Well, I know she's real worried about this pregnancy.*

JLS: *And what have you been feeling yourself?*

Sam: *I don't know what it would do to her if she had another miscarriage. I'm worried for her. She really wants this baby . . . I guess I do too. I was so depressed when she lost the last one.*

The issue is not selfishness. You need to talk about your experience and have people interested in you during such a significant event. Find people you can talk with about your experience (recent fathers are a good bet) and of course talk with your wife about what you are feeling.

Why do I have to be present for the birth?

Many expectant fathers asked this question. The current mode in our culture is that fathers will be involved in the labor and delivery and, if possible, be present at the birth—over 80 percent are. There are several ways to answer this question.

In the first place, it needs to be made clear that there is no absolute rule that fathers have to be present. Indeed, your own father may not have been present for your birth, and your grandfather almost certainly wasn't present for your father's birth. Most expectant fathers do desire to be there but feel both anxious and pressured. The pressure comes from their wives, who understandably want them to be as much a part of the birth as possible, and from the birthing centers and general culture. The anxiety comes from a variety of factors including fear of fainting, being in the way, or otherwise messing up. One way to handle the fear is to avoid the situation altogether.

However, it is important that the couple make this decision together. If it is very important for the mother that the father be present, then his absence could cause resentment and long-term difficulties. Similarly, if it is important for the father (or mother) that he not be present, his insistence on being present could have similar harmful effects.

There is another consideration. Most of the men who were present at the births of their children found the experience most wonderful and meaningful. The opportunity to bond with the infant at the moment of birth can be most important for future relationship between father and child. Also, the moment of birth does tie each person inextricably into the life cycle, linking the generations. It also helps a couple to unite around the new family base—it is something that they are doing together, and it makes a deeper family feeling.

Finally, presence at the birth helps to reintegrate the father into the home environment. Here is an immediate antidote to the continuing cultural pressure that pushes men away from the family and home into work and the larger society.

One father in the survey put it this way:

At first, I was sure. There was no way they were going to get Pedro (himself) *into that room. I found my resolve strong until the childbirth class that Maria got me to attend. All these people were going to do it, and I was ashamed to tell them that I wasn't. Well, as the time came closer and I was more worried about Maria and more learning about the whole thing, I started to soften. Finally, when the moment came, I was so worried about the pain she was going through, I wanted to do anything to help; and then somehow, I was just in there with the gown and hat on, and I was helping my wife. I didn't even think about how it happened. God, it was beautiful. My Felicia came into the world into my hands. I was laughing, crying, and very glad that I was there. I'm glad I didn't miss it. I just wouldn't have ever known what it would be like.*

Where do I go with my concerns?

For many men, this is a prime question. As mentioned repeatedly throughout this text, there exists a paradox that keeps men from fully participating in the pregnancy and at the same time demands their participation. Many men get the clear message that they can bring support, help, and joy to the birth, but they cannot express their fears, concerns, and worries. Many of the men surveyed found no place to go with their personal concerns.

I believe it is important that men share their ambivalence about the pregnancy with their wives. For one thing, your wife is most likely sharing some of the ambivalence herself. Take the opportunity to tell her of your concerns about possibly losing her and the child or losing her to the child. Discuss the timing of the baby and the possibility that the timing is inconvenient in some ways.

Should your wife be unwilling to discuss these factors or should she not be able to provide enough support, find other resources. For example, other men who have been through the experience can be of great help. This is a subject that men frequently do not breech with each other. "It's hard to talk about feelings. It feels disloyal to the spouse. It shows weakness."

Your own father may also be an important source of information. In fact, most men who become expectant fathers begin to think a great deal about their own birth, childhood and especially their own fathers. Sometimes talks with one's own father can be helpful in both getting information and tying the three generations together.

Finally, professional help is of great value. Pastoral counseling, marital counseling, and couple therapy all provide valuable services. Indeed, in my own private practice of psychotherapy, a major focus of much couples therapy is how the couple deals with life transitions as they occur. Pregnancy is certainly one normal life event (crisis) that is transformational. Once it occurs, it changes the relationship forever. In such situations, couple therapy focusing on communication can be an exceptionally positive growth experience and can help the couple grow much closer together.

What's the story with all the childbirth classes? Are they really necessary?

Childbirth classes come in a host of styles, shades, and lengths. First and foremost, a distinction must be made between childbirth education classes and parenting education. The *parenting classes* are designed to help the new parents cope with the infant once it is back home. Segments on such practical issues as proper bathing of an infant, feeding practices, diapering, and the meaning of baby cries are all an integral part of these classes. Parents are given instructions on how to care for the infant and, one hopes, how to care for each other during the difficult, depleted first months of the baby's life. Oftentimes for men, this type of class is the first exposure they get to feeding and diapering infants, and the classes have the function of defusing the situation through knowledge and practice.

Childbirth education classes, on the other hand, are focused on the parents' role in pregnancy, labor, and delivery. The two most popular types of these classes are Lamaze and Bradley. Less common but also quite useful are Leboyer (low lighting, soft music, warm afterbirth baths, and infant massage) and Mongan (also known as hypnobirthing), which are increasing in popularity. These methods use the husband as coach for his wife who is giving birth. He helps to make her comfortable, assists her in regulating her breathing according to the method chosen, deals as much as possible with the hospital staff, helps her practice her birthing skills in class and at home prior to the birth, and accompanies her throughout the labor and delivery. He may also participate in the birthing process itself by "catching the baby," cutting the cord, and generally being part of the delivery team. Many modern dads, often using a smart phone, take pictures or videos of the birth for sharing.

These classes seem invaluable in a couple of ways. By taking the class together, the couple begins to develop the understanding that the pregnancy is "theirs" rather than "hers." The husband can begin to participate in the process more, and in so doing, he feels more connected to the birth and the baby. The classes also demystify the birthing process and let people know clearly what is coming and what all the events mean. This knowledge can be very settling for anxious parents. They also allow the couple to get a greater sense of the universality of their feelings by sharing the class with other expectant couples. Most classes consist of four to ten couples, each in the last trimester of pregnancy.

In lots of the pamphlets and materials they talk about the couple being pregnant, not just the wife. Does that mean that it's normal for him to have morning sickness or what?

There are two parts to that question. In the first place, it is not unusual for men to have some symptoms of a pregnancy along with their wives. This phenomenon called couvade is far more common than is usually believed. Men frequently put on weight during a pregnancy. They also suffer from some gastrointestinal tract discomfort with nausea early in the pregnancy and abdominal pains later. Whatever the explanation—whether men have a subconscious wish to be pregnant or to create life and need to be taken care of themselves or whether they have a subconscious wish to return to the womb—the symptoms all seem to indicate a deep desire on the part of the expectant father to be more involved in the pregnancy and birth process. This desire gets unconsciously transformed into physical symptoms.

But there is even more to the notion that both are pregnant. Even though carried in and delivered from the mother's body, the infant, and later the child, will belong to both parents. Both lives will be inexorably changed. The father who believes that the baby will be for his wife alone will be very surprised. The couple becomes a family, and in that change, there are a host of other significant alterations that must take place. Many sections of this book suggest ways in which the experience of fatherhood changes men intellectually, spiritually, and emotionally.

What about home births? I seem more interested than my wife.

A home birth is an alternative that is favored by some couples. They do it to keep a family (rather than hospital) environment and to have the child enter the world more "naturally." It is a decision that must be favored by both parents and the person delivering the child. This is usually a midwife. Few obstetricians work outside of hospitals or hospital-connected birthing centers. In emergencies, hospitals are far better equipped than homes. If your wife has any doubts about this, go along with her wishes. Homes, freestanding alternative birthing centers, and some small hospitals may have emergency services nearby but are less-well equipped for neonatal intensive care. NICUs are not frequently needed, but when newborns are in distress, the first thirty minutes may be crucial.

I'm very worried about my wife's safety during the birth. I keep having these thoughts that she'll be hurt or die, and I feel helpless. Is there anything I can do about that? Is there anything wrong with me?

It is quite normal to have these fears. Most of the men in the surveys share them with you. I think it is inevitable that when you are close to the beginnings of life, you must reflect on its ending. I interviewed several expectant fathers who were so excited about the wonderful aspects of the event that they began to worry about it being too good. Subsequently, they began to think about how it could go wrong and thought of the worst possible scenario. This may be psychologically protective (i.e., "Prepare for the worst, then you won't be surprised"), or it may be a result of guilt ("I don't deserve something this good. Something will be taken away").

How can you tell if the child will be retarded before birth? Is there a safe test?

The test you have most likely heard about is called amniocentesis. This test involves the removal of a tiny amount of the liquid in which the fetus floats in the uterus. Analysis of this liquid will indicate the presence of mongoloidism, a form of retardation that seems to increase in likelihood as the parents become older. Probabilities for mongolism or other rare inherited metabolic disorders are quite low, but of course for one's own child, it is either present to some degree or absent.

Amniocentesis is a test that allows parents to decide whether or not to induce an abortion if there is presence of mongolism or to prepare emotionally and physically for a disabled child. It is important to note that this procedure is normally safely undertaken during the fourth month of the pregnancy, and test results often take some time to be returned. This is very late for many parents to consider terminating the pregnancy. Other causes of retardation are not detectable by amniocentesis. Specific tests exist for high-risk parents for hereditary disorders such as Tay-Sachs disease.

Amniocentesis (as well as some ultrasound pictures) also provides information as to the sex of the child. Some parents prefer to have this information prior to birth. Others prefer not to know.

What diseases are inherited?

It is natural to be concerned about whether the unborn child will inherit any diseases carried by the parents. It is clear that some disease traits are genetically transmitted. It is always important for both parents to share medical histories with physicians as a way of planning for any possibilities.

Other diseases carried by the parents, while not genetically transmitted to the baby, nevertheless can cause problems for the infant. Most venereal diseases fall into this category, and the obstetrician must be aware of these prior to the birth. Herpes, a communicable disease that has reached epidemic proportions in some segments of the population, can potentially cause great harm to the baby during birth and may necessitate a surgical birth. A mother or father with HIV/AIDS will almost certainly pass it on to the infant unless dramatic anti-retroviral treatment is instituted.[13] Although this is not always fatal, it is very serious and requires many lifestyle changes.

One man who asked about hereditary diseases was trying to ascertain if insanity was hereditary. His brother was diagnosed schizophrenic, and he

---

13. In 2014, there are some very hopeful preliminary reports of early treatments of infants born with HIV that seem to have eliminated the virus within a number of months.

believed that two of his wife's aunts who had been hospitalized for years were also "insane." Answers to questions about these disorders are less clear. Current psychiatric opinion suggests that a *predisposition to schizophrenia* and other disorders may be inherited. Genetics seem to be necessary but insufficient alone to produce a full-blown schizophrenia in the child. A combination of neurobiology, early environment, psychological and social processes appear to be important contributory factors. There is no solid evidence that would suggest that mental disorders are carried by recessive genes. Thus, if the parents and grandparents had no signs, the probability of occurrence in the baby would be the same as in the general population.

There is some evidence that a host of mental diseases, including depression and bipolar illness, do have some hereditary components.

I seem so obsessed with death these days. Almost from the moment I knew that there was life inside my wife, I've been worrying about my own death, my parents, my wife, and the baby.

It is quite normal and expected that being close to and a part of the beginnings of life, one must also face the inevitability of death as well. It is daunting to consider that life itself is a terminal condition and one that is sexually transmitted.

Many men become connected to a deeper sense of the normal life-span cycle as they become a member of the parental (older) generation. In fact, childbirth is dangerous, and the life of one's child becomes so precious that the notion that something could happen to him/her is unthinkable. Similarly, the fears of losing one's partner become far more long reaching once a child is in the picture.

It is normal to worry about the health and safety of your family and to take steps for greater safety. It is not unusual for a man to consider life insurance at this time, to switch to a safer occupation or vocation, to be better about wearing seat belts, to pamper a woman who could previously run a marathon, and to become more concerned with his parents' health.

It is a time of reflection about life and death and a time to take precautions and become more safety conscious. On the other hand, if there are thoughts of suicide or of dread or impending doom, there may be a more serious problem that is being brought to light by the advent of the birth. These problems are best discussed with a qualified psychotherapist.

My wife seems to be very withdrawn and distant since she got pregnant. I find myself getting more and more lonely and angry with her. Is this what the rest of our lives will be like?

It is important for pregnant women to focus inside and begin to bond with the infant growing inside of them. Frequently, a woman will spend a great deal of time with the infant and in her own internal state at the expense of time with the outside world of which her spouse is a large component. A husband cannot focus on the infant by looking within, of course, but it is no less important for you to recognize your own feelings and to find ways of dealing with the rejection and loneliness. One of the most important ways is to discuss the feelings with your wife by stating your own desire for some of her time and a need to share in the pregnancy. If the relationship is in relatively good shape in the first place, your wife will probably be able to make adjustments and include you in some of her musing and dreaming. Take some time to consider either alone or with someone else who is close the implications of your feelings as a husband and father. The most important thing is to keep the lines of communication clear and open. The pregnancy is a time of adjustment to a new member of the family. If you successfully resolve the issues facing you now, there is no reason to fear the rest of your lives together.

I find myself being attracted to other women as my wife becomes more advanced in the pregnancy. I don't know why because I really love my wife and would not act on these strange desires.

The best plan of action, of course, is *not* to act on these desires. There are several reasons men give for attraction to other women during a pregnancy, most of which involve wishes for a different kind of contact with one's wife or for some changes in life. To find out what you are personally lacking in life is also crucial.

Many men, for example, feel very deserted and left out by the pregnancy, fearing that they have emotionally already lost their wives. One indication of this is if the attraction is for women who are close to your wife. In this case, the problem is not necessarily a need for other women as much as it may reflect a need to become closer to your partner. Finding ways of asking her for more time and attention and sharing your feelings of being left out are particularly helpful. If you find it difficult to approach her on your own, try to enlist a third party who is attuned to your feelings, a family member, a trusted clergyperson, or a family therapist.

Another reason you may be leaning toward other women is that you may be finding the responsibility and impending parenthood somewhat stifling. You may be trying to escape from this kind of psychological "entrapment" or trying to recapture a freer younger part of your own life. If this is the case, a professional therapist would be of value. You may need reassurance that your personal freedom will change but not be totally lost by being a father. It may also be very helpful to talk to some other men whom you trust and who experience similar values and feelings.

It can be quite tempting to have a woman you know attracted to you accessible and within reach. Fighting such temptation at a time when you may be feeling needy and aroused (horny) may be difficult. Recognize in advance the serious, long-lasting potential implications of acting on such desires and possibilities during a pregnancy. Consider how you would feel if your pregnant wife were to have an affair with a male friend of yours.

I am surprised that I am much less involved in this pregnancy than I was in the previous two. Does that mean that I don't want this baby?

It *could* mean that you are more ambivalent about a third child. It would be important to explore the differences on how you made the decision to have a third child. A man whose wife became pregnant by stopping birth control without consulting with him or by overriding his objections may quite obviously be more distant from a pregnancy in which he had little or no say.

There are also other explanations, such as finances, age, timing, and the nature of your marriage. Dr. Richard Kleiner's research indicates that experienced expectant fathers are *more* anxious than first-time expectant fathers during a pregnancy. Thus, fathers who have never been through the pregnancy before have some of their anxiety overwhelmed by the excitement and newness, whereas experienced fathers have more of a sense of "I've been through this before," but the reality of all the problems are still present.

I want to have children, and my wife—who is pregnant—doesn't. What rights do I have over her deciding to have an abortion without my okay?

You really do not have the legal right to stop her if she decides to have one. On the other hand, it seems like whatever you do, the two of you need to be more together as a team, and that is the more important issue. This very difficult problem is compounded by the fact that the two of you are so far apart as a couple that issues like this can come up at all. I would suggest that you consult a therapist immediately for marriage counseling that will allow you to work on the relationship itself.

Cal described a painful event from his past that occurred when he was just sixteen:

> We were just two dumb kids, both sixteen. It was the first time for us both and no birth control . . . I planned to pull out, but I guess it was too late . . . She and her parents decided on the abortion, and my religion forbade it. I wanted to keep the baby and have my parents adopt, but she just went ahead, and there was nothing I could do . . . I still feel guilty, and now with my wife pregnant for the first time, I can't get that all out of my mind.

When do you have to give up sex during a pregnancy, and when can you begin again?

You do not have to "give up sex," although intercourse might become uncomfortable. There are rare situations where abstinence might be the only form possible because of medical complications, but generally, it is the couple who decides when, how much, and what kind. You need to talk a great deal to each other and work out compromises during pregnancy and when to resume that are good for both of you.

What about religion? My wife and I are both from different backgrounds, but what about the child?

This is another question that has many answers. The most important thing to discuss is how strong your feelings are about religious practices. In my clinical practice, I saw a Jewish man married to a Protestant woman. The difficulty involved his strong desire to have any male child circumcised. She felt that the practice was "brutal, unnecessary, and a form of mutilation." It was only when he revealed that he could not identify with a son who was different from himself that she was able to listen to the emotional importance of the circumcision for her husband. What is particularly interesting in this family is that they had a daughter. The argument grew again on their daughter's sixth birthday when the wife wanted to have the girl's ears pierced (as was the custom in her family) and they found themselves on exactly opposite sides of the same question.

The only right answer to this question (choose one religion, do both, do neither, join a religion that both can abide, create some new form of spirituality) is very personal to each couple. It is also a matter that might arise many times during their life together.

What is the impact of a child not being wanted by one parent?

There is no way to judge specifically the impact on the child of being unwanted by one parent, except to say that if one parent wants the child and the other doesn't, there is a critical problem in the marital relationship. Unless that is mended, the child will no doubt suffer in some ways and probably grow up with a variety of extra fears that are limiting in the future. Being on different sides of so basic a question is serious. The most important thing to work on here is the relationship between the partners. Therapy is a good alternative.

When Donny and Christine married, he assumed that they would begin a family within five years. She had no interest in children. Because they were both devout Roman Catholics and had similarities in their careers, neither expected a major rift on anything so basic. They did not discuss this in premarital counseling. When he began to press the matter of a child, she withdrew from sexual activity. By the time they came in for marriage counseling, they were well on their way to a divorce.

My parents had nine children, and as soon as the last one left home, they split up. I'm also worried about living only for the children. What can we do about that?

Unfortunately, many people seem to believe that they will fix a deteriorating marriage by having a child (or taking on new financial responsibilities). It almost never works out that way. Parenthood is stressful.

When stress is added to a fragile system, it is even more likely to break down. In clinical practice, I've seen many single parents who conceived the child and separated from their partners during the pregnancy.

The best prevention, of course, is to be careful about strengthening the relationship prior to the decision to have children. Even in the best of relationships, a new child adds to friction simply by the number of new demands. If you are already in this kind of situation, try to strengthen the bonds that brought you and your partner together in the first place. Take some time together to do things you both enjoy and be romantic. It can always be helpful to see a marriage counselor or therapist for help in finding and improving the strengths in your marriage.

I just read in a magazine that a child costs about $240,000, and that doesn't even include college. What's the financial reality of having a child?

Most men have concerns about finances when the child comes along. For one thing, it usually means increased expenses and reduced income from the woman's job. A great number of these concerns involve emotional rather than purely fiscal matters. No matter what figure is given for the cost of raising a child, it represents an average, and you can be sure that it will go up in the future. Wealth is no guarantee of success in child-rearing. What almost every man wants is a sense that he and his wife are a team and are pulling together. He needs to know that as they earn less, they will both economize and cut spending without resentment.

Financial realities are hard to pinpoint because most fathers want the best life for their children and feel a great responsibility to give their children as much or more than they got in their own youth. It's interesting that there seems to be a trade-off between money and energy at different times in life. Fathers who are beginning their families in their twenties are likely to have lower income (they may still be in school) but more energy to deal with kids. Older fathers in their forties usually have better financial resources but less energy. Fortunately, they also usually have more patience for errors.

Another conundrum that fathers face is a conflict between wanting their children's lives to be easier than their own and not wanting the child to be demotivated and fail to develop a good work ethic. This particular tension reemerges at many points as the children grow into adolescence.

Is it normal for men to be uncomfortable with the gynecologists and nurses?

It sure was for the men in the study. Most of the men felt very uncomfortable dealing with health-care professionals. The examining rooms and facilities are all arranged for women. They are not used to having men around and do not do much to make men comfortable in these settings. There is a sense of being treated like a child or being "talked down to" that most men found particularly discomforting. One antidote is to be involved early and to let the physician and other birthing people know that you want information, that you want it presented in normal everyday language (not "medicalese" or "Latin"), and that you want to be treated with respect. What is more important is that your wife be treated with respect in this setting.

In my own experience, the gynecologist initially ignored me and acted as if I were a piece of furniture during my wife's pelvic examinations. When I began asking questions about my concerns, she shifted and treated me as a colleague and ignored my wife. It was close to our daughter's birth date before we were both able to be considered. During such times also, the nurse's aides constantly asked me to stand in one corner or the other (to be out of the way) and then repeatedly bumped into me, often while carrying half-full bedpans, and said "excuse me" in a tone of voice that suggested that I did not belong anywhere in their work space.

My son is twenty-two months old now, and my wife is pregnant with our second. What should we do about the jealousy he feels towards the new baby?

This is called sibling rivalry, and it is almost certain to develop among children in a family. The most important thing is to talk a lot to the older child and explain what is going to happen and what it will be like for him. It is also important to express your continuing love for him during the early days of the new child's entry into the family. The classic advice is for dad to hold the new baby while mom greets and hugs the older child upon her return from the hospital. It is also helpful for both of you to convey the excitement of having a brother or sister. Of course, if the jealousy is very strong, the safety of the infant must be guaranteed. It may also be worth a few sessions of family or play therapy if there is enduring potential danger.

Don't expect to completely overcome or prevent this jealousy, however. Clinical psychologist Jonathon Kellerman offers this illustration: Suppose you planned to bring another woman home to live. You carefully and lovingly explain to your wife that she will like this new person, will be good friends with her, and will enjoy sharing the house, possessions, and you. Your best efforts are unlikely to prevent her jealousy and probably anger. Your child feels similarly about a new brother or sister.

Man to Man: A Few Final Words

I have saved a few choice tidbits for the end of this book. During the interviews, two questions were asked of all of the men: (1) what was the most surprising thing about the pregnancy and birth for you? and (2) what advice would you give a close friend or brother who was going through this experience?

Much of that advice has been incorporated into the text already, but I will close with some of the most heartfelt and welcome advice that these expectant fathers could offer. I hope it will mean as much to you as it has to me. I did not place them in any order. I just took twenty-two of each from the surveys. As you can see, there is a wide range.

Twenty-Two Surprises

1. *When that kid looks into your eyes and you know it's yours, you know what it means to be alive.*
2. *I'm surprised I didn't feel tied down. I thought I'd resent missing restaurants and movies. I guess the kid just means more than that.*
3. *It's the best thing that ever happened to me.*
4. *You're going to learn more, faster than ever before, and still feel stupid.*
5. *How the modern man has no choice but to be with his wife during the childbirth*
6. *How fast the first few months of pregnancy flew by. In no time, it was half over, and we felt we had too much to do.*
7. *How long it actually takes. Pregnancy is really near ten months, and getting prepared felt like it took at least half of that time (preparing the house, baby essentials, care instructions, etc.)*
8. *The emotional lows and highs pre/postbirth—can be the most straining to the most joyous moments of life*
9. *For pregnancy, probably how it affected our relationship, becoming closer, more selfless. For birth, watching the incredible strength and beauty of my partner as our boy was born*
10. *The most surprising thing to me about the pregnancy was when my wife told me that my daughter recognized my voice and moved around a lot when I came home from work and started talking. Talking to her and seeing the belly move was crazy! I felt like this was the first time we communicated.*
11. *Pregnancy surprises: that I would be so concerned about her taking appropriate care of her gestational diabetes and that I would get so good and providing the progesterone shots! Birthing surprises: that I would be as instrumental during the delivery as I was*
12. *Second kid; no real surprises*
13. *The afterbirth*
14. *The intense emotions as my baby was born; seeing her for the first time*
15. *The feeling of helplessness during birth—I felt like I should be doing something but didn't know what.*
16. *How natural it felt*
17. *The huge headache that came from dealing with insurance and the hospital*

18. *That it changes your life*
19. *How unhappy it made my wife*
20. *The amount of stroller, car seat, vaccination, parenting literature*
21. *How it was treated as a medical procedure not a natural process*
22. *How strong I was and how emotional I was. I just started tearing when I saw my son for the first time.*

Twenty-Two Pieces of Brotherly Advice

1. *Talk to lots of other people. If some don't care, find others who do. Sometimes you'll find an understanding ear in the least-expected places.*
2. *Don't do it!*
3. *Go easy on yourself. You will have moments where you're not as good of a father as you envisioned yourself to be. You'll lose your temper. You'll be too tired to play. You'll let your kid eat snacks all day. Don't beat yourself up over those moments. We've all got 'em.*
4. *Be prepared to do a lot of reading.*
5. *Rub her feet and shut the hell up.*
6. *Get ready to change your life for the good.*
7. *Don't trust birth control. We were in the 1 percent that doesn't work even on the pill.*
8. *No returns. So make sure you can spend the rest of your life with your partner before procreating. Get a dog first!*
9. *Realize that you are now responsible for the well-being of another. Also, don't expect your partner to do it all.*
10. *My advice would be to remember that you and your wife are a team in this whole thing.*
11. *Every pregnancy and birth seems different, and no matter how much you prepare, the only way to be ready to be a dad is to be one. I am an advocate for fathers going to big doctor appointments (i.e., ultrasounds) with their wife because: (1) you get to see your child and be involved with the process, and (2) it is good practice for being in a medical setting providing support.*
12. *It boils down to getting involved. The birth and pregnancy will go on without you if you let it. Don't! Be present* (or you'll later regret it).
13. *Be very positive about the way your wife looks.*
14. *Go into counseling! I insisted that Bella and I have relationship counseling to talk about our fears in a neutral setting.*

15. *Get on your wife's case to live a healthy life. Help her cut out the drinking, the smoking, the dope, even if you have to cut it out yourself too.*

16. *I know I can't warn you about this because nobody can understand, but be prepared for more tiredness than you can imagine and for some feelings you didn't know were in you.*

17. *This above all. You and your wife are a team on this, and you've got to decide what you want and how you want it, and for sure, fight to do the birth your way. Don't be put off by relatives, parents, friends, anyone. Do it your way!*

18. *If I can do it, then you can too! Seriously, I was worried, concerned, hesitant, you name it about having a kid. Every thought about what this will do to my life and what I will have to change/stop went through my head. Ultimately, you just go for it, and it ends up being the most amazing experience of your life.*

19. *Every parent says exactly the same thing to people without kids . . . "You won't understand till you have one." Life does change after a kid, and yes, you have less time for yourself, your hobbies, and your friends, but it is all worth it, and it will all come together in time.*

20. *I welcome you in advance to the honorable endeavor of fatherhood. In the future when you face important decisions, always strongly consider what is best for your child first, then try and make that what is best for you.*

21. *Get ready for the best ride of your life and sleep now because you won't get much for the next several years.*

22. *Be there always.*

Bibliography

Annis, L. F. (1978). *The Child Before Birth*. Ithaca: Cornell University Press.

Benson, L. (1968). Fatherhood: A Sociological Perspective. New York: Random House.

Biller, H. B., & Meredith, D. L. (1974). *Father Power*. New York: Mckay.

Bing, E. (1977). *Six Practical Lessons for an Easier Childbirth*. New York: Bantam.

Bittman, S., & Zalk, S. (1978) *Expectant Fathers*. New York: Hawthorn.

Boston Women's Health Book Collective. (1978). *Ourselves and Our Children*. New York: Random House.

Bradley, R. A. (1974). *Husband Coached Childbirth*. New York: Harper and Row.

Brooks, G. R., & Good, G. E. (Eds.). (2001). *The New Handbook of Psychotherapy and Counseling with Men: A Comprehensive Guide to Settings, Problems, and Treatment Approaches*. (Vol. 1) San Francisco: Jossey-Bass. 403-423.

Brott, A. A. & Ash, J. (2013). *The Expectant Father: Facts, Tips and Advice for Dads-to-be. (Third Ed.)* New York: Abbeville Press.

Caplan, F. (Ed.). (1973). *The First Twelve Months of Life*. New York: Grosset & Dunlap.

Cath, S. H., Gurwitt, A. R., & Ross, J. M. (1982). *Father and Child: Developmental and Clinical Perspectives*. Boston: Little, Brown.

Colman, A. D., & Colman, L. L. (1971). *Pregnancy: The Psychological Experience*. New York: Herder and Herder.

Corneau, G. *Absent Fathers, Lost Sons: The Search for Masculine Iden*tity. Boston: Shambhala.

Diamond, M. J. (2007). *My Father Before Me: How Fathers and Sons Influence Each Other throughout Their Lives*. New York: W. W. Norton.

Eiger, M. S., & Olds, S. W. (1972) *The Complete Book of Breastfeeding*. New York: Bantam.

Farrell, W. *The Liberated Man*. (1974). New York: Random House.

Feldman, S. S., Nash, S. C., & Aschenbrenner, B. G. (1983). Antecedents of Fathering. *Child Development, 54*, 1628-1636.

Greenberg, M. (1985). *The Birth of a Father*. New York: Continuum.

Greene, B. (1984). *Good Morning Merry Sunshine*. New York: Atheneum

Grad, R., Bash, D., Guyer, R. et al. (1981). *The Father Book: Pregnancy and Beyond*. Washington, D.C.: Acropolis Books.

Hammer, T. J., & Turner, P. H. (1985) *Parenting in Contemporary Society*. Englewood, NJ: Prentice Hall.

Hanson, S., & Bozett, F. (Eds.). (1985). *Dimensions of Fatherhood*. Beverly Hills, CA: Sage Publications.

Harms, R. W. (Ed.) (2011). *Mayo Clinic Guide to a Healthy Pregnancy: From Doctors Who Are Parents, Too!* New York: HarperCollins.

Jones, C. (1986). *After the Baby Is Born: A Complete Postpartum Guide for New Parents*. New York: Dodd Mead.

—. (1987). *Mind over Labor*. New York: Viking.

—. (1985). *Sharing Birth*. New York: Quill.

Klinman, D. G., & Kohl, R. (1984). *Fatherhood U.S.A.* New York: Garland.

La Leche League International. (1981). *The Womanly Art of Breastfeeding*. Franklin Park, IL.

Lamb, M. (1981). *The Role of the Father in Child Development* (2nd ed.). New York: Wiley.

LaRossa, R. (1986). *Becoming a Parent*. Beverly Hills: Sage.

Lynn, D. B. (1974). *The Father: His Role in Child Development*. Monterey, CA: Brooks/Cole.

May, K. A., & Sollid, D. (1984). *Unanticipated Caesarian Birth from the Father's Perspective. Birth*, 11, 2, 87©95.

McBride, A. B. (1974). *The Growth and Development of Mothers*. New York: Perennial.

Murkoff, H. (2008), *What to Expect When You're Expecting* (4th ed.). New York: Workman.

Nilsson, L. (1977). *A Child Is Born*. New York: Delacorte.

Osherson, S. (2001). *Finding Our Fathers: How a Man's Life Is Shaped by His Relationship with His Father.* New York: McGraw Hill.

Parke, R. (1981). *Fathers*. Cambridge, MA: Harvard University Press.

Pedersen, F. A. (1980). *The Father Infant Relationship*. New York: Praeger Scientific.

Phillips, C. R., & Anzalone, J. T. (1978). *Fathering: Participation in Labor and Birth*. St. Louis: Mosby.

Pollack, W. S. (1999). *Real Boys: Rescuing Our Sons from the Myths of Boyhood*. New York: Henry Holt.

Pruett, K. D. (1987). *The Nurturing Father*. New York: Warner.

Rosno, S. (1981). *A Humanistic Approach to Caesarian Childbirth*. San Jose, CA: Caesarian Birth Council International Inc.

Sachs, B. (1992). *Things Just Haven't Been the Same: Making the Transition from Marriage to Parenthood*. New York: Morrow

Schwartz, A. (1967). *To Be a Father*. New York: Crown.

Selby, J. W., Calhoun, L. G., Vogel, A. W. & King, H. E. (1980). *Psychology and Human Reproduction*. New York: Free Press.

Shapiro, J. L. (1993). *When Men Are Pregnant*. New York: Delta (Paperback).

—. (1993). *The Measure of a Man: Becoming the Father You Wish Your Father Had Been*. New York: Delacorte.

Shapiro, J. L., Diamond, M. J., & Greenberg, M. (1995). *Becoming a Father: Contemporary Social, Developmental and Clinical Perspectives*. New York: Springer.

Shapiro, J. L. (2012). *Finding Meaning, Facing Fears in the Autumn of Your Years (Ages 45-65)*. Atascadero, CA: Impact Publishers.

A Few Recommended Websites

www.pregnancy.com

www.babycenter.com

www.parenting101.com

www.wellnessmama.com

www.webmd.com/baby:

www.webmd.com/men/features/advice-for-expectant-fathers

www.womenshealth.gov/pregnancy

www.nlm.nih.gov/medlineplus/pregnancy.html

www.caesarianrates.com

www.jerroldleeshapiro.com

Please also check out local special interest groups and groups on social media like Facebook. Many communities have magazines such as *Bay Area Baby*.

Index

A

AAP (American Academy of Pediatrics), 206

abandonment, 25, 27, 38–39, 59, 74–75, 137

abortion, 13, 56–58, 60, 79, 91, 99–101, 259, 262

accidental pregnancy, 55–56

ACOG (American College of Obstetrics and Gynecology), 200–202

active labor, 165, 169

Adams, Caren, 219

adjustment, 132, 145, 210, 215, 221, 235, 241, 261

adoption, 36, 62, 71, 83, 235

affair, 34, 37, 41, 135–38, 262

  late-pregnancy, 41, 120, 135–37, 152

afterbirth, 29, 79, 104, 171–72, 192, 266

AIDS (acquired immunodeficiency syndrome), 259

ambivalence, 45, 56, 62, 72, 90, 93, 123, 217–18, 256

amniocentesis, 60, 99, 107, 195, 243, 259

analgesic. *See* pain medication

anesthesia, 21, 98, 168–70, 190–93

announcement, 80, 85, 87, 114, 157–58, 171, 177, 206–7

anxiety, 19, 22, 37, 108, 124–25, 139, 141–42, 153, 157, 159, 199, 223, 247, 255, 262

artificial insemination, 36–37

attachment, 175, 228, 233

  father-child, 116

B

baby blues, 215, 222–23

baby m, 56

birth control, 32, 37, 53–56, 60, 81, 133, 229, 262

birth defects, 107–8, 174

birthing centers, 96–98, 124, 144, 157, 161–63, 165, 169, 173, 205, 233, 236, 255, 258

birthing process, 22, 97, 135–36, 141, 143–44, 151, 155, 157, 161, 175, 191, 222, 250, 257–58

birthing rooms, 142, 163, 184, 187

birthing team, 142, 159–60, 162, 166, 171, 179

birth options, 96, 103, 123, 126

birthplace, 96, 172, 176, 209

Bittman, Sam, 84

bonding, 40, 114–16, 119, 140, 174, 216, 220, 228, 231, 238, 245

Bradley, Robert, 96, 140, 142–43, 176, 195, 257

V

Z

Edwards Brothers Malloy
Thorofare, NJ USA
April 28, 2014